CW00806700

Historical View of the Literature of the South of Europe

by Jean-Charles-Léonard Simonde Sismondi

Address:
HardPress
8345 NW 66TH ST #2561
MIAMI FL 33166-2626
USA
Email: info@hardpress.net

HISTORICAL VIEW

OF THE

LITERATURE

OF THE

SOUTH OF EUROPE;

BY

J. C. L. SIMONDE DE SISMONDI:

OF THE ACADEMY AND SOCIETY OF ARTS OF GENEVA, HONORARY MEMBE
OF THE UNIVERSITY OF WILNA, OF THE ITALIAN ACADEMY, &c. &c.

TRANSLATED FROM THE ORIGINAL,

WITH NOTES,

BY THOMAS ROSCOE, ESQ.

VOL. I.

LONDON:
PRINTED FOR HENRY COLBURN AND CO.
1823.

LONDON:
PRINTED BY S. AND R. BENTLEY, DORSET STREET.

ADVERTISEMENT.

The acknowledged want in our own language of a work exhibiting a comprehensive view of foreign Literature, and the established reputation of M. de Sismondi, as an elegant and accomplished writer, will preclude the necessity of any apology, on the part of the Translator, for presenting to the public the following volumes, which have already, in their original form, acquired an extensive and merited celebrity. It has been the object of the Translator, in the execution of his task, to adhere as closely as possible to the text of the original; no part of which he has taken upon himself either to suppress or enlarge, with the exception of one or two peculiar instances, where the extent of the alteration is pointed out. With regard to the poetical extracts, introduced by M. de Sismondi, and which are generally translated by him into French prose, the Editor has adopted, where practicable, such established English translations as already existed. In other instances he has either been indebted to the kindness of his friends, or has been compelled to insert his own metrical versions.

3d May, 1823.

CONTENTS

OF

THE FIRST VOLUME.

CHAPTER I.

CHAPTER II.

CHAPTER III.

CHAPTER IV.

CHAPTER V.

CHAPTER VI.

CHAPTER VII.

CHAPTER VIII.

CHAPTER IX.

CHAPTER X.

VIEW

OF

THE LITERATURE

OF THE

SOUTH OF EUROPE.

CHAPTER

Introduction—Corruption of the Latin, and Formation of the Romance Languages.

The study of foreign literature does not at all times possess the same importance, or the same degree of interest. At the period when nations, yet in their infancy, are animated by a creative genius, which endows them with a poetry and literature of their own, while it renders them, at the same time, capable of splendid enterprises, susceptible of lofty passions, and disposed to great sacrifices, the literature of other nations is unknown to them. Each draws from its own bosom that which best harmonizes with its nature. Eloquence, in such a nation, is the expression of natural sentiment; poetry, the play of an imagination yet unexhausted. Amongst such a people, no one writes for the sake of writing; no one speaks merely for the sake o speaking. To produce a deep impression, there is no need either of rules or examples. The orator touches the inmost soul of his hearer, because his words proceed from the depths of his own heart. The priest obtains a mastery over the conscience, and in turns awakens love or terror because he is himself convinced of the truth o the dogmas which he inculcates; because he feel the duties he proclaims, and is only the organ o the inspirations within him. The historian place before the eyes of his readers the events of pas times, because he is still agitated by the passion which produced them; because the glory of hi country is the first passion of his heart; and because he wishes to preserve by his writings, tha which his valour has contributed to acquire. Th epic poet adds durability to these historical reco lections, by clothing them in a language mor conformable to the inspirations of his imaginatior and more analogous to those emotions which it his object to awaken. The lyric poet abandor himself to the transports of which he has s deep a sense; while the tragedian places befor our eyes the picture of which his fancy has fir formed a perfect conception. Manner and lar guage, to such a creative genius as this, are merel the means of rendering its emotions more popula

Each seeks, and each discovers in himself th harmonious touch, to which all hearts must r spond; each affects others, in pursuing onl that which affects himself; and art becomes u necessary, because every thing is supplied b nature and by feeling.

Such was Greece in her infancy; such, perhap were the European nations, in their first dev lopement, during the middle ages; and such a all nations which by their native energy rise o of barbarism, and which have not suffered the sp rit of imitation to extinguish their natural vigou At this period of civilization, an acquaintanc with foreign languages, with foreign literatur and with foreign rules, cannot but be perniciou To offer to a people thus gifted with ardent g nius, models which they might, perhaps, attem to imitate, before they are capable of appreciatin them, is much to be deprecated. It is better leave them to themselves. Feeling, with then takes the lead of judgment, and may condu them to the highest results; but they are ev ready to abandon it for art, which, while they a entirely unacquainted with it, appears to them possess superior attractions. They ask with eage ness for rules, while they themselves should b the examples to serve as rules to after-ages. Th more vigour the human mind possesses, the mo disposed it is to submit itself to authority. almost always turns its strength against itself; an the first exertion it makes of its power is too often directed to its own extinction. Fanaticism seems to be the malady peculiar to this period of civil society. The vigour of the political or religious institutions which then arise, is proportioned to the energy of the characters which are at the same time developed; and nations endowed with the most powerful faculties, have failed to occupy a place in the history of the world, or of literature, because they have wasted their best energies in the subjugation of themselves. Many striking examples of this annihilation of the human mind are to be found in the political, and more especially in the religious history of man. The history of literature also presents a few. Thus, the Spartans felt themselves gifted with an extraordinary vigour of character, and passions unusually strong. They were in the full enjoyment of liberty and youth, and for these very reasons they employed the whole energy of their will in subduing themselves. After making themselves acquainted with the most severe codes, like those of the Cretans and the Egyptians, they thought their political labours incomplete, until they had availed themselves of the public liberty to deprive the citizens of all free will. So, also, in the fervour of a recent conversion, the religious feelings display a similar reaction. The monastic orders impose upon themselves more rigorous penances, in proportion to the impetuosity which aith and zeal have awakened in their peculiar character. Thus, too, in that effervescence of oul which produces the poet, we often see oung minds abandon the study of truth and f nature, to encumber themselves with the fetters f a refined versification. We find them designedly lanning the recurrence of certain words, and he return of rhymes which restrict their thoughts; hus proposing as the ornaments of their com osition, the difficulties which they have volunarily imposed upon themselves, instead of inlulging the natural warmth of their imaginations. n the three intellectual occupations which are enerally supposed to be so dissimilar, in politics, eligion, and poetry, the impetuosity of the human haracter thus makes itself manifest by the very ove of confinement and constraint, and the energy f the mind is seen to react continually upon itself.

The literature of other countries has been requently adopted by a young nation with a sort f fanatical admiration. The genius of those counries having been so often placed before it as the erfect model of all greatness and of all beauy, every spontaneous movement has been reressed, in order to make room for the most ervile imitation, and every national attempt to levelope an original character has been sacrificed o the reproduction of something conformable to he model which has been always before its eyes. Thus the Romans checked themselves in the vigour of their first conceptions, to become emulous copyists of the Greeks; and thus the Arabs placed bounds to their intellectual efforts, that they might rank themselves amongst the disciples of Aristotle. So the Italians in the sixteenth century, and the French in the seventeenth, desirous only of imitating the ancients, did not sufficiently consult, in their poetical attempts, their own religion, manners, and character. And thus, again, the Germans, for a period of no long duration, and the Poles and the Russians to the present day, have repressed their own peculiar spirit, in order to adopt the laws of French literature, and to convert themselves into a nation of imitators and translators.

The period, however, during which the human mind is gifted with this degree of energy, is never of long continuance in any country. Reflection soon succeeds to this vehement effervescence; self-examination takes place, and an enquiry is instituted into the effect of the exertions which have been made. The mind feeds upon its own enthusiastic feelings, which withdraw themselves from the observation of others. All the rules of composition are discovered as the faculty of applying them is lost; the spirit of analysis chills the imagination and the heart, and the soaring flight of genius is at an end. We cannot conceal from ourselves that we have long since arrived at this second period. The mind is no longer ignorant of itself. Its course is foreseen, its effects are calculated upon. Genius has lost its wings and its power, and it is in vain to look, in the present age, for any of those inspired productions, in which genius, instead of speculating upon its own powers, advances towards its goal without nicely enquiring into the consequences, with no rules to confine it, and with no guide but its own native superiority. We have arrived at the age of analysis and philosophy; when every thing is matter of observation, even to the mode of observing, and every thing is governed by rules, even to the art of imposing rules. Refinement of intellect has gained the superiority over mere native talent. The latter cannot now advance without the aid of knowledge, which is indispensably requisite in our sentiments, our thoughts, and our conversation. It is necessary to be perpetually comparing ourselves with others, because we are ourselves always the objects of comparison; it is necessary to learn what is known, not merely for the sake of imitation, but of preserving our own position. When habit, education, and imperfect acquisitions, have already given a certain direction to our minds, we shall follow that beaten track more servilely in proportion to the disadvantages of our situation; and, on the contrary, we shall display more originality in proportion to our acquaintance with every kind of knowledge. The genius of man can never again approach its

its noble origin, and recover the station which it held before the birth of prejudices, but by elevating itself sufficiently above them to compare and analyse them all.

To be content with the study of our own literature is to remain in this state of imperfect knowledge. The creators of it were animated with an inspiration which has expired, and they found in their own hearts rules which they never took the trouble of expounding. They produced masterpieces; but we must not confound these masterpieces with models. There are no models but for those who willingly degrade themselves to the wretched condition of imitators. The critics, who succeeded them, discovered in their performances the course most appropriate to their genius, and perhaps to the national genius of the French. They indicated the path by which these great intellects arrived at such extraordinary results, and shewed that any other route would have diverted them from their object. They pointed out the conventional rules which had been observed, and which they have thus rendered essential, in the judgment of the public, for whose benefit they laboured. They have made us acquainted with our prejudices, and they have, at the same time, confirmed us in them. These prejudices are legitimate. They are derived from the authority of our greatest authors. We need only guard ourselves against supposing that these rules are essentially necessary to the productions of the human mind. Other great authors are found in other languages; they have formed the ornaments of the literature of other nations; they, too, have swayed the passions, and produced the same effects, which we are accustomed to consider as the consequences of our own eloquence and poetry. Let us study their manners; let us estimate them not by our own rules, but by those to which they themselves conformed. Let us learn to distinguish the genius of man from the genius of nations, and to raise ourselves to that height whence we may distinguish the rules which are derived from the essential principles of beauty, and which are common to all languages, from those which are adopted from great examples, which custom has sanctioned, refinement justified, and propriety still upholds; but which may, notwithstanding, amongst other nations, give place to other rules, depending upon other notions of propriety and other customs, sanctioned by other examples, and approved by the test of another, and, perhaps, not less perfect, mode of analysis.

It will, therefore, be both useful and interesting to take a review of the modern literature of other countries; to examine its early origin amongst the various nations of Europe; the spirit which animated it, and the different masterpieces which it has produced. In order to render a course like this complete, an extent of knowledge, and a familiar acquaintance with languages, would, no doubt, be necessary, to which I am far from making any pretensions. I am ignorant of the Oriental languages, and yet it was the Arabian which, in the middle ages, gave a new impulse to the literature of Europe, and changed the course of the human mind. I am ignorant, likewise, of the Sclavonic tongues, and yet the Russian and the Polish boast of literary treasures, a brief account of which I could present to my readers only on the authority of others. Amongst the Teutonic languages I am acquainted with the English and the German alone; and the literature of Holland, Denmark, and Sweden, is only accessible to me in an imperfect manner, through the medium of German translations. Still, the languages of which I shall give a summary account, are those in which there exist the greatest number of masterpieces, and which at the same time possess the most original and novel spirit; and, indeed, even with these restrictions, the ground which I intend to traverse is still sufficiently extensive.

I shall divide modern literature into two classes, which I shall make the subject of two courses: one on the Romance, the other on the Teutonic languages. In the first, after casting a glance over the brilliant period of Arabian literature, I shall successively take a review of the nations of the South who formed their poetry in the Oriental schools; and, first of all, the Provençals, who first introduced the poetry of romance into Europe. I shall endeavour to render my readers acquainted with their Troubadours, so renowned and yet so neglected, and to prove how much the poets of all modern ages owe to these, their earliest masters. At the same time I shall take the opportunity of speaking of the Trouveurs, the poets of the country to the north of the Loire, from whom Europe derives her *Fabliaux*, her chivalric romances, and her earliest dramatic representations. From their language, the Romance *Wallon*, or *langue d'oil*, the French was afterwards formed. After these dead, though modern languages, I shall give some account of the literature of Italy, which, amongst all the languages of the South, has exercised the greatest influence over the rest. I shall take it up from its origin about the time of Dante, and shall continue it down to our own times. In the same manner I shall treat of the literature of Spain, of which the earliest remains are anterior, by more than a century, to the first Italian poets, although in the reign of Charles V. the Castilians attempted to imitate the great models which they had learned to value in Italy. We ought, however, to rank the nations, not according to the antiquity of their first attempts, but by the influence which the cultivation of each has exercised over the others. The course will be concluded by the literature of Portugal, with whic perhaps, the majority of my readers are on acquainted through the masterpiece of Camoen but which, in fact, could not have produced great a writer, without at the same time po sessing many distinguished poets and historia worthy of partaking his fame.

I intend in the same manner to take a view, my second course, of the literature of England ar Germany, and to make some observations on th of the other Teutonic nations, as well as on th of the nations descended from the Sclavonian the Poles, and the Russians.

In the execution of a design so extensive, ar so much beyond the capacity of a single indi dual, I shall not have the presumption to affect or ginality. I shall eagerly avail myself of the l bours of the critics and literary historians; and shall, occasionally, be under the necessity of bo rowing from them their opinions on works whic I have not myself read, and which I can do more than point out to the attention of my rea ers *. But as I have proposed rather to make tl

* I am only acquainted with two works which comprehe that portion of literary history of which I purpose to treat this course. The first, the plan of which is very extensive, that of Andres, a Spanish Jesuit, and professor at Mant *Dell' Origine e de' Progressi d' ogni Letteratura*, 5 vols. 4 Parma, 1782. The author has sketched the history of all h man sciences in every language and in all parts of the worl

eader acquainted with the masterpieces of foreign anguages, than to pass a judgment upon them ccording to arbitrary rules, or to give the history f their authors, I have had recourse to the ori-;inals as often as it was in my power, and when-ver their reputation seemed to render them wor-hy of examination; and it is my intention rather o extract and give translations of the most beau-iful pieces I can collect in the languages of the South, than to detail the doubtful opinions of the critics.

---

nd with wonderful erudition has traced, in a philosophical man-ıer, the progress of the human mind. But as he has not given ny examples, and has not analysed the peculiar tastes of each ıation, and as his rapid judgments do not always contain the ;rounds of his decision, he has not succeeded in giving a clear dea of the writers and works of which he has collected the ıames, nor does he enable his readers to form their own opi-ıions. There is much more practical instruction to be found in he work of Professor Boutterwek, of Gottingen, who is em-loyed upon the History of Literature, properly so called, in Modern Europe. (*Friedrich Boutterwek, Geschichte der Schonen Vissenschaften*, 8 vols. 8vo. 1801–1810.) As yet he has only ompiled the literary history of Italy, Spain, Portugal, France, ınd England; but he has executed his task with an extent of rudition, and with a regard to the instruction of his readers, vhich seem peculiar to the German writers. I am more in-lebted to this than to any other critical work. For the par-icular history of each language I have possessed still more ımple resources. Millot (*Histoire Littéraire des Troubadours*) ıas been my principal guide in Provençal literature; Tira-

The languages which are spoken by the inhabitants of the south of Europe, from the extremity of Portugal to that of Calabria o Sicily, and which usually receive the designation of the Romance languages, are all derived from the mixture of the Latin with th Teutonic; of the people who were accountec Romans, with the barbarous nations which overthrew the Empire of Rome. The diversitie which exist amongst the Portuguese, the Spanish the Provençal, the French, and the Italian, aris rather from accidental circumstances than fron any distinction between these different races o

boschi, and in the first three volumes of his excellent work M. Ginguené, in Italian; Nicolas Antonio, Velasquez, with th Commentary of Dieze, and Diogo Barbosa, in Spanish and Portuguese; and Aug. W. Schlegel, in the dramatic literature o every nation. I here beg to acknowledge generally my obligations to all these critics, because in a work from necessity of s condensed a character, and composed to be read as lectures, have frequently availed myself of their labours, and sometime even of their thoughts, without citing them. If I had wished, a in an historical work, to produce my authorities for every fac and opinion, it would have been necessary to have added note to almost every line, and to have suspended, in a fatiguing manner, the delivery of the lecture, or the attention of the audience In critical history it would be ridiculous to attempt never to repeat what has been said before; and to endeavour to separate in every sentence, what belongs to ourselves from what is th property of others, would be little better than vanity and affectation.

men. Each of these tongues is founded upon the Latin, but the form is often barbarous. A great number of the words were introduced into the language by the conquerors, but by far the greater number belong to the vanquished people. The grammar was formed by mutual concessions. More complicated than that of the purely Teutonic nations, and more simple than that of the Greeks and Romans, it has not, in any of the languages of the South, preserved the cases in the nouns; but making a selection amongst the varying terminations of the Latin, it has created a new word from the nominative for the Italian, and from the accusative for the Spanish, while for the French it has contracted the word, and varied it from both of those terminations.* This

---

* This rule more especially applies to the plural. The following are a few examples of these contractions.

Lat.	*Ital.*	*Span.*	*Portug.*	*Proven.*	*French.*
Oculi	occhi	ojos	oilhos	huelhs	yeux (œils)
Cœli	cieli	cielos	ceos	ceus	cieux
Gaudium	godimento / gioia	gozo	gozo	gaug	joie

Since the publication of this work, M. Raynouard, in the grammar prefixed to his *Choix des Poésies originales des Troubadours*, has shewn, that in their language the nouns were formed from Latin substantives, by depriving them of those characterristic terminations which marked the cases; for the barbarians, ignorant of the declensions and the rules of grammar, did not know how to employ them. The termination of *the accusative* was most frequently cut off: thus, *abbatem* became *abbat; infantem, infant; florem, flor*. The examples of this methodical con-

original diversity gives a peculiar character to each language; but it does not prevent us from recognising the common source of all. On the borders of the Danube, the Wallachians and the Bulgarians speak also a language which may be known as a descendant of the Latin, and which its great resemblance to the Italian renders easy to be comprehended. Of the two elements of which it is composed, it has one in common with the Italian—the Latin; the other is entirely different—the Sclavonic instead of the German.

The Teutonic languages themselves are not absolutely exempt from this primitive mixture. Thus the English, which is for the most part a corrupt German dialect, has been mingled partly with the Breton or Gaelic, and partly with the French, which has given it some analogy to the Romance languages. Its character bears a greater impress of harshness than the German; its grammar is more simple, and it might be said more barbarous,

---

traction, which M. Raynouard has collected, are to be found in abundance long before the year 1000; and as this first modification of the Latin is at the same time the most natural and methodical, he concludes not only that the Romance language of the Troubadours is of a date anterior to all the others, but that it was common, in its origin, to all the nations which abandoned the use of the Latin, and that it was not until long afterwards that it was split into various dialects. He supposes too, that all the other languages of the South were formed immediately from this.

if the cultivation which this language has subsequently received, had not educed new beauties even from that very circumstance. The German has not remained what it was, when it was spoken by the people who overthrew the Roman empire. It appears to have borrowed for a period, and afterwards to have lost, a portion of the Latin syntax. When the study of letters began to extend itself over the North, with Christianity, the Germans attempted to give each case of their nouns a different termination, as in the Latin. This rendered their language more sonorous, and admitted more vowels in the construction of their words; but these modifications, which were, no doubt, contrary to the genius of the people, were in the end abandoned, and this distinction between the German and the Latin was again restored.

Thus, from one end of Europe to the other, the encounter of two mighty nations, and the mixture of two mother tongues, confounded all the dialects, and gave rise to new ones in their place. A long period of time now elapsed, during which it might almost be supposed that the nations of Europe were without a language. From the fifth to the tenth century, various races, always new, were mingled, without being confounded. Each village, each hamlet, contained some Teutonic conqueror, with his barbarian soldiers, and a number of vassals, the remains of the vanquished people. The terms upon which they lived, were those of contempt on the one side and hatred on the other. There was no confidence or trust between them. Equally ignorant of every principle of general grammar, they never thought of studying the language of their enemies; but accustomed themselves, merely, to the mutual jargon in which they sought to carry on an intercourse. Thus, we still see individuals transported into a foreign country, forming with those, with whom it is necessary to communicate, a sort of conventional dialect, which is neither their own language nor that of the natives, yet which is comprehended by both, and prevents each from becoming acquainted with the language of the other. Amongst the slaves of Africa and Constantinople, there are Christians, from every part of Europe, mingled with the Moors, who have neither taught the latter their language, nor have themselves acquired the Moorish. They communicate with them in a rude language, called the *Lingua Franca,* which is composed of the most useful European words, despoiled of the terminations which mark the tenses and the cases, and thrown together without any syntax. Thus, also, in the colonies of America, the planters make themselves intelligible to the Negroes by using the Creole language, which is nothing more than the French, adapted to the capacity of a barbarous people, by depriving it of every thing which gives it its precision, force, and pliancy. The want of ideas, the consequence of universal ignorance, left no temptation to augment the number of words of which this jargon was composed, and the absence of communication between village and village deprived it of all uniformity. The continual revolutions which led new nations of barbarians to usurp the place of the former intruders, and which substituted the new dialects of Germany for those with which the people of the South had begun to be familiar, did not suffer the language to acquire any degree of stability. In short, this unformed dialect, which varied with each province and each colony, which changed from year to year, and in which the only rules were imposed by chance or by the caprice of a barbarian people, was never used as a written language, even by the small number of those who were acquainted with the art of writing. It was disdained, as the language of ignorance and barbarism, by all who had the power of polishing it; and the gift of speech, which was granted to man for the purpose of extending and enlightening his ideas by communication, multiplied the barriers which before existed between them, and was only a source of confusion.

During the five centuries which preceded and prepared the way for the rise of the modern languages, it was impossible for Europe to possess any literature. Amongst those barbarous nations, the number of individuals who possessed the talent of reading or writing was small, and indeed the very materials for writing were wanting. Parchment was enormously dear; the Egyptian papyrus, after the victories of the Arabians, had ceased to be imported into Europe; and paper was not yet invented, or had not been introduced by commerce into the West. To tradition alone was committed the preservation of past events; and in order to engrave them on the memory, a metrical form was naturally given them. Such, perhaps, was the origin of versification. Poetry was, at first, nothing more than a mode of assisting the memory. But, amongst the nations of the South, the language which had recently been formed, was confined within very narrow limits. It was too variable to be entrusted with any thing, which was intended to reach another generation. It sufficed, at the utmost, for the purpose of giving and receiving orders, and for the rude communication between the conqueror and the conquered. But as soon as it was desirable to make themselves intelligible at a distant period or in another country, the nations endeavoured to express themselves in the Latin, which, however, they could not effect without difficulty. All the rude chronicles, in which passing events were, at distant intervals, registered, were written in Latin. All contracts of marriage, or of purchase, lending, or exchange, were in the same tongue, or rather in that barbarous jargon which the notaries supposed to be Latin, but which was in fact as far removed from the spoken as from the written language. The excessive price of parchment for their manuscripts compelled them to cover the margins of ancient books with their barbarous contracts, and they often erased the most sublime works of Greece or Rome, for the purpose of substituting some private agreement, or some legendary absurdity.

Amongst all the Romance nations, however, and more especially in France and Italy, there appeared at distant periods during these five centuries, some judicious historians, whose style possesses considerable vivacity, and who have given animated pictures of their times; some subtle philosophers, who astonish us rather by the fineness of their speculations than by the justice of their reasoning; some learned theologians, and some poets. The names of Paul Warnefrid, of Alcuin, of Liutprand, and of Eginhard, are even yet universally respected. They all, however, wrote in Latin. They had all of them, by the strength of their intellect, and the happy circumstances in which they were placed, learned to appreciate the beauty of the models which antiquity had left them. They breathed the spirit of a former age, as they had adopted its language. In them, we do not find the representatives of their contemporaries. It is impossible to recognise, in their style, the times in which they lived; it only trays the relative industry and felicity with hich they imitated the language and the thoughts a former age. They do not belong to modern erature. They were the last monuments of cilized antiquity; the last of a noble race, which, ter a long period of degeneracy, became extinct them.

The popular songs and ballads of every country, hich are the genuine productions of their own e, and belong not to antiquity, are the most rious specimens we possess of national compotions. Some of these songs which have been eserved by chance, are well worthy of observaon, much less for their poetical merit, than for e light which they throw on the strange deruction of national language. They are all of em written in barbarous Latin, and none of them ve been discovered in those dialects, which were on afterwards destined to assume the rank of w languages. Those dialects were scarcely telligible from town to town; and the poet, for e sake of popularity, had recourse to a language hich was generally though imperfectly known, preference to that vulgar tongue which would arcely have been understood beyond the next llage. It is not singular that the hymns of the hurch should have been composed at this period Latin, for that was the language of religion; nor at the learned should frame their poems in the same tongue, for it was the language of study; but, that the songs of the soldiers should have been composed in Latin, shews the impossibility at that time of employing any other medium.

One of these songs was composed in Italy in 871, by the soldiers of the Emperor Louis II. to excite a mutual emulation amongst them to rescue him from his captivity. That monarch, who had been engaged, in the south of Italy, in a war against the Saracens, had become a greater burden to his ally, Adelgizo, Duke of Benevento, than even the enemies whom he had come to repel. Adelgizo, no longer able to endure the exactions and insolence of the army which he had received within his walls, took the rash resolution of arresting the Emperor in his palace, on the 25th June, 871. He was kept in captivity for nearly three months, when the Imperial soldiers, who were scattered throughout all Italy, animating themselves to vengeance by the song which I am about to transcribe, advanced towards the duchy of Benevento, which induced Adelgizo to set his prisoner at liberty. This poem is written in long lines of fifteen or sixteen syllables, without any apparent regard to quantity, but with a cæsura in the middle. The sense terminates at the end of every three lines. It is composed in a barbarous Latin, in which may be found examples of every grammatical error. A translation is subjoined:

* "Listen, all ye boundaries of the earth! listen with horror and sadness, to the crime which has been committed in the city of Benevento. Louis, the holy, the pious Augustus, has been seized. The Beneventines were assembled in council, Adalferio spoke, and they said to the prince, 'If we dismiss him alive, we shall assuredly perish. He has planned a cruel design against this province; he has deprived us of our kingdom; he holds us cheap; he has heaped many evils upon us; it is just that he should die.' They have led this holy saint from his palace; Adalferio has led him to his judgment-seat; but he rejoices as a saint in his martyrdom. Sado and Saducto have departed, invoking the rights of the Empire. And

* The following is the text of this barbarous poem, of which I am not sure that I have always discovered the right sense:

Audite omnes fines terre orrore cum tristitia,
Quale scelus fuit factum Benevento civitas,
Lhuduicum comprenderunt, sancto pio Augusto.
Beneventani se adunarunt ad unum Consilium,
Adalferio loquebatur et dicebant Principi:
Si nos eum vivum dimittemus, certe nos peribimus.
Celus magnum preparavit in istam provintiam,
Regnum nostrum nobis tollit, nos habet pro nihilum,
Plures mala nobis fecit, rectum est ut moriad.
Deposuerunt sancto pio de suo palatio;
Adalferio illum ducebat usque ad Pretorium,
Ille vero gaude visum tanquam ad martyrium.
Exierunt Sado et Saducto, invocabant imperio;
Et ipse sancte pius incipiebat dicere:
Tanquam ad latronem venistis cum gladiis et fustibus.

now the holy saint himself speaks: 'You have come against me with swords and with clubs, as though I were a robber. The time was, when I brought you relief, but now you have taken counsel against me, and yet I know not wherefore you would slay me. I came hither to destroy a cruel generation; I came to worship in the church of God, and to avenge the blood which has been shed upon the earth.' The Tempter has dared to place upon his head the Imperial Crown, and he has said to the people, 'Behold, we are the Emperor, and we will rule you,' and he rejoiced in the work he had done. But the Demon torments him, and has cast him to the earth, and the people have gone forth to behold the miracle. Our

---

Fuit jam namque tempus vos allevavit in omnibus,
Modo vero surrexistis adversus me consilium,
Nescio pro quid causam vultis me occidere.
Generacio crudelis veni interficere,
Eclesie que sanctis Dei venio diligere,
Sanguine veni vindicare quod super terram fusus est.
Kalidus ille temtator, ratum adque nomine
Coronam Imperii sibi in caput ponent et dicebat Populo:
Ecce sumus Imperator, possum vobis regere.
Leto animo habebat de illo quo fecerat;
A demonio vexatur, ad terram ceciderat,
Exierunt multæ turmæ videre mirabilia.
Magnus Dominus Jesus Christus judicavit judicium;
Multa gens paganorum exit in Calabria,
Super Salerno pervenerunt, possidere civitas.
Juratum est ad Sancte Dei reliquie
Ipse regnum defendendum, et alium requirere.

great master, Jesus Christ, has pronounced judgment. A crowd of Pagans have invaded Calabria, they have arrived at Salerno, they have possessed the city; but we have sworn by the holy relics of God to defend this kingdom, and to conquer another."

Another military song has been preserved, later than the former by nearly a century. It was composed about the year 924, to be sung by the Modenese soldiers as they guarded their walls against the Hungarians. The Latin is more grammatical, and the language altogether more correct, than that of the former. It appears to have been the production of a man conversant with antiquity; and yet it approaches more nearly to the style of modern poetry, which was then near its birth. The lines, which consist of twelve syllables, are unequally divided by a cæsura after the fifth. They are all rhymed; or rather, as in Spanish poetry, the rhyme only exists in the terminating vowel, and is continued throughout the whole piece.

*"O thou! who with thine arms guardest these walls, sleep not, I warn thee, but watch. As long as Hector watched in Troy, the crafty Greeks

---

* The text is as follows:—

> O tu qui servas armis ista mœnia
> Noli dormire, moneo, sed vigila!
> Dum Hector vigil extitit in Troia
> Non eam cepit fraudulenta Græcia.

could not capture it; but when she sunk into her first slumbers, the treacherous Sinon opened the perfidious gates, and the hidden bands, gliding down the ropes, seized on the city and burnt Pergama. The watchful voice of the white goose put to flight the Gauls who attacked the Roman Capitol; wherefore, for that deed, a silver bird was fashioned, and adored as a divinity by the Romans. Let us adore the Godhead of Christ, let us sing for him our songs of jubilee. Relying on his powerful guard, let us watch and sing our songs of jubilee. O Christ, king of the world, take into thy powerful keeping these camps in which we watch. Be thou our impregnable rampart, be thou the terrible enemy of our enemies. No force can hurt us while thou keepest guard, for

---

Prima quiete dormiente Troia
Laxavit Sinon fallax claustra perfida:
Per funem lapsa occultata agmina
Invadunt urbem et incendunt Pergama.
Vigili voce avis anser candida
Fugavit Gallos ex arce Romulea,
Pro qua virtute facta est argentea,
Et a Romanis adorata ut Dea.
Nos adoremus celsa Christi numina,
Illi canora demus nostra jubila;
Illius magna fisi sub custodia
Hæc vigilantes jubilemus carmina.
Divina mundi Rex Christe custodia.
Sub tua serva hæc castra vigilia,
Tu murus tuis sis inexpugnabilis,
Sis inimicis hostis tu terribilis;

thou puttest to flight the armies of the warlike. Do thou, O Christ, gird in our walls, do thou defend them with thy powerful lance. And thou, Maria, holy and bright mother of Christ, do thou beseech his assistance for us, with John, whose holy relics we here worship, and to whom these walls are dedicated. Under his conduct, our right-hand shall be victorious in war, and without him our javelins avail not. Valiant youth! bold glory of war! let your songs be heard along the walls; and in our alternate vigils, lest hostile treachery should invade our walls, Echo, our comrade, shall repeat our shout, 'Ho! watch!' and Echo along the walls shall cry 'Watch!'"

These popular songs are not altogether destitute of eloquence, nor of a certain sort of poetry.

Te vigilante nulla nocet fortia,
Qui cuncta fugas procul arma bellica.
Cinge hæc nostra tu Christe munimina
Defendens ea tua forti lancea.
Sancta Maria mater Christi splendida,
Hæc cum Johanne Theotocos impetra,
Quorum hic sancta veneramur pignora,
Et quibus ista sunt sacrata mœnia,
Quo duce victrix est in bello dextera
Et sine ipso nihil valent jacula.
Fortis juventus, virtus audax bellica,
Vestra per muros audiantur carmina:
Et sit in armis alterna vigilia,
Ne fraus hostilis hæc invadat mœnia;
Resultet echo comes: eja vigila.
Per muros eja! dicat echo vigila!

They possess much more life and animation than many of the poems, which the scholars of those times attempted to compose in imitation of the ancients. Literature, however, must be at a low ebb in a nation, when it is necessary, even in its popular songs, to make use of a foreign language.

But at this very time, and in the heart of these very nations, another class of poetry was to be found—the poetry of the conquerors. The people of the North, who possessed a language of their own, which they were confident would continue to exist beyond their own times, and who looked forward to the respect which their posterity would pay to their memory, had yet traditions amongst them, if they could not boast of a written poetry. The most important dogmas of their faith, and the most brilliant events of their history, supplied them with materials for their songs, which were preserved by oral traditions. These poems kept alive that love of glory, that enthusiastic admiration of great actions, that vivacity of imagination, and that belief in the marvellous, which inspired the whole nation with poetical feelings, imposed upon the heroic the duty of seeking adventures, and sowed the seeds of that chivalrous spirit which was developed at a later period. We meet, in history, traces of these songs, which the northern nations carried with them, as though they were a part of their inheritance, into the conquered countries. The victors, however, speedily forgot, amongst their vassals, the language of their fathers, which was not preserved by any regular system of instruction. In two or three generations, these patriotic songs, being forgotten in the South, were only preserved amongst the Northern nations. Charlemagne, who was tenacious of the glory of his family, on the representation of Eginhard, caused these songs, which shed so much glory on the memory of his ancestors, to be collected. Louis le Debonnaire, his son, endeavoured, on the other hand, to consign them to oblivion. The Germans, in our time, have discovered an epic poem of the first class, the composition of which they date as far back as the first conquest of the Roman empire by the Barbarians—the Lay of the Nibelungen. The scene is laid at the court of Attila, the king of the Huns, about the year 430 or 440. The subject is the destruction of the race of the Burgundians, who served in the army of that monarch, and were sacrificed to the vengeance of one of his wives. This woman, herself a Burgundian, drew down this calamity upon her nation, in order to avenge the murder of her first husband, who had been put to death, a considerable time before, by his brothers. Amongst the other heroes who figure in this epic, we find Dietrich von Bern, or Theodoric the Great, the founder of the kingdom of the Ostrogoths in Italy; Siegfried, or Sigefroi, who appears to have been one of the ancestors of the French monarchs of the first race; a Margrave Ruddiger, the ancestor of the first house of Austria; and, in short, the heads of all the conquering dynasties which overturned the Roman empire. The events of this poem are historical, and are related with so much truth, and with such knowledge of the manners which prevailed at the court of Attila, that the poem could not have been written at a period very distant from these transactions. The Lay of the Nibelungen has probably existed since the age which immediately followed that of Attila; perhaps it was one of those compositions which owe their preservation to Charlemagne. Unfortunately, we do not possess it in its antique and original form. Retouched, at different periods, in order to make it conform to the variations in the language, and to gratify by interpolations the pride of new families, it assumed its present shape only about the end of the twelfth or the beginning of the thirteenth century. We shall again refer to this poem, when we treat of the literature of Germany.

It is not easy to assign the exact period, when the German language was abandoned by the conquerors in the south of Europe. In all probability, it was still preserved at the courts of the sovereigns, and in the assemblies of the nations, long after the feudatories, who had retired to their castles and were compelled to hold a communication with the peasantry, had relinquished the use of it. Thus the names of the Lombard kings, in the seventh and eighth centuries, and even of the Dukes of Benevento, in the ninth, indicate a knowledge of the German language, which, at all events, was kept alive at court, whilst all the laws and acts, even of these monarchs, were written in Latin, and the vulgar language of the people was already a Romance dialect. The laws of the Visigoths in Spain, and the mixture of German words with the Latin text, afford room for the same remark. Charlemagne and all his court spoke German, whilst the Romance was, very generally, the dialect of the people throughout all the south of France. Nothing can give a more correct idea of the mode in which a new language is thus formed, by a barbarous nation who inherit the institutions of a civilized people, than the process which we see, at the present day, taking place at St. Domingo. There, the French is what the Latin was in Europe till the eighth century; the African languages are the Teutonic dialects; and the Creole is the Romance. If, in future times, the Creole should become a polished language, abounding in orators and poets, its history in these times will present the same obscurity and the same contradictions which perplex us with regard to the origin of the Romance. We see, in like manner, in St. Domingo, the Jaloff, the Mandingo, and the other African languages, abandoned by the conquerors, whose mother-tongues they are, the Creole universally employed without being written, and the French reserved for the acts of government, its proclamations, and its journals.

It is thus that barbarian invasions, the misery of the people, slavery, civil wars, and all the evils which can afflict society, had destroyed the Latin language and corrupted the German. The most fertile lands, after the massacre of their inhabitants, had become the retreats of wolves and wild-boars; the rivers had overflowed their banks, and converted the plains into marshes; the forests, spreading from the mountains, had covered the face of the country; a few wandering inhabitants, of different races, traversing these vast deserts, fearing and flying from one another, and only meeting in combat, could not preserve any common language. But when the barbarians, as their dominion acquired stability, began to regard as their country the territories which they had conquered, and when they defended their frontiers and cultivated the soil, order was at length restored, and population followed in its train. A few generations filled the immense void which tyranny, war, famine, and pestilence had created. The dawn of more prosperous days appeared with the reign of Charlemagne and his successors. These happy prospects, it is true were disturbed by new barbarian invasions of Normans, Saracens, and Hungarians; but, notwithstanding their devastations, the inhabitants of these countries continued to acquire fresh strength. They rallied in their own defence; they inclosed their towns, their hamlets, and their castles, with walls; they promised one another mutual succour; and their intercourse, becoming frequent, induced them to polish their language. At this time, in the tenth century, it is probable that the languages, which are now spread over the south of Europe, had their origin. During the period which preceded this event, we only recognise two mother-tongues, and the rude progeny which arose from their admixture. As soon as the dialects were separated, they assumed a regular form, even before the languages from which they were derived. Every district, every town, almost every village, had a dialect peculiar to itself, which the inhabitants endeavoured to speak with purity, and to preserve without mixture. In the countries in which these dialects prevailed, their peculiarities are still strongly marked. The Lombards of Milan do not speak the same dialect as the Lombards of Pavia or Lodi, as an experienced ear will immediately discover. Even in Tuscany, where the language is so pure, the dialects of Florence, of Pisa, of Sienna, and of Lucca, are easily distinguishable. In Spain, independently of the Catalan and the

Gallician, which are different languages, there is a clear distinction between the languages of Aragon and Castile, and between the latter and that of Andalusia. In those countries which have distinguished their dialect by the name of the Romance, the same differences were formerly very discernible between the *patois* of Savoy and of Switzerland; but this language having been abandoned for the French by the well-educated classes, the lower orders, by the frequent communication between the two countries, have confounded the dialects, which have thus lost their primitive and local originality.

In former times, that spirit of aggregation and association, which is the consequence of long weakness and of the urgent necessity of uniting for the purpose of resisting aggression, was the means of retaining every family within their native town or village, and every individual within his own family. The countrymen, during the day, went armed to their fields, and at night fortified themselves in their hamlets. They avoided all communication, even by speech, with the neighbouring districts; the inhabitants of which they regarded as enemies. They never united themselves in marriage with them, and they considered all travelling amongst them as dangerous. In fact, since the slightest private injury might give rise to a state of warfare, it was an imprudent step, in any one, to connect himself, by ties of reationship or property, with his neighbours, who night at any moment become his enemies, and render him the sudden victim of an unexpected quarrel, in which he had no personal share. Thus these races were renewed by constant intermarriages amongst themselves, and sometimes for several generations. Whilst the inhabitants of a village were, perhaps, originally déscended from Romans, Greeks, Etruscans, Goths, Lombards, Hungarians, Sclavonians, and Alains, the individuals, thus assembled from the very extremities of the earth, were so well amalgamated by the process of time into one family, that they regarded as strangers all who were born a few miles from themselves; and differed from all the other inhabitants of the country in opinions, manners, costume, and language. This spirit of association has, doubtless, contributed to produce the curious phenomenon, which is observable on the frontiers of the two countries, where the mother-tongues were spoken. The transition from the German to the Romance is as abrupt, as if the two nations had been separated by hundreds of miles. The inhabitants of one village do not understand their neighbours; and there are some, like Fribourg and Morat in Switzerland, where the two races, having accidentally been reunited, have yet never mingled together. They have lived for ages in the same town, without the one ever passing into the quarter occupied by the other, and without the power of making themselves mutually intelligible.

Some of the towns, nevertheless, and some of the provinces, protected by a more firm and just government, succeeded, before the rest, in enlarging the boundaries of what was considered, by their inhabitants, as their country. They forgot their local interests in those of the state, and they abandoned the dialect of their hamlets for the more extended language of the whole community. In this manner arose the first polished languages of Europe. The reign of Bozon, the founder of the kingdom of Arles, may, perhaps, be considered as indicating this happy epoch in the Provençal, which thus advanced before the other languages of Europe. The dukes of Normandy, the successors of Rollo, in the tenth and twelfth centuries, appear to have favoured the birth of the French or Romance-Wallon. The reign of Ferdinand the Great, and the exploits of the Cid, in the eleventh century, by exciting national enthusiasm, formed, in the same manner, a rallying point for the Castilian language, and merged the dialects of the villages in the language of the court and the army. Henry, the founder of the Portuguese monarchy, and his son Alfonso, towards the end of the eleventh century, produced the same benefits in Portugal by their rapid conquests. The birth of the Italian may be referred to a later date, although the way had been prepared for it by the wise and beneficent administration of the dukes of Benevento. It was only at the Sicilian court, in the twelfth century, that this language, which was previously merely a rude dialect, was subjected to the rules of grammar.*

---

* In referring the birth of each language to the reign in which each nation appears to have attained a stable character, the Romance languages will stand in the following order:—

The Provençal, at the court of Bozon, King of Arles - - - - - - - - -	877	887
The Langue d'Oil, or d'Oui, or the Romance-Wallon or French, at that of William Longue-Epee, the son of Rollo duke of Normandy -	917	943
The Castilian, in the reign of Ferdinand the Great	1037	1065
The Portuguese, under Henry the founder of the monarchy - - - - - -	1095	1112
The Italian, under Roger I. King of Sicily -	1129	1154

CHAPTER II.

On the Literature of the Arabians.

The Western world had now sunk into barbarism, and population and riches had disappeared. The inhabitants, who were thinly scattered over those vast countries, found full occupation in struggling against the perpetual recurrence of evils, the invasion of barbarians, civil wars, and feudal tyranny. With difficulty did they preserve their lives, ever menaced by famine or the sword; and, in this constant state of violence or fear, there was little leisure left for intellectual enjoyments. It was impossible that eloquence should exist, deprived of its proper objects. Poetry was unknown, and philosophy was proscribed as a rebellion against religion. Even their very language was destroyed. Barbarous and provincial dialects had usurped the place of that beautiful Latin language, which had so long connected the nations of the West, and which had preserved to them so many treasures of thought and taste. But, at this very period, a new nation, which, by its conquests and its fanaticism, had contributed more than any other to abolish the cultivation of science and literature, having at length established its empire, in its turn devoted itself to letters. Masters of a great portion of the East; of the country of the Magi and the Chaldeans, whence the first light of knowledge had shone over the world; of the fertile Egypt, the storehouse of human science; of Asia Minor, that smiling land, where poetry and taste and the fine arts had their birth; and of the burning plains of Africa, the country of impetuous eloquence and subtle intellect; the Arabians seemed to unite in themselves the advantages of all the nations which they had thus subjugated. Their success in arms had been sufficient to satiate even the most unmeasured ambition. The East and Africa, from their respective extremities, had yielded to the empire of the Caliphs; innumerable treasures had been the fruit of their conquests; and the Arabians, before that time a rude and uncultivated nation, now began to indulge in the most unbounded luxury. With the conquest of those happy countries, over which pleasure had so long held sway, the spirit of voluptuousness was naturally introduced among them. With all the delights which human industry, quickened by boundless riches, can procure, with all that can flatter the senses, and attach the heart to life, the Arabians attempted to mingle the pleasures of the intellect, the cultivation of the arts and sciences, and all that is most excellent in human knowledge—the gratifications of the mind, and the imagination. In this new career, their conquests were not less rapid than they had been in the field, nor was the empire which they founded less extended. With a celerity equally surprising, it rose to as gigantic a height. It rested, however, on a foundation no less insecure, and it was quite as transitory in its duration.

The flight of Mahomet from Mecca to Medina, which is styled the Hegira, corresponds with the year 622 of our æra; and the pretended burning of the library of Alexandria by Amrou, the general of the Caliph Omar, with the year 641. This is the period of the deepest barbarism amongst the Saracens; and this event, doubtful as it is, has left a melancholy proof of their contempt for letters. A century had scarcely elapsed from the period to which this barbarian outrage is referred, when the family of the Abassides, who mounted the throne of the Caliphs in 750, introduced a passionate love of art, of science, and of poetry. In the literature of Greece, nearly eight centuries of progressive cultivation, succeeding the Trojan war, (from 1209 B. C. to 431) had prepared the way for the age of Pericles. In that of Rome, the age of Augustus was, also, in the eighth century after the foundation of the city. In French literature, the age of

Louis XIV. was twelve centuries subsequent to Clovis, and eight, after the developement of the first rudiments of the Romance language, or French. But in the rapid progress of the Arabian empire, the age of Al-Mamoun, the father of letters and the Augustus of Bagdad, was not removed more than one hundred and fifty years from the first foundation of the monarchy.

All the literature of the Arabians bears the marks of this rapid progression; and that of modern Europe, which was formed in their school and enriched by them, occasionally displays the vestiges of too hasty a developement, and of that excitation of spirit which misled the imagination and the taste of the eastern nations.

I propose, in this place, to present a general sketch of Arabian literature, in order to give an idea of its spirit, and of the influence which it has exercised over the nations of Europe; and, at the same time, to enable the reader to comprehend, in what manner that oriental style, which was borrowed by the Spaniards and the Provençals, spread itself over the other Romance languages. If we could penetrate deeper into Arabic literature, if we could unveil those brilliant fictions which have made Asia a fairy-land, and could taste the charms of that inspired poetry, which, in expressing every impetuous passion, employed the boldest yet the most ingenious figures, and communicated an emotion to the soul, of which our timid poets can form no conception, we should discover, in studies so novel and so different from those we have been accustomed to pursue, an ample recompense for any defects which might offend our more fastidious taste. But we can only flatter ourselves with the hope of impressing on the minds of others the beauties of a foreign language, in the same proportion as we are ourselves sensible of them. It is necessary to feel emotion in order to inspire it, and to be convinced of the truth of our own opinions, before we can demand the confidence of others. I am not acquainted with the Arabic, nor, indeed, with any of the languages of the East; and, on the present occasion, I shall confine myself to the selection of extracts from translations.

Ali, the fourth caliph from Mahomet, was the first who extended any protection to letters. His rival and successor, Moawihah, the first of the Ommiades (661—680), was still more favourably disposed towards them. He assembled at his court all who were most distinguished by scientific acquirements; he surrounded himself with poets; and as he had subjected to his dominion many of the Grecian isles and provinces, the sciences of Greece first began, under him, to obtain an influence over the Arabians.

After the extinction of the dynasty of the Ommiades, that of the Abassides bestowed a still more powerful patronage on letters. Al-Manzor, or Mansour, the second of these princes (754—775) invited to his court a Greek physician, whose name was George Backtischwah, and who was the first to present to the Arabians translations of the learned medical works of the Greeks. Backtischwah, or Bocht Jesu, was descended from those persecuted Christians of the Greek empire, who had been compelled, by their attachment to the dogmas of the Nestorians, to seek for safety and tranquillity amongst the Persians, and who had there founded in the province of Gondisapor, a school of medicine, which was already celebrated in the seventh century. Nestorius, patriarch of Constantinople from 429 to 431, and who maintained too strenuously, in opposition to the orthodox faith, the separation of the two persons as well as of the two natures of Christ, had manifested a persecuting spirit, of which he was himself soon afterwards the victim. Thousands of Nestorians, his disciples, had perished by the steel or the faggot, after the Councils of Ephesus and Chalcedon; and they, in their turn, massacred about the year 500, in Persia, seven or eight thousand of their orthodox or monophysitic adversaries. After these first reprisals, however, they devoted themselves to the pursuits of science with more ardour, and at the same time with more charity, than the members of the other Christian churches; and they preserved, in the Syriac language, the literature of

Greece, which was abolished by superstition in the empire of the East. From their school, at Gondisapor, issued a crowd of learned Nestorians and Jews, who, obtaining reputation by their medical knowledge, transported to the East all the rich inheritance of Grecian literature.

The celebrated Haroun-al-Raschid, who reigned from 786 to 809, acquired a glorious name by the protection which he afforded to letters. The historian Elmacin assures us, that he never undertook a journey without carrying with him at least a hundred men of science in his train. The Arabians are indebted to him for the rapid progress which they made in science and literature; for Haroun never built a mosque without attaching to it a school. His successors followed his example, and, in a short period, the sciences which were cultivated in the capital, spread themselves to the very extremities of the empire of the Caliphs. Whenever the faithful assembled to adore the Divinity, they found in his temple an opportunity of rendering him the noblest homage which his creatures can pay, by the cultivation of those faculties with which their Creator has endowed them. Haroun-al-Raschid, besides, was sufficiently superior to the fanaticism which had previously animated his sect, not to despise the knowledge which the professors of another faith possessed. The head of his schools, and the first director of the studies in his empire, was a Nestorian Christian of Damascus, of the name of John Ebn Messua.

But the true protector and father of Arabic literature was Al-Mamoun (Mahomed-Aben-Amer), the seventh Caliph of the race of the Abassides, and the son of Haroun-al-Raschid. Even in his father's lifetime, and during his journey to Khorasan, he had chosen for his companions the most celebrated men of science amongst the Greeks, the Persians, and the Chaldeans. Having succeeded to the throne (813—833) he rendered Bagdad the centre of literature. Study, books, and men of letters, almost entirely engrossed his attention. The learned were his favourites; and his ministers were occupied alone in forwarding the progress of literature. It might be said, that the throne of the Caliphs seemed to have been raised for the Muses. He invited to his court, from all parts of the world, all the learned with whose existence he was acquainted; and he retained them by rewards, honours, and distinctions of every kind. He collected from the subject-provinces of Syria, Armenia, and Egypt, the most important books which could be discovered, and which in his eyes were the most precious tribute he could demand. The governors of provinces, and the officers of administration, were directed to amass, in preference to every thing else, the literary relics of the conquered countries, and to carry them to the foot of the throne. Hundred of camels might be seen entering Bagdad, loade with nothing but manuscripts and papers; an those which were thought to be adapted for th purposes of public instruction, were translate into Arabic, that they might be universally intel ligible. Masters, instructors, translators, and com mentators, formed the court of Al-Mamoun, whic appeared rather to be a learned academy, tha the centre of government in a warlike empir When this Caliph dictated the terms of peace t the Greek emperor, Michael the Stammerer, th tribute which he demanded from him was a co lection of Greek authors. Science, in a peculia manner, experienced the favour of the Calipl notwithstanding the distrustful jealousy of som fanatical Mussulmans, who accused Al-Mamou of shaking the foundations of Islamism. Spec lative philosophy was allowed to indulge in th investigation of the most abstruse questions. Th art of medicine boasted, under his empire, of som of her most celebrated professors. He had bee instructed by the famous Kossa in the science the law, which, in the eyes of the Mussulmans, wa of all the branches of human knowledge, the mo sacred, and that to which they abandoned them selves with the utmost degree of ardour. Th Caliph himself was much attached to the study mathematics, which he had pursued with brillia success. He conceived the grand design of me suring the earth, which was accomplished by his mathematicians at his own expence. The Elements of Astronomy by Alfragan (Fargani), and the Astronomical Tables of Al-Merwasi, were the productions of two of his courtiers. Not less generous than enlightened, Al-Mamoun, when he pardoned one of his relations who had revolted against him and attempted to usurp the throne, exclaimed, "If it were known what pleasure I experience in granting pardon, all who have offended against me would come and confess their crimes."

The progress of the nation in science was proportioned to the zeal of the sovereign. In all parts, in every town, schools, academies, and colleges, were established, from all of which many learned men proceeded. Bagdad was the capital of letters, as well as of the Caliphs; but Bassora and Cufa almost equalled that city in reputation, and in the number of valuable treatises and celebrated poems which they produced. Balkh, Ispahan, and Samarcand, were equally the homes of science. The same enthusiasm had been carried, by the Arabians, beyond the frontiers of Asia. Benjamin Tudela, the Jew, relates in his Itinerary, that he found in Alexandria more than twenty schools for the propagation of philosophy. Cairo also contained a great number of colleges, and that of Betzuaila, in the suburbs of that capital, was so substantially built, that, during a rebellion, it served as a citadel for the army. In the towns of Fez and Morocco, likewise, the most magnificent buildings were appropriated to the purposes of instruction, and these establishments were governed by the wisest and most beneficent regulations. The rich libraries of Fez and Larace preserved to Europe a number of precious volumes, which had been lost in other places. But Spain was, more especially, the seat of Arabian learning. It was there that it shone with superior brightness, and made its most rapid progress. Cordova, Grenada, Seville, and all the cities of the Peninsula, rivalled one another in the magnificence of their schools, their colleges, their academies, and their libraries. The academy of Grenada was under the direction of Schamseddin of Murcia, so celebrated amongst the Arabians. Metuahel-al-Allah, who reigned in Grenada in the twelfth century, possessed a magnificent library; and there are still preserved, in the Escurial, a great number of the manuscripts which were translated for his use. Alhaken, founder of the academy of Cordova, presented six hundred volumes to the library of that town. In various cities of Spain, seventy libraries were opened for the instruction of the public, at the period when all the rest of Europe, without books, without learning, and without cultivation, was plunged in the most disgraceful ignorance. The number of Arabic authors, which Spain produced, vas so prodigious, that many Arabian bibliogra-)hers wrote learned treatises on the authors born n particular towns, as Seville, Valencia, or Cor- lova, or on those, amongst the Spaniards, who levoted themselves to a single branch of study, ıs philosophy, medicine, mathematics, and, more :specially, poetry. Thus, throughout the vast ex- ent of the Arabian empire in the three quarters ıf the globe, the progress of letters had followed hat of arms, and literature, for five or six cen- uries, from the ninth to the fourteenth or fif- eenth, preserved all its brilliancy.

One of the first cares of the Arabians, at the re- toration of letters, would naturally be to carry o perfection the vehicle of thought and imagi- ıation; and, in point of fact, the cultivation of heir language had been amongst the most im- ›ortant labours of the learned. They were di- 'ided into two rival schools, that of Cufa and hat of Bassora, from both of which a number of listinguished men proceeded, who have analyzed, vith the greatest subtlety, all the rules of the Arabic language.

The study of rhetoric was united to that of ;rammar; and, as it always happens in the lite- ature of every country, the precepts of elegant :omposition succeeded the models. The Koran vas not written in pursuance of the rules of the hetoricians. A confusion of ideas, produced by oo elevated an enthusiasm, and an obscurity and contradiction, which were the consequences of the turbulent life and diversified designs of the author, destroyed the unity and even the interest of that volume. The chapters, moreover, were preposterously distributed, not according to their date or connexion with one another, but according to their length, commencing with the longest and finishing with the shortest; and thus a work, in which the ideas might well have been less gigantic and extravagant, became often even more unintelligible by its singular arrangement. Notwithstanding all this, there is scarcely a volume in the Arabic language which contains passages, breathing a more sublime poetry or a more enchaining eloquence. In like manner, the first harangues which were addressed to the people and the armies, to inspire them with the new faith and with a zeal for combat, undoubtedly possessed more true eloquence, than all that were afterwards composed in the schools of the most famous Arabic rhetoricians. The latter, notwithstanding, translated with eagerness the most celebrated works of the Greeks on the art of rhetoric. These they adapted to their own language, though its genius was so dissimilar; and thus they created a new art, which was illustrated by more than one Arabic Quintilian.

After the age of Mahomet and his immediate successors, popular eloquence was no longer cultivated amongst the Arabians. Eastern despotism having supplanted the liberty of the Desert the heads of the state and the army regarded it as beneath them to harangue the people or the soldiers. They no longer relied upon their counsel or their zeal; they only called upon them for their obedience. But, if political eloquence was of no long duration amongst the Arabians, they were, on the other hand, the inventors of that species of rhetoric which is the most cultivated at the present day. They exercised themselves, alternately, in the eloquence of the academy and the pulpit. Their philosophers, so enthusiastic in the belief of the beauty of their language, took the opportunity of displaying, in these learned assemblies, all the measured harmony of which it was susceptible. In this pursuit, Malek was considered as their most fascinating orator, while Schoraïph was thought to unite, more skilfully than any other, the brilliancy of poetry with the vigour of prose, and Al-Harisi was elevated to the same rank with Demosthenes and Cicero. Mahomet, moreover, had ordained that his faith should be preached in the Mosques, and the name of orator, *khateb*, was specially appropriated, by custom, to these sacred orators, and that of an harangue, *khotbah*, to their sermons. Many of these are preserved in the Escurial, and the style of them is very similar to that of the Christian orators. The preachers commenced by offering up thanks; a profession of faith, and prayers for the sovereign and the prosperity of the kingdon followed. Then the orator entered upon his text and opened his subject; and, strengthening him self with the authority of the Koran and the doc tors, he attempted to excite, in the hearts of th people, a love for virtue and a detestation of vice

Poetry, still more than eloquence, was the fa vourite occupation of the Arabians, from thei origin as a nation. It is said that this peopl alone has produced more poets than all other united. Arabic poetry took its rise even befor the art of writing had become general, and, fror remote antiquity, a number of poets had annuall celebrated their academical games in the city o Ocadh. These festivals, Mahomet suppressed a a relic of idolatry. Seven of the most famous o these ancient poets have been celebrated by th Oriental writers under the title of the Arabia Pleiades; and their works were suspende around the Caaba, or Temple of Mecca. Mahome himself cultivated poetry, as well as Ali, Amrou and some others of the most distinguished of his first companions; but after him, the Arabian Muses seem to have been silent until the reign of the Abassides. It was under Haroun-al-Raschid and his successor Al-Mamoun, and more especially under the Ommiades of Spain, that Arabic poetry arrived at its highest pitch of splendour. It is at this period that we find that company of poets, chivalrous lovers, and royal princesses, whom the Oriental writers compare to Anacreon, to Pindar, and to Sappho. Their names, which I have vainly attempted to impress upon my memory, since I am unacquainted with their works, would also probably escape the greater part of my readers. The greatest celebrity to be attained in these languages, so distant from us and so different in their character and orthography, is of such a fugitive nature, that I have been unable to find in D'Herbelot, the names of those authors whom Andres places in the first rank ; as, for instance, Al-Monotabbi of Cufa, whom he calls the prince of poets. I shall not attempt, therefore, to class them according to their merit, since I am not sufficiently versed in those studies even to adopt the opinions of others. I shall prefer presenting, in this place, two fragments translated from other versions of the Arabic and Persian, and I shall accompany them with some general reflections on Asiatic poetry.

The first of the seven poems suspended in the Temple of Mecca, was an idyll, or *casside,* of Amralkeisi. The composition and plan of this ancient specimen of Arabian poetry may give some idea of what was afterwards accomplished.

The hero conducts two of his friends to the place where his harem was formerly situated, but which is now deserted, and there bewails the departure of his mistresses. As he recognises their traces, he sighs in despair, and rejects all the consolations which his friends offer him. "Yo have," say they, "on other occasions, exper enced afflictions not less distressing than this. "I have," replies he; "but then the perfume which waited on the steps of my mistresses, sti delighted my heart and intoxicated my sense My eyes, indeed, then were filled with tears, bu they were the tears of passionate love; the flowed down my cheeks and my bosom, and wit them my breast-plate was bedewed." "At least his friends rejoin, "let the memory of your pa happiness soothe your present griefs. Refle how often they have given new charms to life The hero, solaced by these recollections, recal all the happy hours he had passed, and the deligh he had proved in the company of Oneiza and Fatima, the fairest amongst the fair. He boas of having loved a virgin of unequalled beauty "Her neck," says he, "resembled that of th gazelle, when it raises it to descry a distan object. She was adorned with brilliant neck laces. Her long locks floated over her shoulders black were they as ebony, and clustering as th undulating branches of the palm. Slender an flexible as a thread was her figure, and her coun tenance illumined the shades of night, like th lamp of the lonely sage, who pursues his studiou vigil. Her very garments reflected the azure of th skies, and their fringes of precious stones were lik the Pleiades, when they appear above the hor zon." He adds, that, to obtain her, he had pierce through hostile lances, and braved the most frightful dangers. He then praises his own courage, and the constancy with which he had traversed, by night, dark and savage valleys; and at the same time he takes an opportunity of passing an eulogy upon his horse, which he describes in a strain of the most brilliant poetry. He then presents a picture of a chase, and afterwards of a festival; and the poem is terminated by an admirable description of the showers which refresh the burning desert.

In order, also, to give the reader some idea of the Persian, I shall translate a fragment of the Schah-Namah of Ferduzi, from a Latin version by Frederick Wilken. The lines of this poem are rhymed in couplets, like our heroic verse. The hero speaks, and expresses his love for the daughter of Afrasiab:—

"Behold! how the fields glitter with the red and the yellow rays! What noble heart of man would not beat with joy? How beautiful are the stars! How sweetly does the water murmur! Is not this the garden of an emperor's palace? The colours of the earth are varied, like the tapestry of the kings of Ormuz; the air is perfumed with musk; and the waters of the brooks, are not they the essence of roses? This jasmine, bending under the weight of its flowers, this thicket of roses, shedding their perfume, seem like the Divinities of the garden. The pheasant majestically advances, proud of its beautiful plumage, whilst the turtledove and the nightingale tremblingly descend upon the lower branches of the cypress. As far as the eye can stretch along the stream, a paradise blooms around. The plains and the hills, are they not covered with young girls, more beautiful than the angels? Wherever Menischeh, the daughter of Afrasiab, appears, we find men happy. It is she who makes the garden as brilliant as the sun; the daughter of an august monarch, is she not a new star? It is she who has shed her riches and her splendour over this valley; she is the brilliant star that rises over the rose and the jasmine. Peerless beauty! Her features are veiled, but the elegance of her figure rivals the cypress. Her breath spreads the perfume of amber around her; upon her cheeks reposes the rose. How languishing are her eyes! Her lips have stolen their colour from the finest wines, but their odour is like the essence of roses. Thanks be to God that we have been enabled to reach this blessed place, and that our journey was but of a day's length!"

After introducing these two fragments, which are certainly very inconsiderable, when presented as specimens of a literature as rich as that of all Europe, I shall only add, on the authority of Sir William Jones, that the Orientals, and especially the Arabians, possess many heroic poems, composed for the purpose of celebrating the praises of distinguished men, or of animating the courage of their soldiers. They do not, however, boast of any epics, although Sir William has given that title to the history of Timour, or Tamerlane, written in a poetical kind of prose by Ebn Arabschah. With more reason, it should seem, he has placed, in the rank of epic poems, the work of the Persian poet Ferduzi, called the Schah-Namah, of which I have just given a short specimen. This poem consists of sixty thousand couplets, on all the heroes and kings of Persia. The first half, which can alone be considered as possessing an epic character, describes the ancient war between Afrasiab, king of Transoxian Tartary, and Caikhosru, who is known to us under the name of Cyrus. The hero of the poem is Rustem, the Hercules of Persia.*

With the exception of this single work, the poetry of the East is entirely lyric or didactic. The Arabians have been inexhaustible in their love-poems, their elegies on the death of their heroes, or of their beauties, their moral verses, amongst which their fables may be reckoned, their eulogistic, their satirical, their descriptive, and, above all, their didactic poems, which embrace even the most abstruse science, as grammar, rhetoric, and arithmetic. But, amongst all their

* Ferduzi, the author of the Schah-Namah, died in the year of the Hegira 411, or A. D. 1019.

poems, the catalogue of which, in the Escurial alone, consists of twenty-four volumes, there is not a single epic, comedy, or tragedy.

In these different branches of poetry, the Orientals displayed a surprising subtlety, and great refinement of thought. Their style of expression is graceful and elegant, their sentiments are noble, and, if we may credit the Oriental scholars, there prevails, in the original language, a harmony in the verses, a propriety in the expression, and a grace throughout, which are necessarily lost in a translation. But it cannot escape us that the fame of these lyric compositions rests, in some degree, on their bold metaphors, their extravagant allegories, and their excessive hyperboles. It may justly be asserted that the greatest characteristic of Oriental taste is an abuse of the imagination and of the intellect. The Arabs despised the poetry of the Greeks, which to them appeared timid, cold, and constrained; and, amongst all the books, which, with almost a superstitious veneration, they borrowed from that people, there is scarcely a single poem. None of those relics of classical genius were adjudged worthy of a translation; and neither Homer nor Sophocles, nor even Pindar, was allowed to enter into a comparison with their own poets. The object of the Arabians was always to make a brilliant use of the boldest and most gigantic images. They sought to astonish the reader by the abruptness of their expressions; and they burdened their compositions with riches, under the idea that nothing which was beautiful could be superfluous. They were not contented with one comparison, but heaped them one upon another, not to assist the reader in catching their ideas, but to excite his admiration of their colouring. They neglected natural sentiment, and made an exhibition of art; and the more the ornaments of art were multiplied, the more admirable in their eyes did their work appear. On this account, they were perpetually seeking for difficulties to vanquish, though these added neither to the developement of the idea, nor to the harmony of the verse.

To those nations who possessed a classical poetry, the imitation of nature had discovered the use of the epic and the drama, in which the poet endeavours to express the true language of the human heart. The people of the East never made this attempt. Their poetry is entirely lyric. It ought, indeed, to bear a character of inspiration, to justify it in rising so far above the common language of nature. Under whatever name it be known, and to whatever rules it has been subjected, it will always be found to be the language of the passions.

The poetry of the Arabians is rhymed like our own, and the rhyming is often carried still farther in the construction of the verse, while the uniformity of the sound is frequently echoed throughout the whole expression. Their lyrical poetry is, moreover, subjected to particular rules, either in the form of the strophe, or in the order of the rhymes, or in the length of the poems. They extend to the whole sentence that poetical harmony which already prevailed in each distinct expression or individual verse. Two kinds of versification were in the most general use amongst the Arabians and the Persians, the *ghazèle* and the *casside*. Both these are compositions in couplets, and the second lines of each couplet rhyme with one another throughout the whole poem. The first lines are not rhymed. Thus, in that species of versification which the Spaniards have called *assonant*, and which they have apparently borrowed from the Arabians, the same rhyme, or rather the same terminating vowel, is repeated in every other line for several pages, whilst the first lines of each couplet are not rhymed. The *casside* is an amatory or warlike idyll, the length of which varies from twenty to a hundred couplets. The *ghazèle* is an amatory ode, which cannot comprise less than seven nor more than thirteen couplets. The first may be correctly classed with the *canzoni* of Petrarch, the latter with his sonnets; and as Petrarch composed a *canzoniere*, or collection of *canzoni* and sonnets on different subjects, and as the other Provençal, Italian, Spanish, and Portuguese poets had their *canzonieri*, the principal merit of which was the union of a variety of images with a single sentiment, and of many harmonious changes with only a single measure ; so the Arabians and the Persians had their *divans*, which are collections of *ghazèles*, varying in the termination or the rhyme. A perfect *divan*, in their eyes, was that in which the poet had regularly pursued in his rhymes all the letters of the alphabet, for they had a taste for constraint without harmony ; a taste which we can trace throughout all the Romance poetry, and amongst all the nations who have been formed in their school.

But, if the Eastern nations possess not the epic or the drama, they have been, on the other hand, the inventors of a style of poetry which is related to the epic, and which supplies, amongst them, the place of the drama. We owe to them those tales of which the conception is so brilliant, and the imagination so rich and varied ; tales, which have been the delight of our infancy, and which at a more advanced age we never read without feeling their enchantments anew. Every one is acquainted with the Arabian Nights' Entertainments, but if we may believe the French translator, we do not possess the six-and-thirtieth part of the great Arabian collection. This prodigious collection is not confined merely to books, but forms the treasure of a numerous class of men and women, who throughout the whole extent of the Mahomedan dominion, in Turkey, Persia and even to the extremity of India, find a liveli hood in reciting these tales to crowds who de light to forget, in the pleasing dreams of imagi nation, the melancholy feelings of the presen moment. In the coffeehouses of the Levant, on of these men will gather a silent crowd arounc him. Sometimes he will excite terror or pity but he more frequently pictures to his audienc those brilliant and fantastic visions which ar the patrimony of eastern imaginations. He wil even occasionally provoke laughter, and the se vere brows of the fierce Mussulmans will onl unbend upon an occasion like this. This is th only exhibition of the kind in all the Levant where these recitations supply the place of ou dramatic representations. The public square abound with these storytellers, who fill up th heavy hours of the seraglio. The physician frequently recommend them to their patients, i order to soothe pain, to calm agitation, or t produce sleep after long watchfulness; and thes storytellers, accustomed to sickness, modulat their voices, soften their tones, and gently sus pend them, as sleep steals over the sufferer.

The imagination of the Arabs, which shines i all its brilliancy in these tales, is easily distin guished from the imagination of the chivalri nations, though it is easy to perceive a certai resemblance between them. The supernatura world is the same in both, but the moral world is different. The Arabian tales, like the romances of chivalry, convey us into the fairy-realms, but the human personages which they introduce, are very dissimilar. These tales had their birth, after the Arabians, yielding the empire of the sword to the Tartars, the Turks, and the Persians, had devoted themselves to commerce, literature, and the arts. We recognise, in them, the style of a mercantile people, as we do that of a warlike nation, in the romances of chivalry. Riches and artificial luxuries dispute the palm with the splendid gifts of the fairies. The heroes unceasingly traverse distant realms, and the interests of merchandise excite their active curiosity, as much as the love of renown awakened the spirit of the ancient knights. Besides the female characters, we find in these tales only four distinct classes of persons—princes, merchants, monks or calendars, and slaves. Soldiers are scarcely ever introduced upon the stage. Valour and military achievements, in these tales, as in the records of the East, inspire terror and produce the most desolating effects, but excite no enthusiasm. There is, on this account, in the Arabian tales, something less noble and heroic than we usually expect in compositions of this nature. But, on the other hand, we must consider that these storytellers are our masters in the art of producing, sustaining, and unceasingly varying the interest of this kind of fiction; that they ar the creators of that brilliant mythology of fairie and genii, which extends the bounds of th world, multiplies the riches and the strengtl of human nature, and which, without striking u with terror, carries us into the realms of marvel and of prodigies. It is from them that we hav derived that intoxication of love, that tenderness and delicacy of sentiment, and that reverential awe of women, by turns slaves and divinities which have operated so powerfully on our chivalrous feelings. We trace their effects in all th literature of the South, which owes to this caus its mental character. Many of these tales ha found their way into our poetical literature lon before the translation of the "Arabian Nights." Some of them are to be met with in our ol Fabliaux, in Boccacio, and in Ariosto, and thes very tales which have charmed our infancy, passing from tongue to tongue, and from nation to nation, through channels frequently unknown are now familiar to the memory, and form the delight of the imagination, of half the inhabitants o the globe.

But the influence which the Arabians exercised over the literature of Europe, must not b measured merely by the admiration which thei poetry excited. The rapid progress which the made in the sciences, gave them an universa authority over the kingdom of the mind; an those whom the learned of Europe regarded as their masters in the sciences of arithmetic natural philosophy, history, and geography, appeared equally worthy to be the infallible oracle of taste. In reference, therefore, to European literature, it is important to enquire what was the state of science amongst the Arabians, at the period when our ancestors made their first attempts to emerge from a state of barbarism.

Every branch of history was cultivated with lively interest by the Arabians. Several authors amongst whom the most celebrated was Aboul Feda, prince of Hamah, wrote an universal History, from the beginning of the world to their own days. Every state, every province, every city possessed its individual chronicler and historian Many, in imitation of Plutarch, composed the lives of great men, who had been distinguished by their virtues, their achievements, or their talents. There was, indeed, amongst the Arabians, such a passion for every species of composition, and such a desire to leave no subject untouched, that Ben-Zaid of Cordova, and Aboul-Monder of Valencia, wrote a serious history of celebrated horses; as did Alasueco, of camels which had risen to distinction. Historical dictionaries were invented by the Arabians, and Abdel-Maleck accomplished for the nations which spoke his language, what Moreri has done for the Europeans. They possessed, besides, geographical dictionaries of great accuracy, and others on critical and bibliographical subjects. In short, all those inventions which curtail labour, dispense with the necessity of research, and afford facilities to idleness, were known to the Arabians. The knowledge of coins was familiar to them, and Al-Namari wrote the history of Arabian money. Each art and each science had its history, of which the Arabians possessed a more complete collection than any other nation, either ancient or modern. Al-Assaker wrote commentaries on the first inventors of the arts. Al-Gazel, in his learned work on Arabian antiquities, treated, in a profound manner, of the studies and inventions of his countrymen. Medicine and philosophy had even a greater number of historians than the other sciences; and all these different works were embodied in the historical dictionary of sciences, compiled by Mohammad-Aba-Abdallah of Grenada.

Philosophy was passionately cultivated by the Arabians, and upon it was founded the fame of many ingenious and sagacious men, whose names are still revered in Europe. Averrhoes of Cordova, was the great commentator on the works of Aristotle, and died in 1198. Avicenna, from the neighbourhood of Chyraz, who died in 1037, was a profound philosopher as well as a celebrated physician. Al-Farabi of Farab, in Transoxiana, died in 950. He spoke seventy languages, wrote upon all the sciences, and collected them into an encyclopædia. Al-Gazeli of Thous, who submitted religion to the test of philosophy, died in 1111. The learned Arabians did not confine themselves to the studies which they could only prosecute in their closets. They undertook, for the advancement of science, the most perilous and painful journeys; they became the counsellors of princes, and they were often involved in the revolutions which, in the East, are so violent and generally so cruel. Their private life was thus more varied, more chequered with accidents, and more romantic, than that of the philosophers and learned of any other nation.

Of all the sciences cultivated by the Arabians, philosophy was that which penetrated most rapidly into the West, and which had the greatest influence in the schools of Europe; and yet it was the one, the progress of which was, in fact, the least real. The Arabians, more ingenious than profound, attached themselves rather to the subtleties than to the connexion of ideas. Their object was more to dazzle than to instruct. Their obscurity gave them, in the eyes of the vulgar, an air of profundity. They exhausted their imaginations in search of mysteries; they enveloped science in clouds, instead of penetrating into its real nature, and dissipating the obscurity produced by the grandeur of the subject or the weakness of the human intellect; an obscurity which is not the offspring of philosophy, but th obstacle over which it is the aim of philosophy t triumph. More enthusiastic than enterprising they were willing rather to consider man as th oracle of all human knowledge, than to seek fo it in the primary sources of nature. Aristotl was worshipped by them as a sort of divinity In their opinion, all philosophy was to be foun in his writings, and they explained every meta physical question according to the scholasti rules.

An accurate translation and a subtle com mentary on the work of the Stagyrite, appeare to them the highest pitch to which the genius o a philosopher could attain. With this object the read, they explained, and they compared all th commentaries of the first disciples of Aristotle It is singular, however, that such able men with long study, with so much assistance, an after the industrious application of so many years never succeeded in comprehending and explain ing, with clearness, the authors who were th subject of their labours. They were all of them in error, and sometimes grossly so. Averrhoes in his translations and commentaries, has ofte no sort of connexion with his original. Th mania of discovering mysteries in the most simpl things, and hidden meanings in the cleares phrases, would have rendered the school of Aris totle, amongst the Arabians, if he could have ap peared once more upon earth, quite unintelligible even to the philosopher himself.

The natural sciences were cultivated by the Arabians, not only with more ardour, but with a juster view of the means it was necessary to pursue, in order to master them. Abou-Ryan-al-Byrouny, who died in the year 941, travelled forty years for the purpose of studying mineralogy; and his treatise, on the knowledge of precious stones, is a rich collection of facts and observations. Ibn or Aben-al-Beïthar of Malaga, who devoted himself with the same eagerness to the study of botany, travelled over all the mountains and plains of Europe, in search of plants. He afterwards traversed the burning sands of Africa, for the purpose of collecting and describing such vegetables as can support the fervid heat of that climate; and he subsequently passed into the most remote countries of Asia. In the three portions of the globe then known, he observed with his own eyes every thing strange and rare, which the three kingdoms of nature presented to him. Animals, vegetables, and fossils, all underwent his inspection; and he returned at last to his own country, loaded with the spoils of the East and the South. He published successively three volumes, one on the virtues of plants, another on stones and metals, and the third on animals, which contained more true science than any naturalist had hitherto displayed. He died in 1248 at Damascus, whither he had returned and where he was made superintendent of the gardens to the prince. In addition to these, there were others, amongst the Arabians, who merited the gratitude of posterity, such as Al-Rasi, Ali-Ben-al-Abbas, and Avicenna. Chemistry, of which the Arabians were, in some sort, the inventors, gave them a better acquaintance with nature than the Greeks or the Romans ever possessed; and this science was applied by them most usefully and exclusively to all the necessary arts of life. Above all, agriculture was studied by them with that perfect knowledge of the climate, the soil, and the growth of plants and animals, which can alone reduce long experience into a science. No nation of Europe, Asia, or Africa, either ancient or modern, has possessed a code of rural laws more wise, just, and perfect, than that of the Arabians of Spain; nor has any nation ever been elevated by the wisdom of its laws, the intelligence, activity, and industry of its inhabitants, to a higher pitch of agricultural prosperity than Moorish Spain, and more especially the kingdom of Grenada. Nor were the arts cultivated with less success, or less enriched by the progress of natural philosophy. A great number of the inventions which, at the present day, add to the comforts of life, and without which, literature could never have flourished, are due to the Arabians. Thus, paper, now so necessary to the progress of the intellect, the want of which plunged Europe, from the seventh to the tenth century, into such a state of ignorance and barbarism, is an Arabic invention. In China, indeed, from all antiquity, it had been manufactured from silk; but about the year 30 of the Hegira, A.D. 649, this invention was introduced at Samarcand; and when that flourishing city was conquered by the Arabians, in the year 85 of the Hegira, an Arabian, of the name of Joseph Amrou, carried the process by which paper was made, to Mecca, his native city. He employed cotton in the manufacture; and the first paper, nearly resembling that which we now use, was made in the year 88 of the Hegira, A.D. 706. This invention spread with rapidity throughout all the dominions of the Arabians, and more especially in Spain, where the town of Sativa, in the kingdom of Valencia, now called San-Philippo, was renowned from the twelfth century for its beautiful manufactures of paper. It appears that, at this time, the Spaniards had substituted, in the fabrication of paper, flax, which grew abundantly with them, for cotton, which was much more scarce and dear. It was not until the end of the thirteenth century that, at the instance of Alfonso X, king of Castile, paper-mills were established in the Christian states of Spain, from whence the invention passed, in the fourteenth century only, to Trevisa and Padua.

Gunpowder, the discovery of which is generally attributed to a German chemist, was known to the Arabians at least a century before any traces of it appear in the European historians. In the thirteenth century, it was frequently employed by the Moors in their wars in Spain, and some indications remain of its having been known in the eleventh century. The compass also, the invention of which has been given, alternately, to the Italians and the French in the thirteenth century, was already known to the Arabians in the eleventh. The Geographer of Nubia, who wrote in the twelfth century, speaks of it as an instrument universally employed. The numerals which we call Arabic, but which, perhaps, ought rather to be called Indian, were, undoubtedly, at least communicated to us by the Arabians. Without them, none of the sciences in which calculation is employed, could have been carried to the point at which they have arrived in our day, and which the great mathematicians and astronomers, amongst the Arabians, very nearly approached. The number of Arabic inventions, of which we enjoy the benefit without suspecting it, is prodigious. But they have been introduced into Europe, in every direction, slowly and imperceptibly; for those who imported them did not arrogate to themselves the fame of the invention, meeting, as they did in every country, people who, like themselves, had seen them practised in the East. It is peculiarly characteristic of all the pretended discoveries of the middle ages, that when the historians mention them for the first time, they treat them as things in general use. Neither gunpowder, nor the compass, nor the Arabic numerals, nor paper, are any where spoken of as discoveries, and yet they must have wrought a total change in war, in navigation, in science, and in education. It cannot be doubted but that the inventor, if he had lived at that time, would have had sufficient vanity to claim so important a discovery. Since that was not the case, it may reasonably be presumed that all these inventions were slowly imported by obscure individuals, and not by men of genius, and that they were brought from a country where they were already universally known.

Such, then, was the brilliant light which literature and science displayed, from the ninth to the fourteenth century of our æra, in those vast countries which had submitted to the yoke of Islamism. Many melancholy reflections arise when we enumerate the long list of names which, though unknown to us, were then so illustrious, and of manuscripts buried in dusty libraries, which yet, in their time, exercised a powerful influence over the human intellect. What remains of so much glory? Not more than five or six individuals are in a situation to take advantage of the manuscript treasures which are inclosed in the library of the

Escurial. A few hundreds of men only, dispersed throughout all Europe, have qualified themselves, by obstinate application, to explore the rich mines of Oriental literature. These scholars with difficulty obtain a few rare and obscure manuscripts; but they are unable to advance far enough to form a judgment of the whole scope of that literature, of which they have so partial a knowledge. But the boundless regions where Islamism reigned and still continues to reign, are now dead to the interests of science. The rich countries of Fez and Morocco, illustrious, for five centuries, by the number of their academies, their universities, and their libraries, are now only deserts of burning sand, which the human tyrant disputes with the beast of prey. The smiling and fertile shores of Mauritania, where commerce, arts, and agriculture attained their highest prosperity, are now the retreats of corsairs, who spread horror over the seas, and who only relax from their labours in shameful debaucheries, until the plague periodically comes to select its victims from amongst them, and to avenge offended humanity. Egypt has, by degrees, been swallowed up by the sands which formerly fertilized it. Syria and Palestine are desolated by the wandering Bedouins, less terrible still than the Pacha who oppresses them. Bagdad, formerly the residence of luxury, of power, and of knowledge, is a heap of ruins. The celebrated universities of Cufa and Bassora are extinct. Those of Samarcand and Balkh share in the destruction. In this immense extent of territory, twice or thrice as large as Europe, nothing is found but ignorance, slavery, terror, and death. Few men are capable of reading the works of their illustrious ancestors; and of the few who could comprehend them, none are able to procure them. The prodigious literary riches of the Arabians, of which we have now given only a very cursory view, no longer exist in any of the countries where the Arabians and the Mussulmans rule. It is not there that we must seek, either for the fame of their great men, or for their writings. What have been preserved are in the hands of their enemies, in the convents of the monks, or in the royal libraries of Europe. And yet these vast countries have not been conquered. It is not the stranger who has despoiled them of their riches, who has annihilated their population, and destroyed their laws, their manners, and their national spirit. The poison was their own; it was administered by themselves, and the result has been their own destruction.

Who may say that Europe itself, whither the empire of letters and of science has been transported; which sheds so brilliant a light; which forms so correct a judgment of the past, and which compares so well the successive reigns of the literature and manners of antiquity, shall not, in a few ages, become as wild and deserted as the hills of Mauritania, the sands of Egypt, and the valleys of Anatolia? Who may say, that in some new land, perhaps in those lofty regions, whence the Oronoco and the river of the Amazons have their source, or, perhaps, in the impregnable mountain-fastnesses of New Holland, nations with other manners, other languages, other thoughts, and other religions, shall not arise, once more to renew the human race, and to study the past as we have studied it; nations who, hearing with astonishment of our existence, that our knowledge was as extensive as their own, and that we, like themselves, placed our trust in the stability of fame, shall pity our impotent efforts, and recall the names of Newton, of Racine, and of Tasso, as examples of the vain struggles of man to snatch that immortality of glory, which fate has refused to bestow?

CHAPTER III.

Birth of the Poetry and Language of Provence—Influence of the Arabians on the genius and taste of the Troubadours.

WHEN, in the tenth century, the nations of the south of Europe attempted to give a consistency to the rude dialects which had been produced by the mixture of the Latin with the northern tongues, one of the new languages appeared to prevail over the others. Sooner formed, more generally spread, and more rapidly cultivated than its rivals, it seemed to assume the place of the forsaken Latin. Thousands of poets flourished, almost contemporaneously, in this new language, who gave it a character of originality which owes nothing to the Greeks or the Romans, or to what is called classical literature. They spread their reputation from the extremity of Spain to that of Italy; and they have served as models to all the poets who afterwards succeeded them in other languages, even to those of the North, and, amongst these, to the English and the German. All at once, however, this ephemeral reputation vanished. The voice of the Troubadours was silent; the Provençal was abandoned, and, undergoing new changes, again became a mere dialect, till after a brilliant existence of three centuries, its productions were ranked amongst those of the dead languages. From this period, it received no additions.

The high reputation of the Provençal poets, and the rapid decline of their language, are two phenomena equally striking in the history of the cultivation of the human mind. That literature, which has given models to other nations, yet, amongst its crowd of agreeable poems, has not produced a single masterpiece, a single work of genius destined to immortality, is the more worthy of our attention, as it is entirely the offspring of the age, and not of individuals. It reveals to us the sentiments, the imagination, and the spirit of the modern nations, in their infancy. It exhibits what was common to all and pervaded all, and not what genius, superior to the age, enabled a single individual to accomplish. Thus the return of the beautiful days of spring is announced to us, not by some single wonder of the gardens, in the production of which the artificial exertions of man have seconded the efforts of nature, but by the brilliant flowers of the fields, and by the prodigality of the meadows.

It is, unfortunately, very difficult to obtain the Troubadour poets; and, when obtained, to form a just idea of them. A learned Frenchman, M. de la Curne de St. Palaye, has, it is true, devoted his whole life to collecting, explaining, and commentating upon these works; but his immense collection, consisting of twenty-five folio volumes in manuscript, has not been, nor can be printed. He has left his writings in an unfinished and disordered state. The compositions of hundreds of poets are mingled together in each volume, and the labour of classing them, and of rendering them accessible, still remains to be undergone. The Royal Library of France contains vast treasures of Provençal manuscripts; but of these it is still more difficult to make any use. It is necessary to examine the volumes, from one end to the other, in order to acquire a knowledge of their contents; but the difficulty of the old writing and the contractions render this a painful task, in a language so little known. These manuscripts, moreover, are only within the reach of a few individuals. Several works on the influence of the Troubadours in Europe, have, it is true, been announced by literary men of celebrity; but hitherto none have appeared, nor has the text of any of those poets been given to the public.* We at present only find scattered

* Three years only after the publication of the first edition of this work, M. Raynouard published, in 1816, the first volume of his work, entitled *Choix des Poésies originales des Troubadours.* He has thus begun to supply that blank with the existence of which, for so long a period, in their literature and their history, the French have been so justly reproached. But hitherto this

broad, in works of different kinds, a few fragments, which may convey a knowledge of the Provençal versification, but which are not sufficient to familiarize us with this language, so as to enable us to taste its beauties. We are obliged to content ourselves, in treating of the Troubadours, with extracts from the Abbé Millot, who, taking the labours of St. Palaye as his ground-work, has given us, in three volumes, the Lives of the Provençal Poets, some notices of their works, and short translations of the most striking passages. But his style is, almost invariably, tedious and insipid.

The works on the lives of the Troubadours are much more numerous than the collections of their poems; and, indeed, their lives, independently,

---

volume, which only contains some enquiries into the formation of the Romance language and grammar, has not been followed by the collection of original poems, for which the public is so impatient. The second volume, it is said, will contain many specimens of the Romance language anterior to the year 1000, which have been discovered by M. Raynouard. The third and fourth volumes will contain almost all that remains of the amatory, political, and satirical poetry of the Troubadours. A publication like this can alone enable the literary world to form a judgment of this language and of its poets, which are at present rather matter of conjecture than of study. At the same time, the work must throw much light on the history and manners of ancient France.

[Since the above note was written, the five succeeding volumes of this valuable work have been published.—*Tr.*]

of their verses, present a sufficiently interesting and novel idea of their age, if they were better entitled to our confidence. Unfortunately, they are written without any attention to the rules of criticism, without regard to truth, and with the design rather of striking the imagination by brilliant and romantic adventures, than of adhering to facts, or keeping within the bounds of possibility. With respect to the biography of these poets, there are two original collections made by the monks still remaining in manuscript. One of these was compiled, in the twelfth century, by Carmentiere, a monk of the Isles of Hieres, by the direction of Alphonso II. King of Arragon and Count of Provence; the other by a Genoese of the family of Cibo, who is known by the name of *Monge des Iles d'Or*, or the Monk of the Isles of Gold; and who, at the end of the fourteenth century, corrected and perfected the manuscript of Carmentiere, and dedicated it to the reigning Count of Provence, Louis II. King of Naples, of the second house of Anjou. In 1575, John Nostradamus, Procurator of the Parliament of Provence, published his Lives of the Provençal Poets: a work without the slightest pretensions to critical knowledge, yet which, at the present day, forms the groundwork of their history. He was father of the celebrated physician and astrologer, Michael Nostradamus, whose obscure Centuries have been so often applied to every great event, and uncle of Cæsar Nostradamus, the author of a History of Provence, (fol. 1614) where these lives have been inserted. The Italians, with fewer opportunities than the French of becoming acquainted with the Troubadours, have displayed more zeal regarding them. Crescimbeni has devoted a whole volume to the Lives of the Provençal Poets, which he has selected from Nostradamus. All the Italian poets have mentioned them with respect, and all the literary historians of that country have recognised their powerful influence. The Spaniards have paid them no less homage. Sanchez, Father Sarmiento, Andres, and the Marquis of Santillana, have illustrated their history, and shewn the connexion of the Provençal poetry with that of the Arabians, and of all the Romance nations.

In Italy, on the renewal of the language, each province and each petty district had a dialect of its own. This was owing to two causes: first, to the great number of barbarous nations with whom the Romans had been successively mingled by the frequent invasions of their territories; and, secondly, to the great number of independent sovereignties which were established in that country. Neither of these causes operated upon the Gauls, at the time of the formation of the Romance language. Three nations had settled themselves there, nearly at the same time, the Visigoths, the Burgundians, and the Franks. After the conquest of the latter, none of the barbarous people of the North, with the exception of the Normans, succeeded in effecting a permanent establishment in any of the provinces; nor was there any mixture with the German nations, still less with the Sclavonians or the Scythians, to alter their language or their manners. The Gauls were thus employed for four centuries, in consolidating themselves into one empire and forming one language; during which period, Italy was successively the prey of the Lombards, the Franks, the Hungarians, the Saracens, and the Germans. Thus the birth of the Romance language in Gaul, preceded that of the Italian. It was divided into two principal dialects: the Romance-Provençal, spoken in all the provinces to the south of the Loire, which had been originally conquered by the Visigoths and Burgundians; and the Romance-Wallon, in the provinces to the north of the Loire, where the dominion of the Franks prevailed. The political divisions of the country were conformable to this primary distinction of nations and of languages. Notwithstanding the independence of the great feudatories, the north of France had always formed a single political body. The inhabitants of the different provinces were united in the same national assemblies and in the same armies. Southern France, on the other hand, after having been the inheritance of several of the successors of Charlemagne, was elevated in 879 to the rank of an independent kingdom, by Bozon, who w crowned at Mantes under the title of King Arles, and who reduced under his dominion Pr vence, Dauphiny, Savoy, the Lyonnese, and son provinces of Burgundy. The sovereignty of tl territory exchanged, in 943, the title of King f that of Count, under Bozon II.; but the kingdo of Provence was preserved entire, and continu in the house of Burgundy, of which Bozon I. w the founder. This noble house became extin in 1092, in the person of Gilibert, who left on two daughters, between whom his possessio were divided. One of these, Faydide, marri Alphonso, Count of Toulouse; and the othe Douce, became the wife of Raymond Bereng Count of Barcelona.

The union of Provence, during two hundr and thirteen years, under a line of prince who, though they did not play any brillia part abroad, and are almost forgotten in hi tory, never experienced any foreign invasion, bu by a paternal government, augmented the pop lation and riches of the state, and favoured cor mercial pursuits, to which their maritime situati inclined them, consolidated the laws, the la guage, and the manners of Provence. It was this period, that, without exciting observation, t Romance-Provençal, in the kingdom of Arl completely displaced the Latin. The latter w still employed in the acts of government; but the former, which was universally spoken, soon began to be applied to the purposes of literature.

The accession of Raymond Berenger, Count of Barcelona and husband of Douce, to the throne of Provence, gave a new direction to the national spirit, by the mixture of the Catalans with the Provençals. Of the three Romance languages, which the Christians of Spain at that time spoke, the Catalan, the Castilian, and the Galician or Portuguese, the first was almost entirely similar to the Provençal, and although, eventually, a decided discrepancy appeared, more especially in the kingdom of Valencia, it still retained an appellation borrowed from the name of a French province. The natives called it *Llemosi* or *Limousin*. The Catalans, therefore, were perfectly intelligible to the Provençals, and their union at the same court mutually refined them. The former, it is true, had already received some cultivation, either in consequence of their wars and intercourse with the Moors of Spain, or of the commercial activity of the city of Barcelona. That city enjoyed very ample privileges. The citizens placed a just estimation on the freedom they possessed, and at the same time caused it to be respected by their princes. Their riches, moreover, rendered the imposts exceedingly productive, and enabled the Counts to display a magnificence at their courts, unknown to other sovereigns. Raymond Berenger and his successors introduced into Provence the spirit both of liberty and chivalry, and a taste for elegance and the arts, with all the sciences of the Arabians. The union of these noble sentiments gave birth to that poetical spirit which shone out, at once, over Provence and all the south of Europe, like an electric flash in the midst of the most palpable darkness, illuminating all things by the brightness of its flame.

At the same time with the Provençal poetry, chivalry had its rise. It was, in a manner, the soul of the new literature, and the character which is thus given to the latter, so different from any thing in antiquity, and so rich in poetical invention, is one of the most important matters of observation in the history of modern literature. We must not confound chivalry with the feudal system. The feudal system may be called the real life of the period of which we are treating, possessing its advantages and inconveniences, its virtues and its vices. Chivalry, on the contrary, is the ideal world, such as it existed in the imaginations of the Romance writers. Its essential character is devotion to woman and to honour. But the poetical notions which then prevailed, as to the virtues which constituted the perfection of knights and ladies, were not entirely the fictions of the brain. They existed amongst the people, though perhaps without being carried into action; and when at last they acquired greater stability by the heroic songs in which they were inculcated, they began to assert a more practical influence over the people who had given them birth, and the realities of the feudal system became identified with the fictions of chivalry.

That bold and active life which distinguishes the feudal times was, no doubt, exceedingly attractive. Every lord, enjoying the most complete independence, lived in his own castle, convinced that God was his only judge and master. His trust was in his own strength, which enabled him to brave oppression, and to offer an asylum to the weak and the unfortunate. He divided with his friends the only possessions of the value of which he was sensible, his arms and his horses, looking only to his own prowess for liberty, and glory, and safety. But, at this period, the vices of the human character were developed with a force proportioned to the native vigour of the soul. Amongst the nobility, to whom alone the laws seemed to afford protection, absolute power had produced its usual effects, an infatuation which borders upon insanity, and a ferocity of which modern times no longer afford examples. The tyranny of a baron, it is true, extended not beyond a few leagues around his castle or his town; and, this boundary once passed, the fugitive was in safety. But within his domain, in which he confined his vassals like deer, he gave way, in the consciousness of his omnipotence, to the most ridiculous c: prices, and punished those who displeased hir in the most terrific manner. His vassals, wh trembled at his presence, had forfeited all tl privileges of human nature; and, in this class ‹ society, there perhaps existed not for several cer turies a single individual, who shewed any symp toms of greatness of soul or virtue. Frankne and loyalty, which are essentially chivalric vi: tues, are in general the consequences of strengt and of courage; but, in order to render the practice general, it is necessary that some cha: tisement or disgrace should attend their vi‹ lation. But, in the midst of their castles, tl lords were devoid of all fear, and public op nion had no influence over men to whom soci: life was unknown. The middle ages, conse quently, display more examples of scandalou treachery, than any other period. Love, it is tru had assumed a new character, which preserve the same shape under the operation of the realitie of the feudal system and of the romantic fictior of chivalry. It was not more tender and passionat than amongst the Greeks and the Romans, bu it was more respectful, and something of mys tery was mingled with its sentiment. Som remains of the same religious veneration cont nued to be felt for women, which the Germar evinced towards their prophetesses. They wer considered rather as angelic beings than as de pendants and inferiors. The task of serving and protecting them was considered honourable, as though they were the representatives of the divinity upon earth; and to this worship an ardour of feeling and a turbulence of passion and desire were superadded, little known to the Germans, but peculiar to the people of the South, and the expression of which was borrowed from the Arabians. Amongst the chivalrous, love always preserved this pure and religious character. But, where the feudal system extended its influence, the most extreme disorder prevailed, and, in the literature of that time, we find more scandalous instances, than at any other period, of the corruption of manners. Neither the *sirventes*, nor the *canzos* of the Troubadours, nor the *fabliaux* of the Trouvères, nor the romances of chivalry, can be read without a blush. The licentious grossness of the language is equalled, in every page, by the shameful depravity of the characters, and by the immorality of the incidents. In the south of France, more particularly, peace, riches, and a court life, had introduced, amongst the nobility, an extreme laxity of manners. Gallantry seems to have been the sole object of their existence. The ladies, who only appeared in society after marriage, were proud of the celebrity which their lovers conferred on their charms. They were delighted with becoming the objects of the songs of their Troubadour;

nor were they offended at the poems composed in their praise, in which gallantry was often mingled with licentiousness. They even themselves professed the Gay Science, *el Gai Saber,* for thus poetry was called ; and, in their turn, they expressed their feelings in tender and impassioned verses. They instituted Courts of Love, where questions of gallantry were gravely debated, and decided by their suffrages. They gave, in short, to the whole south of France the character of a carnival, affording a singular contrast to the ideas of reserve, virtue, and modesty, which we usually attribute to those good old times.

The more closely we look into history, the more clearly shall we perceive that the system of chivalry is an invention almost entirely poetical. It is impossible to distinguish the countries in which it is said to have prevailed. It is always represented as distant from us both in time and place; and whilst the contemporary historians give us a clear, detailed, and complete account of the vices of the court and the great, of the ferocity or corruption of the nobles, and of the servility of the people, we are astonished to find the poets, after a long lapse of time, adorning the very same ages with the most splendid fictions of grace, virtue, and loyalty. The Romance writers of the twelfth century placed the age of chivalry in the time of Charlemagne. The period when those writers existed, is the time pointed out by Francis I. At the present day, we imagine we can still see chivalry flourishing in the persons of Du Guesclin and Bayard, under Charles V. and Francis I. But when we come to examine either the one period or the other, although we find in each some heroic spirits, are forced to confess that it is necessary to antedate the age of chivalry, at least three or four centuries before any period of authentic history.

We shall return to the invention of the chivalric fictions, when we speak of the literature of the country where the first romances of chivalry were composed, northern France, and more especially Normandy. The Provençals, at the commencement of their poetical career, were not yet acquainted with them. The compositions of their Troubadours were entirely lyrical, and not epic. They sang, but they did not recite; and chivalry, amongst them, existed rather in gallantry and sentiment than in the imagination. They must necessarily have been acquainted with all the rules of chivalry, before they could form their compositions upon that model. On the most solemn occasions, in the disputes for glory, in the games called *Tensons*, when the Troubadours combated in verse, before illustrious princes, or before the Courts of Love, they were called upon to discuss questions of the most scrupulous delicacy and the most disinterested gallantry. We find them enquiring, successively, by what qualities a lover may render himself most worthy of his mistress; how a knight may excel all his rivals; and whether it be a greater grief to lose a lover by death or by infidelity. It is in these *Tensons* that bravery becomes disinterested, and that love is exhibited pure, delicate, and tender; that homage to woman becomes a species of worship, and that a respect for truth is an article in the creed of honour These elevated maxims and these delicate sentiments were mingled, it is true, with a grea spirit of refining. If an example was wanted, the most extravagant comparisons were employed Antitheses, and plays upon words, supplied the place of proofs. Not unfrequently, as is the case with those who aim at constructing a system o morals by the aid of talent alone, and who do no found it on experience, the most pernicious sentiments, and principles entirely incompatible with the good order of society and the observation of other duties, were ranked amongst the law of gallantry. It is, however, very creditable to the Provençal poetry, that it displays a veneration for the beauties of chivalry, and that it has preserved, amidst all the vices of the age, a respec for honour and a love of high feeling.

This delicacy of sentiment amongst the Troubadours, and this mysticism of love, have a mor intimate connexion with the poetry of the Arabians and the manners of the East than we shoul suspect, when we remember the ferocious jealousy of the Musulmans, and the cruel consequences of their system of polygamy. Amongst the Musulmans, woman is a divinity as well as a slave, and the seraglio is at the same time a temple and a prison. The passion of love displays itself, amongst the people of the South, with a more lively ardour, and a greater impetuosity, than in the nations of Europe. The Musulman does not suffer any of the cares, or the pains, or the sufferings of life, to approach his wife. He bears these alone. His harem is consecrated to luxury, to art, and to pleasure. Flowers and incense, music and dancing, perpetually surround his idol, who is debarred from every laborious employment. The songs in which he celebrates his love, breathe the same spirit of adoration and of worship which we find in the poets of chivalry, and the most beautiful of the Persian *ghazèles* and the Arabian *cassides* seem to be translations of the verses or songs of the Provençals.

We must not judge of the manners of the Musulmans by those of the Turks of our day. Of all the people who have followed the law of the Koran, the latter are the most gloomy and jealous. The Arabians, while they passionately loved their mistresses, suffered them to enjoy more liberty; and of all the countries under the Arabian yoke, Spain was that in which their manners partook most largely of the gallantry and chivalry of the Europeans. It was this country also which produced the most powerful effects on the cultivation of the intellect, in the south of Christian Europe.

Abdalrahman I. who detached Spain from the empire of the Abassides, and founded that of the Ommiades, commenced his reign at a period when the religious fanaticism of the Musulmans was considerably weakened. He introduced literature and the arts into the West, and in Spain they attained greater prosperity than in any other portion of the Musulman dominions. A complete toleration had been granted by the first conquerors to the Christian Goths, who, under the name of Moçarabians (mixed Arabians), lived in the midst of the Musulmans. Abdalrahman, who obtained and merited the name of the Just, respected the rights of his Christian subjects, and only sought to attach them to his empire by that prodigious superiority in arts, letters, sciences, and cultivation, which then distinguished the Arabians. The Christians, living amidst the Arabians, attempted to follow them in the career in which the latter had acquired such celebrity. Abdalrahman, who was the contemporary of Charlemagne, like him was the patron of letters; but, more enlightened than that prince, he pursued, even in the civilization of the Christians themselves, a more beneficent and permanent policy than that of the French monarch. The study of the Arabic language was considered by the Moçarabians as the only means of developing their genius.* As early as the middle of the ninth century, Alvaro of Cordova complains, in his *Indiculus luminosus,* that his countrymen have abandoned the study of their own sacred characters for those of the Chaldæans. John of Seville, for the convenience of those Christians who were better acquainted with the Arabian than the Latin, wrote in the former language an exposition of

* Four princes of the name of Abdalrahman made a distinguished figure in Spain, from the middle of the eighth to the commencement of the tenth century, and are easily confounded with one another. The first, Abdoul-Rahman-Ben-Abdoullah, was only a lieutenant or viceroy of the Caliph Yesid; and yet it was he who endangered France, and after having taken possession of half that country, was defeated in the plains of Tours, by Charles Martel in 733. This is probably the same prince whom Ariosto, in imitation of the ancient Romance writers, has introduced, by an anachronism, as the antagonist of Charlemagne, under the name of Agramante. The second, the individual mentioned in the text, Abdoul-Rahman-Ben-Moawiah, was the only one of his family who escaped being massacred in 749, when the Ommiadan Caliphs, his ancestors, lost the throne of Damascus. He wandered as a fugitive for six years in the deserts of Africa, when Spain declared in his favour. He enjoyed a glorious reign from 756 to 787. Two of his descendants, Abdalrahman II. (822—852) and Abdalrahman III. (912—961) bore with no less virtue and prosperity the titles of Caliph of the West, and of Emin-El-Moumenym (Prince of the Faithful); and thus the most brilliant exploits, and the highest prosperity of the Moors of Spain, are connected with the name of Abdalrahman.

the sacred scriptures. At the same period, a collection of the canons, according to the Church of Spain, was translated into Arabic; whilst, on the other hand, several treatises on the law and religion of the Arabians were composed in Spanish. Thus, throughout the whole extent of the Arabian dominions in Spain, the two languages were universally spoken, and, in this manner, the literature of the Arabians became familiar to the Christians of the West, without the latter being under the necessity of acquiring the Arabic tongue. The colleges and universities, founded by Abdalrahman and his successors, were frequented by all the learned of Europe. One of the most distinguished of these was Gerbert, who appears to have studied at Seville and Cordova, and who had acquired so intimate a knowledge of Arabian literature, and was so superior to his age, that after having been successively the admiration of France and Italy, and having ascended all the steps of the hierarchy, he filled the papal chair, from 999 to 1003, under the name of Sylvester II. Many others, and more particularly the restorers of the exact sciences in France, England, and Italy, in the eleventh century, completed their studies, by a residence of longer or shorter duration, in some of the universities of the south of Spain. Campanus of Novara, Gerard of Carmona, Atelard, Daniel Morley, and many others, confess, in their writings, that they are indebted to the Arabians for all that they have communicated to the public.

The monarchy of the Ommiades gave way, in Spain, to a number of petty Moorish sovereignties, which, ceasing to make war upon one another, became rivals in the cultivation of the arts and of letters. A great number of poets were attached to the courts of the princes of Grenada, of Seville, of Cordova, of Toledo, of Valencia, and of Saragossa; and numbers of astronomers, physicians, and chroniclers enjoyed, at those courts, a distinguished rank and the favour of the sovereign. Amongst these many were Christians and Moçarabians, and many belonged, both by religion and birth, to the two languages and the two countries. Whenever they experienced any mortifications at the courts of the Moorish kings, or whenever they felt any apprehension for their liberty or their property, they fled, carrying with them their talents and their industry, to the Christians, who received them like unfortunate brethren. The petty princes of the growing kingdoms of Spain, more especially those of Catalonia and Arragon, by which, until the year 1112, the Mussulman kingdom of Saragossa was surrounded, attached to their persons, the mathematicians, the philosophers, the physicians, and the Troubadours, or inventors of stories and songs, who had received their first education in the schools of Andalusia, and who entertained those courts by the tales and works of fiction which they borrowed from the literature of the East. The union of the sovereignties of Catalonia and Provence, introduced these men of science and the Troubadours into the states of Raymond Berenger. The various dialects of the Romance were not then so distinct as they are at present, and the Troubadours passed with ease from the Castilian to the Provençal, which was then reputed the most elegant of all the languages of the South.*

---

* In a little work published in 1818, *On the Language and Literature of Provence*, Augustus William Schlegel attempts to disprove the influence of the Arabians on the civilization and poetry of the Provençals. He attributes to the Spaniards of the Middle Ages, and he has done so on other occasions, the intolerance and religious hatred which their descendants evinced, under the three Philips. History does not mention this aversion between the Spaniards and the Moors. Until the time of Alphonso X. of Castile, there was not a single reign in which some Christian prince did not take refuge at a Moorish court, or when a Moorish sovereign did not seek shelter from a Christian king. For a hundred and fifty years, we see at the courts of the two Rogers and the two Williams of Sicily, as well as at that of Frederick II., Arabian courtiers mingled with Italian, and the judges of all the provinces in the two Sicilies selected from amongst the Saracens. The two nations were intimately blended, in the south of Europe, during at least five centuries. M. Raynouard has produced proofs of the existence of the Romance language at Coimbra in Portugal, in the year 734, in an ordonnance of Alboacem, son of Mahomet Alhamar. At this very time, all the provinces of the south of France had been conquered

Thus it was that the nations of modern Europe were taught the art of poetry; and the rules which were imposed enable us to recognise the school from which it proceeded. The first rule, which may be called peculiar to modern poetry, was rhyme. The invention of rhyming the terminations of verses, or the middle of the verse with the termination, was unknown to the Greeks, though it is sometimes to be found in the classical Latin poets, where, however, it appears to have been admitted with a different view than that which we propose to ourselves by the use of rhyme. It was introduced less for the purpose of marking the verses than the sense; and it was formed

---

by Abdalrahman. The taking of Toledo, in 1085, is not, then, the period which the Abbé Andres, M. Ginguené, or myself, have fixed as the æra of the Provençal poetry; nor does the discovery of the Romance poem of Boethius, anterior to the year 1000, give us the *coup de grace*. The taking of Toledo merely placed the most celebrated school of the Arabians in the power of the Christians. This school continued to spread the sciences of the Arabians in the West, long after the mixture of the courts had rendered their poetry familiar.

The influence of the Moors over the Latins is distinguishable in the study of science, philosophy, the arts, commerce, agriculture, and even religion. It would be strange then, indeed, if it did not extend to the songs which enlivened the festivals in which the two nations used to mingle, when we know how passionately fond they both were of music and poetry. The same air adapted by turns to Arabian and Romance words, necessarily required the same time in the stanza and the same distribution of the rhymes.

merely by a coincidence in the construction of the sentence. One verb, or one noun, was placed in opposition to another, and the effect of the repetition was to indicate, by the ear, that the poet was pursuing analogous ideas for three or four verses, after which the rhyming was abandoned. The Latin poems of the Middle Ages are more frequently rhymed, even as early as the eighth or ninth century. But it must be recollected that the mixture of the Arabians and the Latins took place in the eighth century, and it would, therefore, be difficult to prove that the first rhymed Latin poetry was not borrowed from the Arabians. So, also, with regard to the German rhymed poetry, the most ancient poems which we find rhymed in couplets, are not near so early as the first poetical attempts, which were always in rhyme, of the Arabians, or, indeed, as the first known intercourse between the two nations. It is very possible that the Goths, on their invasion of Europe, may have introduced the use of rhyme, from those Eastern countries whence they issued. But the most essential and antique form of versification, amongst the Teutonic nations, was borrowed from the Scandinavians, and consisted in alliteration, and not in rhyme. This alliteration is the repetition of the same letters at the commencement of the words, and not of the same sound at the termination. The Niebelungen, which was written early in the thirteenth century, is rhymed in couplets, and almost, it may be said, in the French style. But the same poem, in the Icelandic traditions, which was versified in the ninth or tenth century, is not rhymed.*

The consonants held a very important place in the languages of the North, which abound in them, as do the vowels in those of the South. Alliteration, therefore, which is but a repetition of the consonants, is the ornament of the Northern tongues; while *assonance*, or the rhyming of the terminating vowels, is peculiar to the popular verses of the nations of the South, although the practice has been reduced into a system only amongst the Spaniards.

Rhyme, then, which was essential to all the poetry of the Arabians, and was combined by them in various ways to please the ear, was introduced by the Troubadours into the Provençal language, with all its variations of sound. The

---

* The following is an example of the alliterations which supplied the place of rhyme. The lines are from the German imitation of Fouqué.

> *H*ell ver*h*eissen
> *H*at's mein o*h*eim,
> *K*urz mein *L*eben *k*ühn mein *L*ust;
> *R*asch mein *r*ache,
> *R*aub de*r* ausgang,
> *Fl*iessend blut im Ni*fl*ungenstam.

most usual form, in Arabic poetry, is the rhyming in couplets; not making the two accordant lines rhyme simply with one another, unconnected with the preceding or subsequent rhymes, as in the poetry of the Nibelungen, or in our heroic verse; but rhyming every other line together, so that the rhyme is continued through the whole stanza, or the whole poem. This is, likewise, the most ancient form of Spanish poetry. A well-known poem of the Emperor Frederick I. proves that the same order of rhymes was employed by the Provençals. This emperor, who spoke almost all the languages of his time, met Raymond Berenger II. Count of Provence, at Turin, in 1154, and bestowed on him the investiture of his fiefs. The count was accompanied by a great number of the poets of his nation, of whom almost all were amongst the principal nobility of his court. They delighted Frederick by the richness of their imaginations, and the harmony of their verses. Frederick repaid their attentions by the following lines:*

A Frenchman I'll have for my cavalier,
And a Catalonian dame,
A Genoese for his honour clear,
And a court of Castilian fame;

---

* Plas mi cavalier Francez,
E la donna Catalana,
E l'onrar del Ginoes,
E la court de Castellana,

The Provençal songs my ear to please,
And the dances of Trevisan,
I'll have the grace of the Arragonese,
And the pearl of Julian ;
An Englishman's hands and face for me,
And a youth I'll have from Tuscany.

In Arabic poetry, also, the second verse of each couplet frequently terminates with the same word, and this repetition has been, likewise, adopted by the Provençals. A remarkable example of it may be found in some verses of Geoffrey de Rudel, a gentleman of Blieux in Provence, and one of those who were presented to Frederick Barbarossa, in 1154. The occasion on which these lines were composed was an extraordinary one, and very illustrative of the wildness of the imagination and manners of the Troubadours. The knights, who had returned from the Holy Land, spoke with enthusiasm of a Countess of Tripoli, who had extended to them

---

Lou cantar Provençalez,
E la danza Trevisana,
E lou corps Aragones,
E la perla Juliana,
La mans e kara d'Angles,
E lou donzel de Toscana.

[The above translation is borrowed from one of the very able articles on the Poetical Literature of Spain, which have appeared in the Retrospective Review, and which are, we believe, correctly attributed to the pen of Mr. Bowring.— *Tr.*]

ne most generous hospitality, and whose grace nd beauty equalled her virtues. Geoffrey Rudel, earing this account, fell deeply in love with her, without having ever seen her; and prevailed upon ne of his friends, Bertrand d'Allamanon, a Troubadour like himself, to accompany him to the Levant. In 1162, he quitted the court of England, whither he had been conducted by Geoffrey the brother of Richard I., and embarked for the Holy Land. On his voyage, he was attacked by a severe illness, and had lost the power of speech, when he arrived at the port of Tripoli. The countess, being informed that a celebrated poet was dying of love for her, on board a vessel which was entering the roads, visited him on shipboard, took him kindly by the hand, and attempted to cheer his spirits. Rudel, we are assured, recovered his speech sufficiently to thank the countess for her humanity, and to declare his passion, when his expressions of gratitude were silenced by the convulsions of death. He was buried at Tripoli, beneath a tomb of porphyry, which the countess raised to his memory, with an Arabic inscription. I have transcribed his verses *on distant love*, which he composed previous to his last voyage. The French version, which I have added to this Provençal fragment, has no pretensions to poetry, but is merely to be considered as an attempt to preserve the measure and rhymes of the original. It is the Provençal itself, with its repetitions, its refinement, its occasional obscurity, though, at the same time, with its simplicity, composed in obedience to rules peculiar to itself but foreign to us, which it is my object to give. If I had wished to translate the Provençal into French verse, I must have paid a very different degree of attention to the construction of our language, and to its poetical character.*

Angry and sad shall be my way,
  If I behold not her afar,
And yet I know not when that day
  Shall rise, for still she dwells afar.
God! who hast formed this fair array
  Of worlds, and placed my love afar,
Strengthen my heart with hope, I pray,
  Of seeing her I love afar.
Oh, Lord! believe my faithful lay,
  For well I love her though afar,
Though but one blessing may repay
  The thousand griefs I feel afar.
No other love shall shed its ray
  On me, if not this love afar,
A brighter one, where'er I stray
  I shall not see, or near, or far.

* [The original Provençal, and M. de Sismondi's version, are both given below. The attempt which the Translator has made to present these singular verses in an English dress, is, he is aware, a very imperfect one.—*Tr.*]

Irat et dolent m'en partray
S'ieu non vey cet amour de luench,
Et non say qu' oura la veray
Car sont trop noutras terras luench.

But the Troubadours did not always adhere to this form, which is essentially of Arabic invention. They varied their rhymes in a thousand different ways. They crossed and intertwined

---

Dieu que fez tout quant van e vay
Et forma aquest amour luench
My don poder al cor car hay
Esper vezer l'amour de luench.
Segnour, tenes mi pour veray
L'amour qu'ay vers ella de luench
Car pour un ben que m'en esbay
Hay mille mals, tant soy de luench.
Ja d'autr'amour non jauzirai
S'ieu non jau dest'amour de luench
Qu'una plus bella non en say
En luez que sia ny prez ni luench.

Irrité, dolent partirai,
Si ne vois cet amour de loin,
Et ne sais quand je le verrai,
Car sont par trop nos terres loin.
Dieu, qui toutes choses as fait,
Et formas cet amour si loin,
Donne force à mon cœur, car ai
L'espoir de voir m'amour au loin.
Ah! Seigneur, tenez pour bien vrai
L'amour qu'ai pour elle de loin,
Car pour un bien que j'en aurai,
J'ai mille maux, tant je suis loin.
Ja d'autr'amour ne jouirai,
Sinon de cet amour de loin,
Qu'une plus belle je ne'n sçais,
En lieu qui soit ni près ni loin.

their verses, so that the return of the rhyme was preserved throughout the whole stanza; and they relied on their harmonious language, and on the well exercised ears of their readers, for making the expectation of the rhyme, and its return after many verses, equally productive of pleasure. In this manner, they have always appeared to me to have been completely masters of rhyme, and to have treated it as their own peculiar property; whilst the Germans, who pretend to have communicated it to them, managed it in the most timid manner, even in the twelfth century, rhyming their lines together, two and two, when they ought to have rhymed them alternately; as though they feared that, in a language so heavy as their own, two rhymes, not immediately connected, would be lost. Still less did they attempt to restore the rhyme after an interval of several lines. It is true, that at a later period, in the thirteenth century, the Minne-singers, or reciters of love-songs, the Troubadours of Germany, imitated this play upon the rhymes, and all the difficult variations which they saw in use amongst the Provençals.

Rhyme was the very groundwork of the Provençal poetry, whence it crept into the poetry of all the other nations of modern Europe. But it did not constitute all the requisites of verse. The number and the accentuation of the syllables were substituted by the Provençals, in imitation of the Arabians, as far we can judge, in the place of the quantity or the emphasis, which formed the basis of Greek and Latin verse. In the languages of antiquity, each syllable had, in the pronunciation, a sound, the duration of which was invariably fixed. The relative duration of these sounds was likewise determined by an exact standard; and, all the syllables being distributed into two classes of long and short, the versification was founded on this primary classification, and very much resembled the measure in music. The verse was formed of a certain number of measures which were called feet, and which marked the rise and fall of the tune, which always comprised the same time, and, whatever variation there might be in the sound of the pronunciation, the line still preserved the same uniform measure. This mixture of different feet gave the Greeks and Romans a prodigious number of verses, of various lengths and measures, in which it was essentially necessary to arrange the words in such a manner, that the ear might be struck by the equality of the time, and by the uniform cadence of the sounds. In none of the Romance languages can the ear distinguish the syllables into long and short, or assign them a precise and proportionate quantity. Accent, in them, supplies the place of quantity. In all of them, with the exception of the French, there is some one syllable, in every word, upon which the stress of pronunciation is laid, and which seems to determine the predominant sound of the word. The Provençal in particular, is strongly accentuated. The Troubadours, perceiving this, and being probably unacquainted with the harmony of Latin verse, produced something analogous to it in their own poetry, by mixing accentuated with unaccentuated syllables. The ear alone was their guide, for they did not, in their poetry, attempt to imitate the classical authors. Indeed they ill understood the rules which they themselves obeyed, and would have found it difficult to communicate them. The organization of their verse was more simple than that of the ancients. They only employed a measure which consisted of two syllables unequally accentuated, and that of two kinds, the trochee, consisting of a long and a short syllable, and the iambic, of a short and a long; and they preferred for constant use, and for the groundwork of their verse, the iambic, as did afterwards the Italians. The Spaniards, on the contrary, in their ancient poetry, made choice of the trochee, and preserved also, in their heroic poetry, *los versos de arte mayor*, the dactyl, consisting of a long and two short syllables, or the amphibrach, of a long syllable between two short ones. But it must not be supposed that the Provençals, the Spaniards, and the Italians, or even the Greeks and Romans, took any extraordinary pains in the selection of the syllables, so as to place the long and short syllables alternately and in the requisite order. Certain parts of the line required an accent or a long syllable. There were thus two or three syllables in each verse, as the fourth or the sixth, the eighth and the tenth, the quantity and position of which were fixed ; and, in consequence of the regular proportion in the modern languages, between the accentuated and the unaccentuated syllables, the former naturally drew the others into their proper places and communicated the measure to the verse.

These syllables, the quantity of which is fixed in the modern languages, are those which mark the cæsura, those which correspond with it, and those which terminate the verse. The cæsura is that point of rest which the ear, in accordance with the sense, determines in the middle of the line, dividing it into two parts of uniform proportion. In the verse of ten syllables, which is most frequently met with in the Romance languages, this point, which ought naturally to occur after the fourth syllable, may, according to the taste of the poet, be deferred to the sixth ; and it is one branch of the art, so to intermix these unequal proportions as to prevent the ear from being fatigued with the too great monotony of the verse. When the cæsura is placed regularly after the fourth syllable, that syllable ought to be strongly accentuated ; so ought the eighth, with which it corresponds at an equal distance ; and the same is to be observed with regard to the tenth syllable, upon which the voice dwells, at the end of the verse. In those verses, in which this disposition of the accents is varied, and the first hemistich is longer than the second, the cæsura falls upon the sixth syllable, which ought to be accentuated as well as the tenth. When all the equal syllables are accentuated, it almost necessarily happens that the unequal ones are not so, and the verse naturally divides itself into five iambics. The poet has only the power of sometimes substituting a trochee in the place of the first and third foot, or of the first and second; and the quantity of the line cannot be false, unless when the fourth, the eighth, and the ninth, or the sixth and the tenth, are not accentuated.*

* However fatiguing these details may appear, I have thought it necessary to add, in a note, some examples, drawn from different languages, for the benefit of those only who are desirous of seriously studying the laws of versification, in foreign languages. In fact, the prosody which the Provençals invented, is universally adopted in the modern languages, with the exception of the French. The French, who are strangers to these rules, are inclined to deny their existence. They judge of the verse of other nations by their own. They count the syllables and observe the rhyme, but whilst they neglect the study of the prosody, it is impossible for them to feel that harmony of language to which poetry owes its most powerful effects.

In prosody, two marks are employed; the one (–) distinguishes the long or accentuated syllables; the other (˘) the short syllables. These I have placed over the corresponding syllables in the verse, and I have divided the hemistich after the cæsura by this mark (=).

I must claim the indulgence of the reader, for these dry and fatiguing details, into which I am compelled to enter. The laws of versification which the Troubadours discovered, are of very

---

Lo jorn que us vi = o donna primament
Quant a vos plac = que us mi laisest vezer
Parti mon cor = tot autre pensamen,
E forum ferm en vos = tuit mei voler
Que sim passez = Donna en mon cor l'enveia
A un dolz riz = et ab un dolz esgard
Mie quant es = mi fezes oblidar.

Arnaud de Marveilh.

In the Provençal verses, at least in those of ten syllables, the quantity is more difficult to fix, since the poet has the choice of such a variety of measures, and has only one, or at most two feet, in the verse, the quantity of which is determined. Still, it is always the variation of the accent which gives the verse its harmony.

The same rules apply, without exception, to all the other modern languages; and the Italian verses, for instance, ought to be scanned, on the Provençal principle, thus:

Miser chi mal o pran = do si con fida
Ch' ognor star deb = bia il maleficio occulto,
Che quando ogn' altro tac = cia intorno grida
L'aria e la terra stes = sa in ch' è sepulto.

Ariosto.

It should be remarked, that the cæsura often divides a word in the middle, but, in this case, the accent is on the first syllable; and thus, the mute syllable which follows, being scarcely sounded, re-attaches itself to the first hemistich. The lines, in Italian,

by some secret and mysterious associations, with our feelings and our emotions, and with all that speaks to our imaginations and our hearts. It would be wrong, in studying the divine language of poetry, to regard it merely as the trammels of thought. Poetry excites our emotions, and awakens or captivates our passions, only because it is something which comes more home to our bosoms than prose; something, which seizes upon our whole being, by the senses as well as by the soul, and impresses us more deeply than language alone could do. Symmetry is one of the properties of the soul. It is an idea which precedes all knowledge, which is applicable to all the arts, and which is inseparable from our perceptions of beauty. It is by a principle, anterior to all reflection, that we look, in buildings, in furniture, and in every production of human art, for the same proportion which the hand of Nature has so visibly imprinted on the figure of man and of the inferior animals. This symmetry, which is founded on the harmonious relation of the parts to the whole, and is so different from uniformity, displays itself in the regular return of the strophes of an ode, as well as in the correspondence of the wings of a palace. It is more distinguishable in modern poetry than in that of antiquity, in consequence of the rhyme, which harmonizes the different parts of the same stanza. Rhyme is an appeal to our memory and to our expectations. It awakens the sensations we have already experienced, and it makes us wish for new ones. It encreases the importance of sound, and gives, if I may so express myself, a colour to the words. In our modern poetry, the importance of the syllables is not measured solely by their duration, but by the associations they afford; and vowels, by turns, slightly, perceptibly, or emphatically marked, are no longer unnoticed, when the rhyme announces their approach and determines their position. What would become of the Provençal poetry, if we perused it only to discover the sentiment, such as it would appear in languid prose? It was not the ideas alone which gave delight, when the Troubadour adapted his beautiful language to the melodious tones of his harp; when, inspired by valour, he uttered his bold, nervous, and resounding rhymes; or, in tender and voluptuous strains, expressed the vehemence of his love. The rules of his art, even more than the words in which he expressed himself, were in accordance with his feelings. The rapid and recurring accentuation, which marked every second syllable in his iambic verses, seemed to correspond with the pulsations of his heart, and the very measure of the language answered to the movements of his own soul. It was by this exquisite sensibility to musical impressions, and by this delicate organization, that the Troubadours became the inventors of an art, which they themselves were unable to explain. They discovered the means of communicating, by this novel harmony, those emotions of the soul, which all poets have endeavoured to produce, but which they are now able to effect, only by following the steps of these inventors of our poetical measures.

CHAPTER IV.

On the State of the Troubadours, and, on their Amatory and Martial Poems.

The Counts of Provence were not the only sovereigns, amongst those of the south of France, at whose court the Langue d'Oc, or Romance-Provençal, was spoken, and where the reciters of tales, and the poets, who had been formed in the Moorish schools, found a flattering reception and sure protection. At the conclusion of the eleventh century, one half of France was governed by independent princes, whose only common bond was the Provençal language, which was spoken alike by them all. The most renowned of these sovereigns were, the Counts of Toulouse, the Dukes of Aquitain, of the house of Poitou, the Dauphins of Viennois and of Auvergne, the Princes of Orange, of the house of Baux, and the Counts de Foix. After these, came an infinite number of viscounts, barons, and lords, who in some petty province or town, or even castle, enjoyed the prerogatives of sovereignty. To these inferior courts, the physicians, the astrologers, and the reciters of tales, resorted, in pursuit of fortune, and introduced into the North an acquaintance with the learning and the arts of Spain. Their highest ambition, probably, was to amuse the leisure of the great, and to please them by their flatteries. The recompense which they promised themselves, and which they received alike from the Christian and Moorish princes, was the permission to take a part in the festivals, to which they gave animation by their recitals and their songs, and to accept the presents of rich habits and of horses which were there bestowed upon them. But it was to heroes they addressed themselves; and as they sang of love and glory, their verses, penetrating to the inmost hearts of their hearers, communicated to them the deep emotion which swelled within the poet's own bosom. It was thus that the subject of their songs gave an elevation to their characters, and that the fugitives from the Moorish territories became the instructors of princes. Scarcely had the art of song been introduced into southern France, and the rules of versification been invented, when poetry became the recreation of the most illustrious men. The lyric form, which it had received from the Arabians, rendered it proper to convey only the noblest sentiments. In verse, the poet sang his love, his martial ardour, and the independence of his soul; and no sovereign sate upon so proud a throne, as not to think himself honoured in the capacity of expressing such sentiments. The amorous monarchs celebrated their mistresses in verse; and when the first sovereigns of Europe had thus assumed their rank, amongst the poets or Troubadours, there was not a single baron or knight, who did not think it his duty to superadd to his fame, as a brave and gallant man, the reputation of a gentle Troubadour. To these poetical pursuits, nothing more was necessary, than a perception of what is musical and harmonious. In obedience to this faculty, the words naturally fell into the order most agreeable to the ear, and the thoughts, the images, and the sentiments, acquired that general accordance and melodious congruity which seem to proceed from the soul, and to which study can add nothing. It is astonishing to observe what very slight traces of learning, the poetry of the Troubadours displays. No allusion to history or mythology; no comparison, borrowed from foreign manners; no reference to the sciences or the learning of the schools, are mingled with their simple effusions of sentiment. This fact enables us to comprehend, how it was possible for princes and knights, who were often unable to read, to be yet ranked amongst the most ingenious Troubadours.

Several public events materially contributed to enlarge the sphere of intellect of the knights of the Langue d'Oc; to make enthusiasm, rather than interest, their spring of action; to present a new world to their eyes, and to strike their imaginations with extraordinary images. Never does a nation display a more poetical character, than when some great and uncommon circumstances operate upon minds, yet endowed with all the vigour of youth.

The first of these events was the conquest of Toledo, and of all New Castile, by Alfonso VI. King of Castile. That monarch, who was then seconded by the hero of Spain, the Cid Rodriguez, or Ruy Diaz de Bivar, invited a number of French, Provençal, and Gascon knights, who were connected with him by his marriage with Constance of Burgundy, to take part in the expedition, in which he was engaged from 1083 to 1085, and the result of which more than doubled his territories, and confirmed the preponderance of the Christians in Spain. This was the first war against the infidels, in which, for two hundred years, the French had been engaged, and it preceded, by forty years, the preaching of the first crusade. The warriors, gathered together in one army from various states, finding themselves thus in the midst of stranger nations, became still more deeply attached to glory. The fame of the Cid was pre-eminent above that of every other man of his age. The Moorish and Castilian poets had already begun to celebrate it, and to prove how well their popular songs were calculated to spread the renown of their heroes. The conquest of Toledo, also, mingled the Moors and the Christians in a more intimate manner. A complete toleration was granted to such of the Moors as remained subject to the King of Castile; and Alfonso engaged, even by oath, to permit them to use the cathedral as a mosque. Of this, however, he afterwards deprived them, at the solicitation of his wife, and in obedience to a pretended miracle. From this period, even until the reign of Philip III., for the space of 530 years, Toledo always contained a numerous Moorish population, intermingled with the Christians. This city, one of the most celebrated universities of the Arabians, retained its schools and all its learned institutions, and spread amongst the Christians, the knowledge of Eastern letters. The Moçarabians assumed a rank in the court and the army, and the French knights found themselves residing amongst men, whose imagination, intellect, and taste, had been developed by the Saracens. When, after the capture of Toledo, on the 25th of May, 1085, they returned from this glorious expedition, they carried back with them, into their own country, a portion of that cultivation of mind, which they had witnessed in Spain.

The second circumstance, which contributed to impress a poetical character on the eleventh and twelfth centuries, was the preaching of the crusade in 1095, and the continued communication which was in consequence established, between Christendom and the Levant. The crusade appears to have been preached with much zeal in the countries of the Langue d'Oc. Clermont d'Auvergne, where the council was held, was within that territory. The Pontifical Legate at the crusade, the Bishop of Puy, the Count of Toulouse, Raymond de Saint-Gilles, and the Duke of Acquitain, William IX. Count of Poitou, were at that time the principal sovereigns of the south of France, and amongst the most distinguished of the Crosses. Of all the events recorded in the history of the world, there is, perhaps, not one of a nature so highly poetical as the crusades; not one, which presents a more powerful picture of the grand effects of enthusiasm, of noble sacrifices of self-interest, which is ever prosaic in its nature, to faith, sentiment, and passion, which are essentially poetical. Many of the Troubadours partook of the enthusiasm of their countrymen, and accompanied them to the crusade. The most distinguished of these poets as well as warriors, was William IX. Count of Poitou, and Duke of Acquitain, the oldest of the poets, whose works M. de la Curne de Sainte-Palaye has collected. He was born in 1071, and died in 1127. The famous Eleanor, Queen of France, and afterwards of England, who, when divorced by Louis le Jeune, transferred the sovereignty of Guienne, Poitou, and Saintonge, to Henry II. of England, was grand-daughter to this prince.

The succession of the Kings of England to the sovereignty of a considerable part of the countries where the Langue d'Oc prevailed, was the third great political event which influenced the manners and opinions of the people, and consequently of the Troubadours also, by mingling the different races of men, introducing poets to the courts of the most powerful monarchs, and extending to literature something of that national interest, to which the long rivalry between the Kings of France and England had given rise. On the other hand, the encouragement given to the Troubadours, by the kings of the house of Plantagenet, had a great influence on the formation of the English language, and furnished Chaucer, the father of English literature, with his first model for imitation.

This language was adopted, at one and the same time, by the sovereigns of one half of Europe. We find Provençal verses composed by the Emperor of Germany, Frederick Barbarossa, Richard I. of England, Alfonso II. and Peter III. of Aragon, Frederick III. of Sicily, the Dauphin of Auvergne, the Count de Foix, the Prince of Orange, and the Marquis of Montferrat, King of Thessalonica. It well deserved the preference which it obtained over all other languages. The grammar was regular and complete; the verbs had the same inflexions which the Italian verbs have at the present day, and even more.* The regularity of their moods allowed the suppression of the pronouns, and thus added to the rapidity of the expression. The substantives had a quality peculiar to this language, of being employed either as masculines or as feminines, at the option of the writer.† The flexibility of the substantives gave the language a more figurative character. Inanimate beings were clothed with a sex at the will of the poet, and were by turns masculine and fierce, or sweet and voluptuous, according to the gender which was assigned to them. The substantives, as well as the adjectives, had terminations which expressed all the modifications, both of augmentation and diminution, which denoted either agreeable or disagreeable

---

* As, for instance, a peculiar gerund—*tout-barjan*, signifying the duration of the act of speaking; *espandiguen*, the duration of the act of extending.

† Thus they said *lou cap*, or *la capa*, the head; *l'os*, or *l'ossa*, the bone; *un fais*, or *una faissa*, a burden; *lou rusc*, or *la rusca*, the bark; *lou ram*, or *la rama*, the foliage; *un fielh*, or *una fielha*, a leaf, &c.

Another peculiarity of this language, which is not to be found in any other, is its having preserved, instead of declensions, a sign which distinguishes the nominative and the vocative from the other cases. In general the nominative singular has its termination in *s*, which is abandoned in the other singular cases; whilst the nominative plural wants the *s*, and the other plural cases have it. Some words have their termination in *aire* in the nominative, and in *ador* in other cases: *El Trobaire diz al Trobador*—the Troubadour said to the Troubadour.

ideas, contempt, ridicule, or approbation. This is still the case in the Italian and Spanish; whilst, in French, the diminutives have become solely expressive of the ridiculous, and augmentatives are no longer known. The Provençal language, as we now find it written, appears to us to be studded with consonants, but most of those which terminated the words were suppressed in the pronunciation. On the other hand, almost all the diphthongs were pronounced with the two sounds united in the same syllable (for example, *daürada*, and not *dorada)*, which gave greater fulness and richness to the language. A great number of the words were figurative, and expressed their signification in their sound. Many were peculiar to the language, and can only be translated by employing a periphrasis.*

This beautiful language was exclusively employed, for a long time, in those compositions to which it was so peculiarly appropriate—in amatory and martial songs. The multitude of Provençal poems which are extant, may be classed under one or the other of these two divisions; and although they bear different names, they all of them equally belong to the lyrical style of composition. Love and war furnished the only occupation, the only delight of all the kings and soldiers, of the most powerful barons and the most humble knights of

* See M. Fabre D'Olivet, Preface to his *Poésies Occitaniques.*

the age. Now kneeling at the feet of their mistresses, whom they often addressed in language applicable only to the Deity, and now braving their enemies, their verses bear the double imprint of their pride of character and of the power of their love. The poems of the Provençals, according as they expressed the one or the other of these passions, were divided into *chanzos* and *sirventes.* The object of the former was gallantry; of the latter war, politics, or satire. The structure of both was the same. The Provençal songs were, in general, composed of five stanzas and an envoy. The form of the stanza was perfectly regular, and often so uniform, that the same rhyme was repeated in the same place in each stanza. These rhymes were distinguished, as in the French, into masculine and feminine; that is to say, into those accentuated on the last syllable, and those on the penultimate; and were dextrously interwoven, not so as to follow one another in the regular order of our poetry, but in such a manner that their disposition always produced a harmony, conformable to the sense of the verse and the feelings of the hearer. This original perception of harmony afterwards gave place, it is true, to the refinement of affecting to vanquish difficulties, and the Troubadours, by imposing upon themselves rules which were both ridiculous and difficult to obey, with regard to the return of the same rhymes, or of the same words at the termination of the verses, contracted a puerile habit of playing with words, to which they too often sacrificed both the idea and the sentiment. They displayed a more delicate and correct taste in the choice of the different metres which they employed; in the mixture of long and short verses, from the heavy Alexandrine to the lines of one or two syllables; and in the skilful use of the regular terminations in the stanza. All our knowledge upon this subject is derived from their experience. It was they who invented those varied measures of the stanzas, which give so much harmony to the *canzoni* of Petrarch. We are likewise indebted to them for the forms of the French ode, and particularly for the beautiful stanza of ten lines, in one quatrain and two tercets, which J. B. Rousseau has employed in his most elevated subjects. Some sonnets are also found in their language, but, at the same time, it appears to me, that they are posterior to the earliest Italian sonnets, and even to those of Petrarch. Lastly, the ballad, the first verse of which is converted into a burthen for the others, and in which the return of the same thought produces such a graceful and pleasing effect, is of Provençal origin.

It is my wish rather to familiarize my readers with the Troubadours themselves, and to make them acquainted with their poems, than to detail the opinions which have been entertained respecting them, and the romances of which they have been the heroes. But of all the poems which it will be necessary for us to notice, these are the least likely to produce an impression in a translation. We must not look, in them, for that wit and that faculty of invention, which in modern poetry shed such brilliancy upon the ideas, by ingenious contrasts and by happy reflections of light. Nor must we look for profound thoughts. The Provençals were too young a nation, they had seen too little, and they had not sufficiently analyzed and compared what they saw, to entitle them to lay any claim to the empire of thought. Invention seems to have been out of the question in so narrow a field, and in compositions which never dwelt on more than two sentiments. Their merit entirely consists in a certain harmony and simplicity of expression, which cannot be transferred to another language. I have therefore been obliged, whenever I have wished to give an idea of their imagination and their sensibility, or of the charm and elegance of their style, to direct the attention of my readers to their personal character. It is not in my power to awaken, for their talents, an admiration which can only be felt by those who thoroughly understand their language; but without judging of them as poets, their adventures may yet excite our interest. The connexion, between a romantic life and the wild imaginations of the poet, is not altogether ideal. Such of the Troubadours as were regarded as the most celebrated men of their day, wer likewise those who had met with the most renowned adventures. The poet has always been a hero to his biographer. The latter has ever persuaded himself that the most beautiful verses were addressed to the most beautiful women and as time has passed away, our imaginations have invested the Troubadour knight with new glories.

No one has experienced this good fortune in an equal degree with Sordello of Mantua*, whose real merit consists in the harmony and sensibility of his verses. He was amongst the first to adopt the ballad-form of writing, and in one of those, which has been translated by Millot, he beautifully contrasts, in the burthen of his ballad, the gaieties of nature, and the ever-reviving grief of a heart devoted to love †. Sordel, or Sordello, was born at Goïto, near Mantua, and was, for some time, attached to the household of the Count of S. Bonifazio, the chief of the Guelph party, in the march of Treviso. He afterwards passed into the service of Raymond Berenger, the last Count of Provence of the house of Barcelona. Although a Lombard, he had adopted, in his compositions, the Provençal language, and many

* [See *Parnasse Occitanien*, I. 145. *Tr.*]

† Aylas e que m'fan miey huelh
Quar no vezon so qu'ieu vueilh.

of his countrymen imitated him. It was not, at that time, believed that the Italian was capable of becoming a polished language. The age of Sordello was that of the most brilliant chivalric virtues, and the most atrocious crimes. He lived in the midst of heroes and monsters. The imagination of the people was still haunted by the recollection of the ferocious Ezzelino, tyrant of Verona, with whom Sordello is said to have had a contest, and who was, probably, often mentioned in his verses. The historical monuments of this reign of blood were, however, little known, and the people mingled the name of their favourite poet with every revolution which had excited their terror. It was said that he had carried off the wife of the Count of S. Bonifazio, the sovereign of Mantua, that he had married the daughter or sister of Ezzelino, and that he had fought this monster, with glory to himself. He united, according to popular report, the most brilliant military exploits to the most distinguished poetical genius. By the voice of Saint Louis himself, he had been recognized, at a tourney, as the most valiant and gallant of knights; and, at last, the sovereignty of Mantua had been bestowed upon this noblest of the poets and warriors of his age. Historians of credit have collected, three centuries after Sordello's death, these brilliant fictions, which are, however, disproved by the testimony of contemporary writers. The reputation of Sordello is owing, very materially, to the admiration which has been expressed for him by Dante; who, when he meets him at the entrance of Purgatory, is so struck with the noble haughtiness of his aspect, that he compares him to a lion in a state of majestic repose, and represents Virgil as embracing him, on hearing his name. M. de la Curne de Sainte-Palaye has collected thirty-four poems of Sordello's. Fifteen of these are love-songs, and some of them are written in a pure and delicate style. Amongst the other pieces, is a funeral eulogium on the Chevalier de Blacas, an Aragonese Troubadour, whose heart, Sordello says, should be divided amongst all the monarchs in Christendom, to supply them with the courage of which they stand in need. At the same time, we find amongst the compositions of Sordello, some pieces, little worthy of the admiration which has been bestowed upon his personal character, and not altogether in accordance with the delicacy of a knight and a troubadour. In one, he speaks of his success in his amours, with a kind of coarse complacency, very far removed from the devotion which was due to the sex from every cavalier. In another, he thus replies to Charles of Anjou, who pressed him to follow him to the crusade. "My lord Count, you ought not to ask me, in this manner, to affront death. If you want an expert seaman, take Bertrand d'Alamanon, who understands the winds, and who wishes for nothing better than to be your follower. Every one is seeking his salvation by sea; but, for my own part, I am not eager to obtain it. My wish is, to be transported to another life as late as possible." In a *tenson*, in which he is an interlocutor, he sustains the least heroic side of the question. The *Tensons*, or *jeux partis*, were songs, in dialogue, between two speakers *, in which each interlocutor recited successively a stanza with the same rhymes. The other party who, in this *tenson*, disputes with Sordello, is the same Bertrand d'Alamanon, whom, as I have just related, he recommended as a crusader.

"SORDELLO. If it were necessary either to forego the delight of lady-love, and to renounce the friends whom you possess or may possess, or to sacrifice to the lady of your heart, the honour which you have acquired, and may acquire, by chivalry, which of the two would you choose?"

"BERTRAND. The mistresses whom I have loved, have despised me so long, and so little have I gained by them, that I cannot compare them to

---

* [Sometimes, the interlocutors were more than two, in which case it was called a Torneyamen. A specimen of this species of composition is given by M. Raynouard, vol. ii. p. 199. The interlocutors are, Savari di Mauleon, Hugues de la Bachelerie, and Gaucelm Faidit. A paraphrase is given by Millot. *Tr.*]

chivalry. Yours may be the folly of love, the enjoyment of which is so frail. Still continue to chase the pleasures, which lose their value as soon as tasted. But I, in the career of arms, ever behold before me new conquests and new glories.

"SORDELLO. What is glory without love? How can I abandon joy and gallantry for wounds and combats? Thirst and hunger, a burning sun or piercing frost, are these to be preferred to love? Ah! willingly do I resign to you these benefits, for the sovereign joys which my mistress bestows.

"BERTRAND. What! dare you then appear before your mistress, if you dare not draw your sword for the combat? Without valour, there is no real pleasure; it is valour which elevates man to the highest honours, but love is the degradation and the fall of those whom he seduces.

"SORDELLO. Let me but be brave in the eyes of her I love, and I heed not the contempt of others. From her, all my happiness flows; I seek for no other felicity. Go then, overthrow your castles and your walls, while I enjoy the sweet kisses of my mistress. You may gain the esteem of all noble Frenchmen; but, for my part, I prize more her innocent favours, than all the achievements of the lance.

"BERTRAND. But, Sordello, to love without valour, is to deceive her whom you love. I would not wish for the love of her I serve, did not at the same time merit her esteem. A treasure, so ill acquired, would be my grief. Do you, then, be the protector of the follies of love, whilst the honour of arms is mine; since you are so deluded as to place false joys in the balance against real happiness."

This *tenson* may, perhaps, give an idea of those poetical contests, which were the great ornament of all festivals. When the haughty baron invited to his court the neighbouring lords and the knights his vassals, three days were devoted to jousts and tourneys, the mimicry of war. The youthful gentlemen, who, under the name of pages, exercised themselves in the profession of arms, combated the first day; the second was set apart for the newly-dubbed knights; and the third, for the old warriors. The lady of the castle, surrounded by youthful beauties, distributed crowns to those who were declared, by the judges of the combat, to be the conquerors. She then, in her turn, opened her court, constituted in imitation of the seignorial tribunals, and as her baron collected his peers around him, when he dispensed justice, so did she form her Court of Love, consisting of young, beautiful, and lively women. A new career was opened to those who dared the combat, not of arms but of verse, and the name of *Tenson*, which was given to these dramatic skirmishes, in fact signified a contest*. It frequently happened that the knights, who had gained the prize of valour, became candidates for the poetical honours. One of the two, with his harp upon his arm, after a prelude, proposed the subject of the dispute. The other then advancing, and singing to the same air, answered him in a stanza of the same measure, and very frequently having the same rhymes. This extempore composition was usually comprised in five stanzas. The court of love then entered upon a grave deliberation, and discussed not only the claims of the two poets, but the merits of the question; and a judgment or *arrêt d'amour* was given, frequently in verse, by which the dispute was supposed to be decided. At the present day, we feel inclined to believe that these dialogues, though little resembling those of Tityrus and Melibæus, were yet, like those, the production of the poet sitting at ease in his closet. But, besides the historical evidence which we possess of the Troubadours having been gifted with those improvisatorial talents, which the Italians have preserved to the present times, many of the *tensons* extant bear evident traces of the rivalry and animosity of the two interlocutors. The mutual respect, with which the refinements of civilization have taught us to regard one another, was at this time little known. There existed no

* [According to Raynouard, it was derived from CONTENTIO.—*Tr.*]

the same delicacy upon questions of honour, and injury returned for injury was supposed to cancel all insults. We have a *tenson* extant, between the Marquis Albert Malespina and Rambaud de Vaqueiras, two of the most powerful lords and valiant captains, at the commencement of the thirteenth century, in which they mutually accuse one another of having robbed on the highway and deceived their allies by false oaths. We must charitably suppose, that the perplexities of versification and the heat of their poetical inspiration compelled them to overlook sarcasms, which they could never have suffered to pass in plain prose.

Many of the ladies, who sate in the Courts of Love, were able themselves to reply to the verses which they inspired. A few of their compositions only remain, but they have always the advantage over those of the Troubadours. Poetry, at that time, aspired, neither to creative energy, nor to sublimity of thought, nor to variety. Those powerful conceptions of genius which, at a later period, have given birth to the drama and the epic, were yet unknown; and, in the expression of sentiment, a tenderer and more delicate inspiration naturally endowed the productions of these poetesses with a more lyrical character. One of the most beautiful of these songs is written by Clara d'Andusa, and is unfinished. A translation is subjoined, which can give but little idea of a poem, the excellence of which so essentially consists in the harmony of the verse.*

Into what cruel grief and deep distress
  The jealous and the false have plunged my heart,
  Depriving it by every treacherous art
Of all its hopes of joy and happiness:
For they have forced thee from my arms to fly,
  Whom far above this evil life I prize;
  And they have hid thee from my loving eyes.
Alas! with grief, and ire, and rage I die.

Yet they, who blame my passionate love to thee,
  Can never teach my heart a nobler flame,
  A sweeter hope, than that which thrills my frame,
A love, so full of joy and harmony.
Nor is there one—no, not my deadliest foe,
  Whom, speaking praise of thee, I do not love,
  Nor one, so dear to me, who would not move
My wrath, if from his lips dispraise should flow.

---

* [The French prose translation given by M. de Sismondi, is by M. Fabre d'Olivet, *Poésies Occitaniques*, vol. vii. p. 32. The original, which follows, is extracted from the *Parnasse Occitanien*, vol. i. p. 252. *Tr.*]

En greu esmai et en greu pessamen
An mes mon cor, et en granda error
Li lauzengier el fals devinador,
Abaissador de joi e de joven;
Quar vos, qu ieu am mais que re qu'el mon sia
An fait de me departir e lonhar
Li qu' ieu nous posc vezer in remirar,
Don muer de dol e d' ir' e de feunia.

Cel que m blasma vostr' amor ni m defen
No podon far en re mon cor melhor,
Ni'l dous desir qu'ieu ai de vos major,
Ni l'enveja, ni 'l dezir ni 'l talen.

Fear not, fair love, my heart shall ever fail
  In its fond trust—fear not that it will change
  Its faith, and to another loved one range;
No! though a hundred tongues that heart assail—
For Love, who has my heart at his command,
  Decrees it shall be faithful found to thee,
  And it *shall* be so. Oh, had I been free,
Thou, who hast all my heart, hadst had my hand.

Love! so o'ermastering is my soul's distress,
  At not beholding thee, that, when I sing,
  My notes are lost in tears aud sorrowing,
Nor can my verse, my heart's desires express.

We have already said that the *Sirventes*, which constitute the second class of Provençal poems, were martial and political songs. At a period, when almost all the poets were knights likewise, and when the love of combats, and the infatua-

---

E non es hom, tan mos enemics sia,
Si'l n'aug dir ben, que no'l tenha en car;
E si'n ditz mal, mais no m pot dir ni far,
Neguna re quez à plazer me sia.

Ja nous donets, bels amics, espaven
Quez ieu ves vos aia cor trechador,
Ni queus camge per nul autr' amador
Si m pregavon d'autras domnas un ceu;
Qu 'amors que m te per vos eu sa bailia,
Vol que mon cor vos estuj'e vos gar;
E farai o: e s'ieu pogues emblar
Mon cors, tals l'a que jamais no l'auria.

Amics, tan ai d'ira e de feunia
Quar no vos vei, que quant ieu cug cantar
Plang e sospir; per qu' ieu no posc so far
A mas coblas que 'l cor complir volria.

tion of dangers, were the prominent passions o: the soul, we naturally look to the martial songs for instances of the noblest inspiration. Thus Guillaume de Saint-Gregory, in an harmonious *sirvente*, in stanzas of ten lines, like those of our odes, celebrates his love of war, and seems to feel the inspiration of the field of battle.*

The beautiful spring delights me well,
   When flowers and leaves are growing;
And it pleases my heart, to hear the swell
   Of the birds' sweet chorus flowing
         In the echoing wood;
And I love to see all scatter'd around,
Pavilions and tents, on the martial ground;
         And my spirit finds it good
To see, on the level plains beyond,
Gay knights and steeds caparison'd.†

* [This *Sirvente* is attributed by M. Raynouard to Bertrand de Born, *Poésies de Troubadours*, ii. 209, and in the *Parnasse Occitanien*, i. 65, where a different version of it is given. The text is taken from M. Raynouard, and for the translation the editor is indebted to the kindness of a friend.—*Tr.*]

† Be m play lo douz temps de pascor,
   Que fai fuelhas e flors venir;
E play mi quant aug la vaudor
   Dels auzels que fan retentir
         Lor chan per lo boscatge;
E plai me quan vey sus els pratz,
Tendas e pavallos fermatz;
         E plai m'en mon coratge,
Quan vey per campanhas rengatz
Cavalliers ab cavals armatz.

It pleases me, when the lancers bold
  Set men and armies flying;
And it pleases me, too, to hear around
  The voice of the soldiers crying;
    And joy is mine,
When the castles strong besieged shake,
And walls uprooted totter and quake,
    And I see the foe-men join
On the moated shore, all compass'd round
With the palisade and guarded mound.

* * * *

E play mi quan li corredor
  Fan las gens els aver fugir;
E plai me quan vey aprop lor
  Gran ren d'armatz ensems brugir;
    E ai gran alegratge,
Quan vey fortz castels assetjatz,
E murs fondre e derolatz;
    E vey l'ost pel ribatge
Qu'es tot entorn claus de fossatz,
Ab lissas de fortz pals serratz.

Atressi m play de bon senhor,
  Quant es primiers a l'envazir,
Ab caval armat, çes temor;
  C'aissi fai los sieus enardir,
    Ab vallen vassallatge;
E quant el es el camp intratz,
Quascus deu esser assermatz,
    E segr el d'agradatge,
Quan nulhs hom non es rea prezatz
Tro qu'a manhs colps pres e donatz.

Lances and swords, and stained helms,
  And shields dismantled and broken,
On the verge of the bloody battle-scene,
  The field of wrath betoken;
      And the vassals are there,
And there fly the steeds of the dying and dead;
And where the mingled strife is spread,
      The noblest warrior's care
Is to cleave the foeman's limbs and head,
The conqueror less of the living than dead.

I tell you that nothing my soul can cheer,
  Or banqueting or reposing,
Like the onset cry of "charge them" rung
  From each side, as in battle closing;
      Where the horses neigh,
And the call to "aid" is echoing loud,
And there, on the earth, the lowly and proud
      In the foss together lie;
And yonder is piled the mingled heap
Of the brave that scaled the trench's steep.

Lansas e brans elens de color,
  Escutz trancar e desguarnir,
Veyrem a l'intrar, de l'estor,
  E manhs vassalhs ensems ferir
      Don anaran a ratge,
Cavalhs dels mortz e dels nafratz;
E la pus l'estorn er mesclatz,
    Negus hom d'aut paratge
Non pens mas d'asclar caps e bratz
Que mais val mortz que vius sobratz.

Je us die que tan no m'a sabor
  Mangars ni beure in dormir,

Barons! your castles in safety place,
Your cities and villages, too,
Before ye haste to the battle-scene:
And, Papiol!* quickly go,
And tell the Lord of "*Yes and No,*"†
That peace already too long hath been!

This warlike ode is dedicated to Beatrix of Savoy, the wife of Raymond Berenger V. the last Count of Provence. Beatrix was the mother of four queens, of France, of Germany, of England, and of Naples. Like her husband, she was a great patroness of the Troubadours, and some verses of this illustrious couple are still preserved, which are wanting neither in poetical skill nor in delicacy. The lines written by the countess are

---

Cum a quant aug cridar; a lor!
D'ambas las partz; et aug agnir!
Cavals voitz per l'ombratge,
Et aug cridar: aidatz! aidatz!
E vei cazer per los possatz
Paues e grans per l'erbatge;
E vei los mortz que pels costazt
Au los tronsons outre passatz.

Baros, metetz en gatge,
Castels e vilas e ciutatz,
Enans q'usquecs no us guerreiatz
Papiol, d'agradatge,
Ad oc e no, ten vai viatz,
Dic li que trop estan en patz.

---

* The name of the Troubadour's *Jongleur*, or page.
† Richard Cœur de Lion.

ldressed to her lover, in which she reproaches m with being too reserved and timid. For the onour of the princess, we must suppose that is reproach is a mere sally of wit.

But the war, of all others, most fitted to inspire poet, was the crusade. Whilst the preachers, om every pulpit, announced salvation to those ho should shed their blood to deliver the tomb f Christ, the Troubadours, who partook of the ame enthusiasm, were still more strongly in-uenced by the new and strange adventures hich the fairy realms of the East promised them. heir imaginations wandered with delight over ose romantic countries, and they sighed as well or the conquest of that terrestrial paradise, as or that which was promised them in heaven. Many f them were, however, detained in Europe by he bonds of love; and the contests between these wo passions, these two religions of their hearts, equently gave an interesting character to the oems which were composed to animate the cru-aders. This conflict is no where more agreeably lescribed than in a *tenson* between Peyrols and ove. Peyrols was a knight of slender fortune, rom the neighbourhood of Roquefort in Auvergne.* His distinguished talents for poetry introduced im to the court of the Dauphin of Auvergne.

* [Three poems by Peyrols are given in the *Parnasse Occitaien*, i. 88, and six, in Raynouard, iii. 268.—*Tr.*]

He there fell passionately in love with the sister of that prince, the Baroness de Mercœur, and the Dauphin prevailed upon his sister to return the passion of his Troubadour, in order to encourage those poetical talents which were the ornament of his court. Neither the Baroness nor the Troubadour were able rigorously to preserve the strict bounds of a poetical attachment; and Peyrols, who for a considerable time had only celebrated, in his verse, the cruelty of his mistress, at length sang the victories and the exultation of a happy lover. The Baron de Mercœur was offended. The Dauphin resented the injury which he believed his brother-in-law had sustained, and Peyrols was banished. Other attachments succeeded this first love, which are also celebrated in his verses. The preaching of the second crusade changed, at once, his mode of life. The following is his dialogue with Love, the original of which has been published by M. Fabre d'Olivet, who has happily mingled in his "Court of Love" many ancient fragments with his own verses.*

Love! I long have been your slave,
Till my heart is broken;
What is the reward I have?
Where, my duty's token?

* [The original of this curious poem is not given by M. de Sismondi. It is to be found, with some variations, in the *Parnasse Occitanien*, vol. i. p. 90. and likewise in Raynouard, iii. 279. *Tr.*]

yrols! can you then forget
That same blooming Beauty,
hom with such delight you met,
Swearing love and duty?
at 's the way I paid the debt!
t me tell you, your light heart
Tender thoughts disperses;
hen you act the lover's part
You falsify your verses.

ve! I 've still been true to you,
And if now I leave you,
s what I am forced to do;
Do not let it grieve you.
aven will see me safely through!
aven, too, make the kings agree!
Keep them both from fighting!
st Saladin their folly see
Which he 'll take delight in.

yrols! do the best you will,
You alone can't save it;
ery Turk you cannot kill,
That storms the Tower of David;
re remain and sing your fill!
u 're not wanted by the kings;
Stay then and amuse you,
ey 're so fond of quarrelings
They can well excuse you.

ve! I 've felt your power depart;
Though my fair one's beauty
ngers still about my heart,
Yet I 'll do my duty.
ny a lover now must part;
ny hearts must now begin
To feel their sad griefs springing,
hich, but for cruel Saladin,
Had joyously been singing.

Peyrols did, in fact, visit the Holy Land, and a *sirvente* composed by him in Syria, after the Emperor Frederic Barbarossa had lost his life, and the Kings of England and France had abandoned the crusade, is still preserved.

I have seen the Jordan river,
I have seen the holy grave;
Lord! to thee my thanks I render
For the joys thy goodness gave,
Shewing to my raptured sight,
The spot wherein thou saw'st the light.

Vessel good, and favouring breezes,
Pilot trusty, soon shall we
Once more see the towers of Marseilles
Rising o'er the briny sea.
Farewell, Acre! farewell, all
Of Temple or of Hospital!

Now, alas! the world's decaying—
When shall we once more behold
Kings like lion-hearted Richard—
France's monarch, stout and bold—
Montferrat's good Marquis—or
The Empire's glorious Emperor!

Ah! Lord God, if you believed me,
You would pause in granting powers
Over cities, kingdoms, empires,
Over castles, towns, and towers;
For the men that powerful be
Pay the least regard to thee.*

* [The Translator has been unable to discover the original of his *Sirvente;* the lines in the text are, therefore, only a version of the French prose translation.]

The poem terminates with a violent invective against the reigning Emperor. This was caused by the treacherous conduct of Henry VI. who detained in his prisons Richard Cœur de Lion, when on his return from the crusade, after having been shipwrecked on the coast of Istria, he was seized, as he traversed Germany, in the disguise of a pilgrim by Leopold, Duke of Austria, in 1192. Richard, who was the hero of the age; who had humbled Tancred and Philip Augustus; who, in a short space of time, had conquered the island of Cyprus, and had bestowed that kingdom on the unfortunate Lusignan; who had vanquished Saladin in a pitched battle, and had dispersed the innumerable armies of the East; who had inspired such terror into the infidels, that his name alone was long the signal of affright; who had remained, after the return of all the other sovereigns from the crusade, and had alone commanded the Christian host; and who had signed the treaty, in virtue of which the pilgrims were allowed to accomplish their long journey to the Holy Sepulchre—Richard was equally dear to all the Crosses. They pardoned the vices and the ferocity, which were inseparable from the manners of the age. They reproached him not with the odious massacre of all the prisoners whom he had captured from Saladin; and, in short, they seemed to think that so much valour might dispense with all other virtues. But, above ıll, Richard was dear to the Troubadours. Himself a royal poet and knight, he united in his own person all the brilliant qualities of the age. He was a bad son, a bad husband, a bad brother, a bad king; but he was the most valiant and intrepid warrior in the army. His companions in arms oved him with a kind of idolatry. The devotion of William des Préaux, one of his followers, saved him, contrary to all expectation, from a Saracen prison. He was sleeping under the shade of a tree in Syria, with six of his knights, when he was surprised by a troop of the enemy. He had only time to mount his horse and defend himself with his accustomed bravery; and four of his companions having fallen, he was on the point of being taken prisoner, when William des Préaux, seeing his master's danger, exclaimed in Arabic, "Spare me! I am the King of England!" The Saracens, who had not suspected that a prisoner of such importance was in their power, threw themselves immediately on Des Préaux, that they might all claim a share in the capture, and paid no attention to Richard, who gallopped away. Fauchet asserts, that he likewise owed his liberty in Germany to the zeal of his minstrel, Blondel; and this is the story which has been dramatised. We cannot help regretting that this tale has been ranked amongst the apocrypha of history. Henry VI. according to Fauchet, carefully concealed the fact of his having detained the King of Eng-

and as a prisoner, lest he should incur the excommunication of the Crusaders. Blondel, who had been shipwrecked with him on the coast of Istria, and who had sought him in all the fortresses of Germany, sang, beneath the tower in which he was confined, a *tenson* which he and Richard had composed in common. Scarcely had he finished the first stanza, when Richard commenced the second. Blondel, having discovered his master, carried into England the tidings of his captivity, and engaged his brother to treat for his ransom. If this *tenson*, which delivered the King of England from captivity, had been preserved, it might have been some confirmation of an anecdote to which we are so willing to give credit. We do, however, possess a *sirvente* which he composed in prison, after fifteen months captivity *. The uniform and masculine rhymes, no doubt, augmented, to the ear of Richard, the melancholy of his verses.

---

* It is not known in what language this song was originally written, for the different manuscripts in which we find it, with many variations, give it in the Provençal and Langue d'Oil. It seems to me an agreeable task to compare, in the words of the brave King Richard, the two languages which so long divided France between them. Below, I have given the two first verses in Provençal, from a manuscript of M. de la Curne de Sainte-Palaye, and also the entire song in old French, together with the sixth stanza, and an envoy, from a manuscript in the Royal Library.

SONG, BY RICHARD I.

Written during his imprisonment in the Tour Ténébreuse, or Black Tower.

No wretched captive of his prison speaks,
  Unless with pain and bitterness of soul,
Yet consolation from the Muse he seeks,
  Whose voice alone misfortune can control.
Where now is each ally, each baron, friend,
  Whose face I ne'er beheld without a smile?
Will none, his sovereign to redeem, expend
  The smallest portion of his treasures vile?

Jà nul hom près non dirà sa razon
Adreitamen, se come hom doulen non;
Mas per conort pot el faire canson.
Prou ha d'amicz, ma paûre son li don!
Honta y auran se por ma rehezon
    Souy fach dos hivers prez.

Or sachan ben miei hom e miei baron,
Anglés, Norman, Peytavin et Gascon,
Qu'yeu non hai ja si paûre compagnon
Que per avé, lou laissesse en prezon;
Faire reproch, certas yeu voli non,
    Mas souy dos hivers prez.

La! nus homs pris ne dira sa raison
Adroitement, se dolantement non,
Mais por effort puet-il faire chançon;
Moût ai amis, mais poure sont li don,
Honte i auront se por ma reançon
    Sui ca dos yvers pris.

Though none may blush that, near two tedious years,
Without relief, my bondage has endured,
Yet know, my English, Norman, Gascon peers,
Not one of you should thus remain immur'd:
The meanest subject of my wide domains,
Had I been free, a ransom should have found;
I mean not to reproach you with my chains,
Yet still I wear them on a foreign ground!

Too true it is—so selfish human race!
"Nor dead nor captive, friend or kindred find;"
Since here I pine in bondage and disgrace,
For lack of gold my fetters to unbind;
Much for myself I feel, yet ah! still more
That no compassion from my subjects flows:
What can from infamy their names restore,
If, while a prisoner, death my eyes should close?

Ce sevent bien mi home et mi baron
Ynglois, Normans, Poitevin et Gascon,
Que je n'ai nul si pauvre compaignon
Que por avoir je lessaisse en prison.
Je vous di mie por nule retraçon.
Car encore sui pris.

Or sai-je bien de voir certeinement
Que je n'ai pu ne ami ne parent,
Quand on me faut por or ou por argent,
Moût m'est de moi, mais plus m'est de ma gent
Qu'après lor mort aurai reprochement.
Si longuement sui pris.

N'est pas mervoilh, se j'ai le cuer dolent
Quand mes sire mest ma terre en torment,
S'il li membrast de notre sacrement
Que nos feismes à Deus communement,
Je sai de voir que ja trop longuement
Ne seirie ca pris.

But small is my surprise, though great my grief,
To find, in spite of all his solemn vows,
My lands are ravaged by the Gallic chief,
While none my cause has courage to espouse.
Though lofty towers obscure the cheerful day,
Yet, through the dungeon's melancholy gloom,
Kind Hope, in gentle whispers, seems to say,
"Perpetual thraldom is not yet thy doom."

Ye dear companions of my happy days,
Of Chail and Pensavin, aloud declare
Throughout the earth, in everlasting lays,
My foes against me wage inglorious war.
Oh, tell them, too, that ne'er, among my crimes,
Did breach of faith, deceit, or fraud appear;
That infamy will brand to latest times
The insults I receive, while captive here.

Know, all ye men of Anjou and Touraine,
And every bach'lor knight, robust and brave,
That duty, now, and love, alike are vain,
From bonds your sovereign and your friend to save:

Que sevent bien Angevin et Lorain,
Al Bacheler qui or sont riche et sain,
Qu'encombrés suis loing d'eux en autre main,
Fort moût m'aidessent, mais il n'en vient grain
De belles armes sont ore vuit et plain,
Porce que je suis pris.

Mes compagnons que j'amoie et que j'am,
Ces de Chacu, et ces de Percheram,
Di lor chançon qu'il ne sunt pas certam,
C'onques vers eux ne vi faus cuer ne vam,
S'ils me guerroient il feront que vilam,
Tant com je serai pris.

Remote from consolation, here I lie,
The wretched captive of a powerful foe,
Who all your zeal and ardour can defy,
Nor leaves you aught but pity to bestow.

We have only two *sirventes* by Richard, and the second is not very worthy of remark. But a knight, who was intimately connected with that monarch, and whose ungoverned passions had a powerful influence over the destiny of the royal family of England, Bertrand de Born *, Viscount of Hautefort, in the diocese of Périgeux, has left a number of original poems, which, it is much to be regretted, have never been printed in the original language. The most ardent and impetuous of the French knights, he breathed nothing but war. Exciting and inflaming the pas-

Contesse suer votre pris soverain,
Vos saut et gart, al acunement claim,
Et porce suis-je pris.
Je ne di mie a cele de chartain
La mere Loeys.

[The English translation given in the text is taken from Burney's History of Music, vol. ii. p. 238. The original, as given by him, which frequently varies from the copy in the foregoing note, is to be found in the preface to the *Roman de la Tour Tenebreuse*, printed at Paris in 1705. *Tr.*]

* [Three poems, by Bertrand de Born, are given in the *Parnasse Occitanien*, i. 65, two of which are likewise given by *Raynouard*, i. 135. In addition to these, a number of other poems by Bertrand de Born, will be found in the fourth volume of M Renouard's work, which has been recently published.—*Tr.*]

sions of his neighbours or of his superiors, in order to rouse them to combat, he agitated, by intrigues and arms, the provinces of Guienne during the latter half of the twelfth century, and in the reigns of the English monarchs, Henry II. and Richard I. In every new war in which he engaged, he animated his soldiers, encouraged his allies, and sustained his own hopes, by disburdening his mind, in a *sirvente,* of those passions which had prompted him to take up arms. Having attempted to despoil his brother Constantine of his share of their paternal inheritance, Richard Cœur de Lion, who was then only Count of Poitou, took the latter under his protection; and Bertrand de Born, on account of this war, composed the first of those *sirventes,* in which he has, with such truth, pourtrayed that inflexible soul, which no dangers could cast down, nor any violence subdue. "What," says he, "are happy or evil days to me? What are weeks or years? At all times my desire is to destroy those who offend me. Let others embellish their mansions, if they will; let them surround themselves with all the conveniences of life—but, for me, my sole desire is to collect lances and casques, and swords and horses. . . . . . I am disgusted with the advice they give me; and, by Jesus, I know not to whom to listen. They tell me I am imprudent in refusing peace, but were I to accept it, who is there that would not call me coward?" At the conclusion of this war, Bertrand de Born, being irritated against Richard, who had ravaged his territories, attached himself to the eldest brother of that prince, Henry Duke of Guienne, the heir apparent to the crown of England. On all sides, he roused the enemies of Richard, and formed powerful leagues against him, while, with all the martial ardour of Tyrtæus, he sang anew the combats to which he was leading his allies. "Ventadour and Comborn, Ségur and Turenne, Montfort and Gordon, have made a league with Périgueux. The citizens labour at the intrenchments of their towns. The walls are rising around them. Let me strengthen their resolution with a *sirvente!* What glory awaits us..... Should a crown be offered me, I should blush not to enter into this alliance or to desert it." Being soon afterwards abandoned by Henry, he composed a *sirvente* against him, and addressed another to Richard, who, after having besieged him in his castle, and forced him to capitulate, had generously restored to him his property. Shortly after this time, Henry died, in 1183; and Bertrand, who had again leagued himself with him, and had engaged him in a second revolt against his father, celebrated his praises in some *sirventes,* which breathe the tenderest affection. "I am devoured," says he, "with a grief, which will end but with my life. There is no longer any joy for me; I have lost the best of princes. Great God! you have snatched him from the age, and our wickedness has but too well merited it. Noble Henry! it was reserved for you, to be the king of the courteous and the emperor of the brave!" The death of his friend, the prince, left Bertrand exposed to great danger. Henry II. with the forces of two kingdoms, besieged the lord of a little castle in Hautefort. Bertrand defended himself to the last extremity, until, the walls falling around him, he was taken prisoner with his garrison. But, when he was led before the king, and reminded the monarch, by a single word, of the tender friendship which he had enjoyed with the young prince, the unfortunate father burst into tears, and in the name of the son whom he had lost, restored to him his castle, his fief, and his riches.

These reverses could not discourage the high spirit of Bertrand de Born. Scarcely had he escaped one danger, when he provoked new enemies. He wrote many *sirventes* against Alfonso II. of Aragon, in which he endeavoured to excite his subjects to rebellion. He likewise took an active part in the war between Richard and Philip Augustus; and when it appeared to relax, he rekindled it with his verses, in which he alternately roused the shame of the one sovereign or the other, by imputations of cowardice.

This ardent warrior, whose whole life was spent in the field, was not, however, insensible to the passion of love; and here his success was not unworthy of his glory in arms. He was attached to Helen, the sister of King Richard, who afterwards married the Duke of Saxe, and was the mother of the Emperor Otho IV. Richard beheld, with pleasure, his sister, celebrated by so valiant a warrior and so illustrious a Troubadour. Nor was Helen insensible to the homage of a man, who was even more distinguished by his talents than by his rank. Only one of the songs, which Bertrand composed in honour of this princess, has survived. It was written in the camp, at a time when the army was without provisions; and the Troubadour endeavoured to forget his hunger, in poetry and love. He was afterwards passionately attached to Maenz de Montagnac, the daughter of the Viscount de Turenne, and wife of Taleyrand de Périgord. His love was returned, and he was recognized by the lady as her knight; but jealousy disturbed their enjoyments. To her, in order to exculpate himself from a charge of infidelity, he addressed a song, which appears to possess much originality. It places before us the real knight of former times, all busied in war and the chase, the labour and the delight of our fathers, successively appealing to every thing that is dear to him in life, to every thing which has been the study of his youth and of his riper age, and yet esteeming them all light, in comparison with love.

* I cannot hide from thee, how much I fear
The whispers breathed by flatterers in thine ear,
Against my faith. But turn not, oh! I pray,
That heart so true, so faithful, so sincere,
So humble and so frank, to me so dear,
Oh lady! turn it not from me away.

So may I lose my hawk, ere he can spring,
Borne from my hand by some bold falcon's wing,
Mangled and torn before my very eye,
If every word thou utterest does not bring
More joy to me than Fortune's favouring,
Or all the bliss another's love might buy.

So, with my shield on neck, mid storm and rain,
With vizor blinding me and shorten'd rein,
And stirrups far too long, so may I ride,
So may my trotting charger give me pain,
So may the ostler treat me with disdain,
As they who tell those tales have grossly lied.

---

* The following is the original apology of Bertrand de Born:—unfortunately, many of the verses have been corrupted by the transcribers, to the injury both of the sense and the prosody.

Jeu m' escondic que mal non mier
De so qu' eus an de mi dig lauzengier.
Per merce' us pres c' om nom puezca mezclar
Lo vostre cor fin lial vertadier
Humilz e francz e plazentier
Ab mi Dona per messonjas comtar.

Al premier get perd'ieu mon esparvier,
Que'l m'ausian al ponh falcon lanier
E porton l'en qu'iel lor veya plumar,
Si non am mais de vos lo cossirier
No faz d'autra jauzir lo desirier
Que 'm don s' amor ni' m retenh 'al colcar.

When I approach the gaming board to play,
May I not turn a penny all the day,
Or may the board be shut, the dice untrue,
If the truth dwell not in me, when I say
No other fair e'er wiled my heart away,
From her I've long desired and loved—from you.

Or, prisoner to some noble, may I fill
Together with three more, some dungeon chill,
Unto each other odious company;
Let master, servants, porters, try their skill,
And use me for a target if they will,
If ever I have loved aught else but thee.

Autr' escondig vos farai pus sobrier,
E non m' en puesc onrar, pus encombrier,
S' ieu anc falli ves vos, veys, del pensar.
Can serem sols en cambro dins vergier,
Falham poders de vos mon companhier
De tal guiza que nom puesc aiudar.

Escut al col cavalq' ieu al tempier,
E port salat capairon traversier,
E regnas brevs que non puesc alongar,
Et estrueps loncs, e caval mal trotier,
Et al ostal truep irat lo stalier,
Si no us menti quien o aves comtar.

S' ieu per jaugar m' asseti al taulier
Ja no y puesca baratar un denier,
Ma ab taula presa non puesca intrar,
Anz giet a dez lo reir azar derrier;
S' ieu mais autra dona am ni enquier
Mais vos, cuy am, e dezir, e tem car.

So may another knight make love to you,
And so may I be puzzled what to do;
So may I be becalmed 'mid oceans wide;
May the king's porter beat me black and blue,
And may I fly ere I the battle view,
As they, that slander me, have grossly lied.

Bertrand de Born was reconciled to Maenz de Montagnac, by another celebrated woman of that time, Dame Natibors, or Tiberge de Montauzier, herself a poetess, and one whose praises had frequently been sung by the Troubadours. Disgusted with the world, he, at last, retired into a monastery, where he died, after having assumed the habit of a Cistercian monk. But the history of the great men of this age does not terminate with their lives. The terrible fictions of Dante, before whom they are, as it were, placed in judgment,

---

Senher sia ieu de Castel parsonier,
Si qu'en la tor siam quatre parsonier,
E l'un l'autre noc aus pusiam amar,
Anz m'aion obs tos temps albalestrier
Mètre, sirvens, e gaitas, e portier,
S'ieu anc ai cor d'autra dona amar.

Ma Don'aim lais per autre cavayer
E pueis no say a que m'aia mestier,
E falham vens quant iray sobre mar;
En cort de Rey mi batan li portier,
En encocha fasa l'fogir primier,
Si no us menti quien m'an ot encusar.

A als envios se mentitz lauzengier
Pus ab mi dons m'aves encombrier
Ben lauzera quen laisaretz estar.

seem to possess a sort of reality: and Bertrand de Born, who, as a poet and warrior, had played so brilliant a part, and exercised such noxious influence over his contemporaries, was not likely to be passed over in neglect, by the bard of the *Divina Comedia*. The poet, in fact, meets him in hell. He beholds, with horror, a body advancing without a head, or rather holding its head by the hair, in its right hand. The severed head is raised by the hand, and thus addresses the poet:

——— "Now, behold
This grievous torment, thou, who breathing goest
To spy the dead: behold, if any else
Be terrible as this. And that on earth
Thou may'st bear tidings of me, know that I
Am Bertrand, he of Born, who gave King John
The counsel mischievous. Father and son
I set at mutual war. For Absalom
And David, more did not Ahitophel,
Spurring them on maliciously to strife.
For parting those so closely knit, my brain
Parted, alas! I carry, from its source,
That in this trunk inhabits. Thus the law
Of retribution fiercely works in me."

Inferno, Canto xxviii.

NOTE.

M. de Sismondi has announced his intention of devoting his attention, hereafter, to the production of a similar work on the Literature of the North. He will, probably, there give an account of the poets who, in Germany, under the name of Minnesingers, were equally prolific with the Troubadours, during precisely the same æra. The emperors of the Suabian line were great patrons of the Muses. M. de Sismondi has cited a little piece, usually attributed to Frederic Barbarossa. Their connexion with Italy, Sicily, and Provence, unites the German literature of that age so intimately with that of the southern dialects, that it would have been very desirable if all could have been brought under one view, to illustrate their mutual affinities and influences. So popular was the German Muse, that there are even instances of Italian poets composing in that language, as well as in the Provençal.

In comparing the poetic merits of the Troubadours and Minnesingers, it seems impossible to avoid differing from the opinion expressed by M. de Sismondi, and awarding the palm to the latter. They partake very little of the metaphysical speculations, and refinements of the Troubadours, while the harmony and grace of their versification are pre-eminent. The unbounded gaiety with which it revels in the charms of nature, and the spirit of tenderness and affection which it displays, give their poetry charms which very seldom adorn that of their rivals.

The Translator trusts that he may be excused for adding two specimens of the lighter pieces of these "singers," for which, as well as for a few of the translations of the Troubadours, inserted in this work, he is indebted to the papers of a friend, who, for the purpose of bringing all the contemporary songsters of this age into one view, is preparing a volume for publication. It is entitled 'Specimens selected and translated from the lyric poetry of the

German Minnesingers or Troubadours of the twelfth, thirteenth and fourteenth centuries, illustrated by similar Selections and Translations from the Poets of the Provençal and other Southern Dialects."

The following Song is the production of Dietmar von Aste.

There sate upon the linden tree
  A bird, and sang its strain;
So sweet it sang, that as I heard
  My heart went back again.
It went to *one* remember'd spot,
  It saw the rose-trees grow,
And thought again the thoughts of love
  There cherish'd long ago.

A thousand years to me it seems,
  Since by my fair I sate;
Yet thus to be a stranger long,
  Is not my choice, but fate:
Since then I have not seen the flowers,
  Nor heard the bird's sweet song:
My joys have all too briefly past,
  My griefs been all too long.

The following song of Earl Conrad of Kirchberg, is translated very closely, and in the same measure as the original:

May, sweet May, again is come;
May, that frees the land from gloom:
Children, children, up and see
All her stores of jollity!
O'er the laughing hedgerows' side
She hath spread her treasures wide;

She is in the greenwood shade,
Where the nightingale hath made
Every branch and every tree
Ring with her sweet melody:
Hill and dale are May's own treasures,
Youth, rejoice in sportive measures;
Sing ye! join the chorus gay!
Hail this merry, merry May!

Up, then, children, we will go
Where the blooming roses grow,
In a joyful company
We the bursting flowers will see;
Up! your festal dress prepare!
Where gay hearts are meeting, there
May hath pleasures most inviting,
Heart, and sight, and ear delighting:
Listen to the bird's sweet song,
Hark! how soft it floats along!
Courtly dames our pleasures share,
Never saw I May so fair;
Therefore, dancing will we go:
Youths rejoice, the flowrets blow;
Sing ye! join the chorus gay!
Hail this merry, merry May!

Our manly youths,—where are they now
Bid them up, and with us go
To the sporters on the plain;
Bid adieu to care and pain,
Now, thou pale and wounded lover!
Thou thy peace shalt soon recover:
Many a laughing lip and eye
Speaks the light heart's gaiety.
Lovely flowers around we find,
In the smiling verdure twined,

Richly steep'd, in May dews glowing :
Youths! rejoice, the flowers are blowing ;
    Sing ye! join the chorus gay!
    Hail this merry, merry May!

Oh, if to my love restored,
Her, o'er all her sex adored,
What supreme delight were mine!
How would Care her sway resign!
Merrily, in the bloom of May,
I would weave a garland gay ;
Better than the best is she,
Purer than all purity!
For her spotless self alone,
I will sing this changeless one ;
Thankful or unthankful, she
Shall my song, my idol, be.
    Youths, then, join the chorus gay!
    Hail this merry, merry May!

CHAPTER V.

On some of the more celebrated Troubadours.

In examining the literature of Provence, we have not the same advantages which we enjoy in enquiring into that of other countries. We are not directed, by public opinion, to a few celebrated authors; to a few compositions, which have been ranked amongst the masterpieces of the human intellect. All the Troubadours, on the contrary, have nearly an equal title to fame. We find them, it is true, divided into two very distinct classes; the Troubadours, and the *Jongleurs* or minstrels. But it is in their rank rather than in their talents; in their employment rather than their renown, that the distinction consists. The Troubadours, as their name imports, were men *qui trouvaient*, who composed, new poems; just as the *Poets*, a name which has passed, from the Greek, into all other languages, were those who *made* or *created*: for at the origin of poetry, invention was always considered as the essence of the art. The Troubadours often themselves sang their *treuves* in courts and festivals, but more frequently these were sung by their Jongleurs. It was the duty of the latter, who were altogether of an inferior rank, to entertain the companies into which they were admitted, by the recitation of tales and verses which they had learned, and which they accompanied on different instruments, and even by juggling tricks and buffoonery. Even though thus degraded, they learned to compose verses, in imitation of those which they recited from memory. The Provençal poetry was founded on the sentiment of harmony, and required no previous knowledge in the poet; and those, therefore, who lived by reciting verses, soon learned to compose them. Thus the corruption and degradation of the Jongleurs, who, as soon as they began to rhyme themselves, assumed the name of Troubadours, contributed, more than any thing else, to the destruction of the fraternity. Giraud de Calanson, a Troubadour, or rather a Jongleur, of Gascony, has given, in a curious *sirvente,* the following advice to a Jongleur.

He tells him that he must know how to compose and rhyme well, and how to propose a *jeu-parti.* He must play on the tambourine and the cymbals, and make the symphony resound. To throw and catch little balls, on the point of a knife; to imitate the song of birds; to play tricks, with the baskets; to exhibit attacks o castles, and leaps (no doubt, of monkeys) through four hoops; to play on the citole and the mandore; to handle the claricord and the guitar; to string the wheel with seventeen cords, to play on the harp, and to adapt a gigue so as to enliven the psaltry, are indispensable accomplishments*. The Jongleur must prepare nine instruments with ten cords, which, if he learns to play well, will be sufficient for his purpose; and he must know how to sound the lyre and the bells.

After an enumeration of the romances and the tales, which the Jongleur ought to be able to

---

* [It is difficult to determine what was the nature of all these various musical instruments. The gigue seems to be unknown. Burney, *Hist. of Music*, vol. ii. p. 270. The mandore was a species of lute, about two feet long, and strung with four cords. The manicord, or claricorde, was a sort of spinet resembling the virginals, and is said, by Scaliger, to be more ancient than the harpsicord or the spinet. The psaltry is described by Burney, vol. i. p. 519. and in the *Essai sur la Musique*, vol. i. p. 302. Burney likewise gives a fragment, in which all the accomplishments of a Jongleur are catalogued.

"All the minstrel art I know:
  I the viol well can play;
I the pipe and syrinx blow,
  Harp and gigue my hand obey;
Psaltry, symphony, and rote,
  Help to charm the listening throng,
And Armonia lends its note
  While I warble forth my song.

recite, the poet tells him, that he must know how Love runs and flies, how he goes naked and unclothed, and how he repulses Justice with his keen darts, and his two arrows, one of which is made of dazzling gold, and the other of steel, which inflicts wounds so deep that they cannot be healed. He must learn the ordinances of Love, its privileges and remedies; and be able to explain its different degrees; how rapid its pace; on what it lives; how it departs; the deceptions it then exercises; and how it destroys its worshippers. He then tells him, that, when he knows all this, he must seek the young king of Aragon, for that no one can better appreciate such accomplishments; and that if he there plays his part well, and distinguishes himself amongst the foremost, he will have no occasion to complain of that monarch's want of liberality. And lastly, that if he does not rise above mediocrity, he will deserve an ungracious reception from the best prince in the world.

I have tales and fables plenty,
Satires, past'rals, full of sport,
Songs to Vielle I've more than twenty,
Ditties, too, of every sort.
I from lovers tokens bear,
I can flowery chaplets weave,
Amorous belts can well prepare,
And with courteous speech deceive."—*Tr.*]

But whilst Giraud de Calanson, in this *sirvente*, prepares the Troubadours for the lowest arts and the most degrading occupations, other poets felt and expressed a lively indignation at the decay of this sublime art, and at the corruption of taste and the confusion of ranks, which gave the name of Jongleurs to men who played legerdemain tricks and exhibited apes. Giraud Riquier and Pierre Vidal have both expressed the same sentiments.

Amongst the Troubadours, some were raised above their fellows, less by their talents than by the distinguished rank which they held in society. In the number of those whose manuscripts have been collected by M. de la Curne de Sainte-Palaye, and analyzed by Millot, we find several sovereigns, the first of whom is William IX. Count of Poitou and Duke of Acquitaine. Nine of his compositions in verse have been preserved, remarkable for the harmony of their versification and for the elegant mixture of their measures and rhymes. His life was divided between devotion to the ladies and to religion, for he was engaged in the first crusade. In the midst of the Holy War he still preserved his gay and somewhat licentious humour; and in his verses, we find traces of his love, his pleasures, and his devotion. We have already mentioned two *sirventes* of Richard I. of England. There is likewise a love-song of Alfonso II. of Aragon, one of the most illustrious warriors of the eleventh century, an age fertile in great men. We also possess many other poems, both political and amatory, by the Dauphin D'Auvergne, the Bishop of Clermont, and the last Count and Countess of Provence, Raymond Berenger V. and Beatrix; by Peter III. of Aragon, the celebrated instigator of the Sicilian Vespers, and by his youngest son, Frederic II. the hero and the avenger of the Sicilians. The works of these sovereigns merit our observation as historical monuments, which throw a light on the interests by which they were governed, on their personal character, and on the manners of the times in which they lived. In a literary point of view, however, there were but few Troubadours, whose names were still renowned, at the period when Dante and Petrarch flourished; and to these we shall now proceed.

In the first rank, we shall place Arnaud de Marveil; although Petrarch, in giving the preference to Arnaud Daniel, calls the former *il men famoso Arnaldo.* He was born at Marveil, in Perigord, in a humble rank of life, from which his talents fortunately raised him; and he was attached to the court of Roger II. Viscount of Beziers, called Taillefer. The love which he conceived for the wife of his master, the Countess Adelaide, daughter of Raymond V. Count of Toulouse, was the means of developing his talents and directing the destiny of his life. His versification is easy, and full of nature and tenderness. Amongst the Provençals he well deserves to be called the Great Master of Love, a name which Petrarch has reserved for Arnaud Daniel.

All I behold recalls the memory
Of her I love. The freshness of the hour,
Th' enamell'd fields, the many coloured flower,
Speaking of her, move to me melody.
Had not the poets, with that courtly phrase,
Saluted many a fair of meaner worth,
I could not now have render'd thee the praise
So justly due, of "Fairest of the Earth."
To name thee thus had been to speak thy name,
And waken, o'er thy cheek, the blush of modest shame.*

Arnaud de Marveil, when exiled from Beziers, by the jealousy, not of the husband of the lady he loved, but of a more illustrious and happy rival, Alfonso IX. King of Castile, thus delicately sang the torments of absence.

"They tell me that the heart is only touched by the intervention of the eyes; but I, though I see not the object of my passion, am but the more deeply sensible of the loss I have sustained. They may bear her from my presence, but they can never untie the knot which attaches my heart to her. That heart, so tender and so constant, God alone divides with her; and the portion

* [The Translator has been unable to discover the originals of this, and of the following extracts. A translation of the first is given by M. Raynouard, vol. ii. p. xxiv. *Tr.*]

which God possesses, *he holds as a part of her domain, if God could be a vassal, and hold a fief.* Happy scenes, in which she dwells! when shall I be permitted to revisit you? When shall I behold some one who comes thence? A herdsman from thence would be a noble in my eyes. Oh! that I inhabited a desert, were she but with me! That desert should then be my paradise."

Arnaud de Marveil has left many poems, some of which are very long*. One of his pieces contains four hundred verses, and many of them, two hundred. His language is clear and easy, and his text appears to have suffered but little alteration. He is, therefore, a Troubadour whose works might be separately printed, to try the taste of the public for Provençal poetry, and at the same time to gratify the wishes of the

---

* [A number of his poems are given by *Raynouard*, iii. 199, and in the *Parnasse Occitanien*, i. 15. As the specimens of this poet, given by M. de Sismondi, are so very short, the insertion of the following lines, for which the Translator is indebted to the kindness of a friend, will perhaps be excused. The original may be found in *Raynouard*, iii. 208.—*Tr.*]

Oh! how sweet the breeze of April,
  Breathing soft as May draws near!
While, through nights of tranquil beauty,
  Songs of gladness meet the ear:
Every bird his well-known language
  Uttering in the morning's pride,
Revelling in joy and gladness
  By his happy partner's side.

earned throughout all Europe, who regret the oss of these monuments of our earliest literature and civilization *. The Countess of Beziers died in 1201, and there is reason to believe that Arnaud de Marveil died before her.

Next to a Troubadour, who sang nothing but love, we shall place a valiant knight, who acquired as much glory by his sword as by his lyre.

When, around me, all is smiling,
When to life the young birds spring,
Thoughts of love, I cannot hinder,
Come, my heart inspiriting—
Nature, habit, both incline me
In such joy to bear my part:
With such sounds of bliss around me
Who could wear a sadden'd heart?

Fairer than the far-famed Helen,
Lovelier than the flow'rets gay,
Snow-white teeth, and lips truth-telling,
Heart as open as the day;
Golden hair, and fresh bright roses,—
Heaven, who form'd a thing so fair,
Knows that never yet another
Lived, who can with her compare.

* The following commencement of an epistle from Arnaud de Marveil to his mistress, possesses beauty, grace, and sensibility:

Cel que vos es al cor pus près
Don' am preguet qu' eus saludes,
Sel qu'eus amet pus anc nos vi
Ab franc cor et humil e fi;
S que autra non pot amar
Ni auza vos merce clamar,

Rambaud de Vaqueiras * was the son of a poor knight, of the principality of Orange. He attached himself, in his youth, to the person of Wil-

---

E vien ses joy ab grant dolor;
Sel que non pot son cor partir
De vos sin s' abia a morir;
Sel que tos temps vos amara
May c' autra, tan can vievra,
Sel que ses vos non pot aver
En est segle joy ni plazer,
Sel que no sap cosselh de se
Si ab vos non troba merce,
Vos saluda; e vostra lauzor,
Vostra beutat, vostra valor,
Vostre solatz, vostre parlar,
Vostr' aculhir e vostr' onrar,
Vostre pretz, vostr' essenhamen,
Vostre saber, e vostre sen,
Vostre gen cors, vostre dos riz,
Vostra terra, vostre pays.
Mas l'erguelh que avetz a lui
Volgra ben ayzas ad altrui:
Quel erguelh Dona e l'espavens,
Quel fezes lestal marrimens
C' anc pueys non ai joy ni deport,
Ni sap en cal guizas conort;
Mas lo melhos conort que a
Es car sap que por vos morra,
E plaits li mais morrir per vos
Que per autra vivre joyoz.

* [Five poems, by this author, are given in the *Parnasse Occitanien*, i. 75. and three, in *Raynouard*, iii. 256. One of the poems is to be found in both.—*Tr.*]

iam de Baux, first Prince of Orange, within whose allegiance he was born. Whilst he acted the part of a valiant soldier beneath that prince's banners, he at the same time celebrated his victories, and attacked his enemies in his verses, commemorating even the trophies which he bore away in the tourneys. From the service of the Prince of Orange, Vaqueiras passed into that of Boniface III. Marquis of Montferrat, who led, with Baldwin and Dandolo, the fourth crusade, and who, after having disputed the throne of Constantinople, was raised to that of Thessalonica. By Boniface, Vaqueiras was dubbed a knight. That excellent judge of bravery and military talent, bestowed many honours on the poetical warrior, who had rendered him such important services in his various wars. He beheld, with pleasure, his attachment to his sister Beatrix, and he himself took the trouble of reconciling them, after a serious quarrel. Vaqueiras composed many *chanzos* in honour of Beatrix, whom he called his *Bel Cavalier*, from having once seen her gracefully managing a sword. In these verses, we find the impression of the manly haughtiness and loyalty of his character. But all love-poems lose their identity, when translated into prose, and, perhaps, are all equally tiresome. Vaqueiras was more remarkable for his warlike imagination. The preaching of the third crusade inflamed him with new enthusiasm. He sang the Holy War in a *sirvente*, addressed to his princely protector and friend, when, on the death of the Count of Champagne in 1204, the former was chosen leader of the Christian forces.

"It is clear that God delights to recompense the brave. He has raised the reputation of the Marquis of Montferrat so high above the most valiant, that all the crusaders of France and Champagne have demanded him from heaven, as the man best qualified to recover the holy sepulchre. This brave marquis, God has given him courageous vassals, a large territory, and great riches, to ensure him success.

"He who made the air, the heavens, the earth, the sea, the heat, the cold, the rain and the thunder, wills, that we should pass the seas in his train, as the Magi, Gui, Gaspard, and Melchior, sought Jerusalem. May St. Nicolas guide our fleet! May the Champagners raise their banner! May the marquis cry, Montferrat! May the Count Baldwin cry, Flanders! May every one strike so stoutly, that swords and lances may shiver, and we shall soon put the Turks to flight. May the brave King of Spain extend his conquests over the Moors, while the marquis carries on the campaign, and besieges the Saracen.

Envoy. "Fair knight, for whom I compose these verses and songs, I know not whether, for you, I shall assume or quit the cross; so much you please me, when I see you, and so much I suffer in your absence.

Vaqueiras followed the Marquis Boniface into Greece, and combated, like a brave cavalier, by his side, before the palace of Blachernæ, and afterwards at the assault of Constantinople. After the division of the Greek empire, he followed Boniface into his kingdom of Thessalonica, and received from him fiefs, seignories, and other magnificent rewards. Still, ambition could not make him forget his love; and in the midst of his conquests in Greece, he thus bewailed his absence.

"What avail my conquests, my riches, and my glory! How much richer was I, when I was loved, myself a faithful lover! I know no other pleasures than those of love. Useless are all my goods and my lands, and the more my power and riches increase, the more deeply does my heart feel its distress, parted from my Fair Knight."*

But, by far the most curious poem by Vaqueiras, is that in which, retracing the history of his own life and of that of Boniface, the dangers they had confronted in common, the services they had

* [The Translator has been unable to discover the original of these two fragments. He has, therefore, given a prose translation only of the French prose version.]

rendered, and the conquests they had made, he demands, with noble confidence, the recompense due to his fidelity and his valour. I regret that this poem is too long for insertion, since no production of the kind bears a deeper impress of the chivalric character of that faithful vassalage, which did not chill friendship, and of that subordination, which did not hinder the souls of both lord and vassal from attaining the same elevation. Vaqueiras praises his master, as he recalls his victories and his dangers. He brings to mind their numerous adventures in Piedmont, in the States of Genoa, in Sicily, and in Greece, where he was ever by his side; and he frankly claims a portion of the glory and the gratitude which were due to him. The following anecdote, which he relates amongst others, seems to give a good picture of the manners of the times:—

"Do you remember," says he, "the Jongleur Aimonet, who brought you news of Jacobina, when she was on the point of being carried into Sardinia, and married to a man she disliked? Do you also remember how, on bidding you farewell, she threw herself into your arms, and besought you, in such moving terms, to protect her against the injustice of her uncle? You immediately ordered five of your bravest esquires to mount. We rode all night, after supper. With my own hand, I bore her from the domain, amidst an universal outcry. They pursued us, horse and foot; we fled, at full speed; and we alread thought ourselves out of danger, when we wei attacked by the knights of Pisa. With so mai cavaliers pressing close upon us, so many shielc glittering around us, and so many banners wavir in the wind, you need not ask us whether w were afraid. We concealed ourselves betwee Albenga and Final, and, from the place of oi retreat, we heard on all sides the sound of hoi and clarion, and the signal-cries of pursui Two days, we remained without meat or drinl and when, on the third day, we recommenced oi journey, we encountered twelve banditti, and w knew not how to conduct ourselves; for to attac them on horseback was impossible. I dismounte and advanced against them on foot. I wa wounded by a lance; but I disabled three ‹ four of my opponents, and put the rest to fligh My companions, then, came to my assistance we drove the robbers from the defile, and yo passed in safety. You, no doubt, recollect ho merrily we dined together, although we had onl a single loaf to eat and nothing to drink. In th evening, we arrived at Nice, and were receive by our friend Puiclair, with transports of joy The next day, you gave Jacobina in marriage t Anselmo, and recovered for him his county ‹ Vintimiglia, in spite of his uncle, who er deavoured to despoil him of it."

The Marquis Boniface III., of Montferrat, wa

slain in 1207, at the siege of Satalia. We are not informed whether Vaqueiras survived him.

Pierre Vidal of Toulouse, a Troubadour who followed King Richard to the third crusade, was no less celebrated for his extravagant actions than for his poetical talents. Love and vanity, amongst the poets, seem by turns to assume such an empire over the feelings, as almost to shake the reason. None, however, have been known to display more perfect madness than Pierre Vidal. Persuaded that he was beloved by every lady, and that he was the bravest of all knights, he was the Quixote of poetry. His ridiculous amours, and his extravagant rhodomontades, heightened by the treacherous pleasantries of pretended friends, led him into the strangest errors. During the crusade, he was persuaded, at Cyprus, to marry a Greek lady, who asserted that she was allied to one of the families which had filled the throne of Constantinople; and this circumstance furnished him with sufficient grounds for believing that he was himself entitled to the purple. He assumed the title of Emperor, and bestowed that of Empress upon his wife. He had a throne carried before him, and he destined the produce of his savings and his songs, to assist him in the conquest of his empire. Notwithstanding this affair, he still remained much attached to the wife of Barral des Baux, Viscount of Marseilles, whom he had selected as the lady of his thoughts, and to whom, rom Cyprus, he addressed some verses remarkable for their harmony. On his return into Provence, a new amour led him into a still wilder piece of extravagance. He fell in love with a ady of Carcassonne, called Louve de Penautier, nd, in honour of her, he assumed the surname of *Loup*. To give himself a better title to the appellation, he clothed himself in a wolf's skin, and persuaded the shepherds to chase him, with dogs, over the mountains. He had the perseverance to uffer this strange pursuit to the last extremity, nd was carried half-dead to his mistress, who vas not much moved by so singular a piece of levotion. Yet, with a head apparently so badly rganized, Pierre Vidal possessed an exquisite ensibility, and great harmony of style; and, what vill appear still more strange, a sound and ealthy judgment on all matters not relating to is own vanity, or to his own attachments. The ollection of his works contains more than sixty pieces, and amongst them, three long poems of he kind to which the Provençals gave the simple ppellation of *verses*. The most remarkable of he three is that, in which he gives advice to a Troubadour, as to the mode of exercising his noble profession.* Poetry, he considers to be the ultivation of high sentiment, the storehouse of niversal philosophy, and the Troubadours to be

* The whole poem is translated by *Millot*, vol. ii. p. 283.

the instructors of nations. He recalls the glorious days of his youth, when Heaven permitted all Europe to be governed by heroes: when Germany possessed the Emperor Frederic I.; England, Henry II. and his three sons; Toulouse, Count Raymond; and Catalonia, Count Berenger and his son Alfonso. He shows how poetry was the common bond of union amongst these heroës, and he declares it to be his belief, that it is the duty of the Jongleurs to awaken, in the next generation, the high sentiments which had been the glory of their fathers. He inculcates, at the same time, maxims of modesty, decency, and morality, honourable alike to his character and to his judgment: thus displaying a nobility of language, and a depth of thought, strangely at variance with the extravagance of his conduct.

Another of his *verses*, or long poems, is a new allegory, in which the principal personages whom he introduces are Love, Mercy, Modesty, and Loyalty; some of the allegorical beings, which the East had given to the Provençals, and such as afterwards figured in the Triumphs of Petrarch. The poet relates, that once, when he was in the country, he saw a young cavalier, fair as the morning, advancing towards him, with whose mien he was unacquainted. His eyes were soft and tender; his nose was beautifully formed; his teeth, shining like the purest silver; his mouth, blooming and smiling, and his figure, slight and graceful.

His robe was embroidered with flowers, and his head was adorned with a crown of roses. His palfrey, which was white as snow, was marked with spots of black and purple. His saddle-bow was of jasper, his housings were of sapphire, and the stirrups, of chalcedony. Addressing himself to the poet, he said, "Know, Pierre Vidal, that I am Love; this lady is called Mercy; that damsel is Modesty; and my esquire, here, is Loyalty." This poem proves that the Love of the Provençals was not Cupid, the son of Venus, and that these romantic allegories are not borrowed from the Pagan mythology. The *Cavalier Love* of Pierre Vidal, is clothed in the costume of the chivalric age, which gave him birth. His palfrey is described with the same minuteness as his own person. His suite is composed of the chivalric virtues, and not of joys and smiles. The whole idea bears the character of another age. Love, indeed, amongst the poets of the East, was mounted in a manner, very different from that, in which our Troubadour represents him. Most frequently, he was seated, by them, on the wings of a parroquet; whence the Provençals, in imitation of the Arabians, have often introduced that richly-plumaged bird into their songs, as the messenger of Love.

It is said, that Pierre Vidal, in his old age, wrote a treatise *On the art of holding one's tongue.* He made a second voyage to the Levant, where, we are assured, he again indulged the ridiculous idea of becoming Emperor of the East, then under the dominion of the Latins. He died in 1229, two years after his return.

We have seen that Petrarch gives the first rank, amongst the Troubadours, to Arnaud Daniel, whom he places above Arnaud de Marveil. Dante pays him no less a compliment, in his treatise *De Vulgari Eloquentiâ*. He looks upon him as the Troubadour who possessed the greatest mastery over his language, and surpassed all the other writers in the Romance languages, both in the tenderness of his verses, and in his prose compositions. He introduces him in the twenty-sixth canto of the Purgatorio, and puts some lines, in the Provençal language, into his mouth, which have a singular effect in a poem entirely Italian. But the seventeen pieces, by this poet, which survive, do not bear out all these eulogies. The invention of the stanza in six lines, which is attributed to him, does not confer so much honour upon him, in our eyes, as it appears formerly to have done.* There is reason to believe that his

* The stanzas of six lines, which were afterwards imitated by Petrarch, and by the principal Italian, Spanish, and Portuguese poets, are songs in six stanzas, of six lines each. The lines of the first stanza are terminated by six substantives, of two syllables each, which ought likewise to form the termination of the lines of all the other stanzas, with this variation, that in each stanza the words ought to change their place. The same word ought to

better productions are lost, and we ought not, therefore, to judge him too severely, by those which remain.

Amanieu des Escas, who flourished at the end of the thirteenth century, under the dominion of the Kings of Aragon, has left us, amongst various amatory effusions, two *verses,* or long poems, on the education of young ladies and gentlemen; which, without being remarkable for poetical invention, are interesting from the *naïveté* of the descriptions, which they contain, of the manners of the times. The lady, who, in the course of the poem, is twice or thrice addressed by the title of Marchioness, applies herself to Des Escas, who was himself a powerful lord, for his counsel, as to the proper mode of conducting herself in the world. We are not a little surprised, when we find that the first advice he gives her, is more fitted for a domestic than for a lady of rank. He tells

---

be found successively at the end of the first, the sixth, the fifth, the fourth, the third, and the second lines of each stanza; so that by the end of the piece it will have occupied all the places in the stanza. No harmony, perceptible to the ear, results from this order of words, so difficult to observe; and the sense is almost always sacrificed to the constrained versification. The constant return of six words, necessarily forming the groundwork of the ideas, and compelling the poet, as they recur, to avail himself of all their significations, has, however, something pensive and melancholy about it; and the poets have occasionally clothed, in this stanza, some very touching reflections.

her that, in the first place, after attending to her toilet (and, here, the poet enters into the most minute details), she must prepare to assist her lady in rising, and that she must bring her all she requires for dressing her head, adjusting her robe, and washing her hands.* It was, at this time, regarded as an essential part of female education, that a young lady should learn to obey, before she presumed to command; and she, therefore, willingly attached herself to some noble dame, to learn from her, whilst she performed these menial offices, politeness and the art *de beau parler*. Des Escas then instructs the damsel on her duties, when she is addressed by a suitor. He tells her that it is

* E cosselh vos premier
Que siatz matiniera,
Cascu jorn que premieira
Vos levetz que vostra dona,
En asi que si eus sona
Vos truep gent adobada,
E vestida e caussada;
Et enantz que eus cordetz
Lau qu'el bras vos lavetz
E las mas, et la cara.
Après amiga cara
Cordatz estrechamen
Vostre bratz ben e gen,
I es las onglas dels detz
Tan longuas non portetz
Que i paresca del nier.

quite proper that she should make choice of some obedient admirer; provided that, instead of selecting him merely for his handsome person or his riches, she accept the services of a courteous lover, of honourable birth. He permits her both to give and to receive presents; but he admonishes her not to trespass beyond certain boundaries: "For, if he loves you," continues he, "he ought to ask you for nothing, *whilst you continue unmarried*, which can be prejudicial or dishonourable to you." We perceive, from this, that the Provençals were of opinion, as are the Italians and the Spanish at the present day, that gallantry after marriage was a venial offence, whilst, in an unmarried woman, it was accounted highly disreputable; and the consequences of this false morality are easily foreseen.*

The advice to the young gentlemen is much of the same nature, intermingled with domestic details and maxims of gallantry. Such young men as were not rich enough to support themselves at court, at their own expense, and yet wished to educate themselves to gallantry and arms, usually attached themselves to some lord, whom they

* E si eus ama fort bela
De mentre qu'es pieusela
El no us deu requerer
Qu' eus torn a desplaser
Ad onta ni a dampnatje
De tot vostre linhatje.

erved as pages at court, or as esquires in the eld. The counsels of Des Escas to the youth, re those of an honourable man, of good sense, ut exceedingly verbose, as if he thought that he ad never said enough. He takes occasion, from a ompliment which the young gentleman had addressed to him, to caution him against the habit of flattering his superiors. He shews him what an injury it is to his own character, and how he only heaps ridicule upon the man to whom he wishes to render himself agreeable. He enlarges very much on the subject of love, that most important affair, the great duty of all young cavaliers, and the science in which the Troubadours may be said to have taken their degrees. The advice which he gives him, with regard to the elegance of his dress, his demeanour during tourneys, his reserve, and his discretion, is conformable to the manners of a chivalrous age, but does not possess sufficient novelty for insertion in this place. The following exhortation, as to his conduct towards his mistress, we are certainly unprepared for. "In case she should give you real grounds for jealousy, and should deny that, of which your own eyes have given you proof, say to her, 'Lady, I am persuaded that what you tell me is true, but I did really believe that I had seen it.'"* This reminds us of the lady of fashion, who,

* E se la us fa gelos
E us en dona razo,

when surprised, by her lover, with another, thus answered his furious reproaches: "I am persuaded you do not love me, for you believe your own eyes, in preference to my word."

Pierre Cardinal,* of an illustrious family at Puy in Velay, who died when almost a century old, occupied, at the commencement of the thirteenth century, a distinguished place amongst the Troubadours, less on account of the harmony of his style than of the vigour and asperity of his satirical powers. He is the Juvenal of the Provençals. The obstinacy of his character, his frankness, often degenerating into rudeness, and his bitter raillery, were not calculated to promote his success amongst the ladies. He, therefore, quitted gallantry, at an early age, to become a writer of *sirventes;* for the Troubadours gave this name to their satires also, from the time that they were divided into stanzas like their *chanzos.* These *sirventes* are levelled, by turns, against all ranks of society; the elevated clergy, the military orders, the monks, the barons, and the ladies. Pierre Cardinal sees nothing around him

---

E us ditz c' ancre no fo
De so que dels huelhs vis,
Diguatz Don: Eu suy fiz
Que vos disetz vertat,
Mas yeu vay simiat.

* [See *Raynouard*, iii. p. 436. *Parnasse Occitanien*, i. p. 306. *Tr.*]

but corruption of manners, cupidity, egotism, and baseness. His observations, although they exhibit but little acuteness, have yet an air of truth about them. Vice excites his anger, which is occasionally eloquent; and, in his rapid invectives, he seldom mingles either idle details or ill-judged reflections. His boldness astonishes us, at a period when the Inquisition might have called him to account, for his offences against the church. "Indulgences and pardons, God and the Devil," says he, speaking of the priesthood, "are all put in requisition. Upon these, they bestow Paradise, by their pardons; others, they condemn to perdition, by their excommunications. They inflict blows which cannot be parried; and no one is so skilful in imposition, that they cannot impose upon him. ......There are no crimes, for which the monks cannot give absolution. For money, they grant to renegades and usurers that sepulture which they deny to the poor, because they are unable to pay for it. To live pleasantly, to buy good fish, the whitest bread, and the finest wine, this is their object, the whole year round. God willing, I would be of this order, if I could purchase my salvation at this price."

We, likewise, possess a *sirvente*, by the same writer, against the priests; another, against the barons; and a third, on the general depravity of the times. "From the East to the West, I will nake a new covenant with all the world. To every loyal man I will give a *bezant*,* if the disoyal will give me a nail. To all the courteous I will give a mark of gold, if the discourteous will give me a penny. To all that speak the truth I will give a heap of gold, if every liar will give me in egg. As to all the laws that are obeyed, I could write them on a piece of parchment, no larger than half the thumb of my glove. A young turtledove should nourish all the brave, for I should be ashamed to offer them a scanty entertainment. But if I had to invite the wicked, I would cry, without regard to the place, 'Come and feast, all honest people!'"†

* A coin, current in Constantinople, of about the value of ten shillings.

† D'aus aurien tro al solelh colgan
Fauc a la gen un covinen novel;
A lial hom donarai un bezanh
Si'l deslial mi dona un clavel;
Et un marc d'aur donarai al cortes
Si'l descauzit mi dona un tornes.
Al vertadier darai d'aur un gran mont
Si ay un huovs dels messongiers que son.

Tota la ley qu'il pus de la gen an
Escrieur 'ieu en un petit de pel,
En la meitat del polgar de mon gan;
El pros homes paisserai d'un tortel,
Car ja pels pros no fara car con res;
Mais si fos uns que los malvats pogues,
Cridar ferai, e no gardassen on,
Venetz manjar, li pro home del mon.

These satires drew down, upon Pierre Cardinal, the hatred of all whom he had attacked, and he thus describes his desolate condition.—"There was once a city, I do not remember where, in which such a shower fell, that it drove every one mad whom it touched. All the inhabitants were thus affected, except one; and he escaped, in consequence of having been asleep in a house when the shower happened, and when he awakened, he perceived that it had ceased. When he walked out, one man ran after him, another ran away from him. This man stood stupified, that threw stones at the stars, and another was tearing off his clothes. This man strikes him, that offers him money. Here, a man imagines himself a king, and walks magnificently with his arms a-kimbo; while, there, another is sitting on the ground. One man uses menaces, another vents abuse; one weeps, and another laughs; one speaks without understanding what he says, and another is entirely occupied with himself. The man, who had retained his senses, is prodigiously astonished; he sees that they are wide awake, and he eyes them from head to foot. But, though he is thus astonished, their surprise is much greater, at seeing him in his sound mind. They believe that he has lost his senses, because he does not act as they do. They all think that it is they who are wise and prudent, and that it is he who is mad. One of them strikes him on the body, another on the neck; and he cannot stir, without being attacked. This man seizes him; the other pushes him, as he strives to escape from the crowd. One man menaces him; another drags him along. Now, they raise him up, and again, they let him fall; and each plays his pranks upon him. He takes refuge in his house, covered with mud, bruised, and half-dead, rejoicing in his escape from them.

"This fable is very applicable to the world at large. This present age represents the city, which possesses so many madmen. The highest wisdom of man is, to love God and his mother, and to keep his commandments; but that wisdom is now lost. The shower which fell is the covetousness, the pride, and the malice, with which the whole race of man is perplexed; and if God has preserved any from this misfortune, the others regard them as madmen, and despise them, because they differ from themselves, and because the wisdom of God appears to them folly. The friend of God knows that they are senseless, when they have lost the wisdom of God; and they hold him to be mad, because they have forsaken the wisdom of God."*

---

* It has been thought proper to give a literal translation of this specimen of Provençal poetry; as it will enable those, who read the original, to comprehend it with greater ease, and to those who, without making that attempt, content themselves with the version, it will give a better idea of the turn and spirit of the original. The text has been translated, word for word, as far as my very imperfect acquaintance with a language, which I

Giraud Riquier, of Narbonne,* was a follower
f Alfonzo X., King of Castile, and flourished

ave been able to study only in a few manuscript fragments,
as enabled me so to do.

Yssy comensa la faula de la pluya.

Una ciutat fo, no say quals
Hon cazee una plueya tals
Que tuy li home de la ciutat
Que toque, foro forcenat.
Tuy desse n'ero mals, sols us,
Et aquel escapet, ses pus,
Que era dins una mayzo
Que dormia quant aysso fo.
E vet, quant at dormit
Del plueya diquit,
E foras entre la gens
Fero d'essenamens
Arroquet, l'autre foueis,
Utre estupit versus,
E trays peras contre estelas,
L'autre esquisset las gonelas,
Us feric, el autrem peys,
E l'autre cuyet esser Reys,
Et tenc se riquement pels flancx,
E l'autre s'asset per los bancx.
L'us menasec l'autre maldisz,
L'autre plorec et l'autre riz,
L'autre parlec e no saup que;
L'autre fe meteys de se.
Aquel que avia so sen,
Meravilha se molt formen,

* [Six of his pieces are given in the *Parnasse Occit.* i. 329, and the same number, in *Raynouard,* iii. 461. Three of the latter are the same as those given in the *Parnasse.—Tr.*]

at the end of the thirteenth century. He is one of the Troubadours, of whose works we have the

---

Que vee que be destatz son,
E garda ad aval ed amon,
E grans meravelha a de lor.
Mas mot l'hau ilh de lui mayor;
Qu' el vezon estar saviamen
Cuio que aia perdut so sen,
Car so qu' elh fan no lh vezo fayre
Que a cascu de lores veyaire
Que ilh son savi e assenatz.
Mas lui teno por dessenat
Qui 'l fer en gansa, qui en col;
Nos pot mudar que nos degol;
L' us l' empenh, e l' autre le bota,
El cuya isshir de la rota,
L' us l' esquinsa, l' autre li tray,
E pren colos, e leva, e chay;
Cascu 'l leva a gran gabantz,
El fuy a sa mayzo deffantz,
Fangos e battutz e mieg mort,
E ac gaug can lor fo estort.
Sest fable es en aquest mon
Semblans als homes que i son.
Aquest seigles es la ciutat
Que es tot ples de forsennatz;
Que el mager sen qu' om pot aver
So es amar Dieu et sa mer,
E gardar sos comendamens,
Mas arra es perdutz aquels sens.
La pluya say es casuda,
Una cobeytat qu' es venguda,
Us erguelh et una maleza
Que tota la gent a perpreza.

most numerous remains. He lived at a period, when the poets sought, by novel attempts, to distinguish themselves from the crowd of their predecessors. He has left pastorals, *aubades*, serenades, *retrouanges*, epistles, and discourses in verse.* He has varied, as far as lay in his power, the form of his verses, but he has not succeeded in infusing into them any substantial novelty. His discourses in verse, and his didactic poems, contain little, beyond common-place ideas and trite moral maxims. Yet we recognize, in them, the spirit of an honourable man, not deficient in a proper pride. The longest of his poems, by far, is a pe-

---

E si Dieu n'a alcu gardatz,
L'autru ils teno por dessenat,
E menon lo de tomp en vilh,
Car no es del seu que son illi.
Qu'el sen de Dieu lor par folia,
E l'amiers de Dieu on que sia
Conoys que dessenatz son tug
Car le sen de Dieu an perdut;
E els an lui per dessenat
Car le sen de Dieu an layssat.

* These different names do not indicate much real variety in the poems. The pastorals were eclogues, which more frequently contained conversations between the writer and the shepherds, than dialogues between the shepherds themselves. The *aubades* and the serenades were love-songs, for the morning and the evening. The *retrouanges* and the *redondes* were ballads of a more complicated construction, in which the burthen was introduced in such a manner as to render the composition more laborious. All these poems, even the pastorals, were of a lyrical cast.

tition addressed to Alfonso of Castile, to raise the profession of the Jongleurs from the degradation into which it had fallen, on account of the Charlatans, who amused the people by their buffooneries, exhibiting dancing apes and goats, and singing the grossest songs in public, under the same name as the poets of the courts. He demands that, by his royal authority, Alfonso shall separate all the men who are thus confounded together, into four distinct classes—the professors of the art of poetry, the simple Troubadours, the Jongleurs, and the buffoons. This poem, which bears date in the year 1275, is one of the last sighs, breathed by the expiring poetry of Provence.* The Troubadour had already witnessed the fall of his art: he had survived his

* This long poem is, properly, an epistle to the King of Castile. Giraud Riquier wrote many of the same kind, and seems to have been very successful in catching the epistolary style. Still, he is difficult to be understood, and this difficulty appears to me, generally, to arise from the corruption of the text of the Troubadours. After having shewn how each state in society divides itself into several classes, distinguished by name, he adds:

Per quem ai albirat
Que fora covinen
De noms entre joglars,
Que non e ben estars.
Car entr' els li melhor
Non an de noms honor
Atresi com de fach
Qu' ieu ne teng a maltrags

glory, the literature which he loved, and the language in which he had distinguished himself. His situation reminds us of that of Ossian, in the last of his poems, where he renounces his harp, whose harmony the new race of men knew not how to appreciate. But, how different are the two poems! The Jongleur of Narbonne thinks only of his own vanity; while the bard of Morven is insensible to every thing but the loss of Oscar and Malvina, and of the country and the glory which he has survived.

We shall not attempt to make the reader acquainted with any of the other poets, who form the multitude of Troubadours, and who all hold nearly the same rank, and possess

---

Cus homs senes saber
Ab sotil captener,
Si de qualqu' estrumen
Sab un pauc a prezen
S'en ira el tocan
Per carrieiras sercan
E queren c'omz li do
O autre sez razo.
Cantara per las plassas
Vilmen et en gens bassas;
Metra queren sa ponha
E totas ses vergonha
Privadas et estranhas,
Pueys iras si en tavernas.
Ab sol qu' en puesc aver
E non auzan parer
En deguna cort bona.

equal pretensions to that celebrity, which none of them have been able to obtain. An extreme monotony reigns throughout all their works; and, when the features are similar in all, it is difficult to paint a portrait so as to present any individuality of character. We have seen how the Provençal poetry, taking its rise in the eleventh century, and spreading throughout the south of France, and over a portion of Spain and Italy, was the delight of every court, animated all the festivals, and was familiar to all classes of the people; and we have seen how, at the middle of the thirteenth century, it had made no perceptible progress. All that we find in the earliest songs of William IX., Count of Poitiers, meets us again in the latest productions of Giraud Riquier, or of Jean Estève. The language was almost always the same, and seems only to vary, according to the greater or less negligence of the copyists; or, perhaps, in consequence of the pretensions of the later poets, who, to gain the reputation of employing singular and difficult rhymes, corrupted their language, by augmenting its obscurities and irregularities. We find the same gallantry, expressed in the same hyperbolical terms; the same tenderness, proceeding from the ingenious conceits of the brain, rather than from the real feeling of the heart; the same love-songs, presenting the portrait of a beauty like all other beauties, and destitute of expression; with the same exaggerations of her merit, her birth, and her character; the same tears, the same submission, the same prayers, each undistinguishable from the other, and all of them equally tedious. We have satirical *sirventes*, in which grossness and abuse supply the place of novelty and of wit; and *tensons*, in which all the common-places of gallantry are debated, without exciting our interest, and without ability. We find *sextines*, *retrouanges*, and *redondes*, in which sense gives place to rhyme, without a single fine poetical conception, or a single attempt at the epic or tragic style. No trace of true feeling is discoverable; no gaiety proceeding from the frankness of the heart, or founded upon any thing better than trespasses against decency. This result is really surprising, after examining the productions of nearly two hundred poets, whose works have been collected by M. de Sainte-Palaye, and extracted by Millot. The enthusiastic love of poetry, which seized the whole nation, leads us to expect far different things. The harmonious ear which had presided at the invention of so many varied forms of verse; the sensibility, the fancy which displayed themselves in the earlier songs of the Troubadours; the richness of the images, which they had borrowed from the East, or which were created by the effort of their own imaginations, all gave a hope that some true poet would soon rise up amongst them. The art of versification amongst the Italians, the Spanish, and other nations, had not nearly so brilliant an origin. As we advance, however, we are gradually undeceived, and are disgusted with all that at first promised us pleasure. We feel inclined to concur in opinion with the public, who, even without a knowledge of the Troubadours, have rejected their claims to celebrity, leaving their works buried in manuscripts, rarely to be met with, and in danger of perishing for ever; and who have condemned their language, the earliest of the European dialects, notwithstanding its sonorous harmony, its flexibility, equal to the Italian, and its majesty of sound which rivals the Spanish, because no writer of true genius has arisen, to redeem it from the charge of sterility. This poverty in the literature of Provence, and this sudden decay, succeeding so splendid an era, demand some explanation. After the thirteenth century, the Troubadours were heard no more, and all the efforts of the counts of Provence, who had then assumed the title of king of Naples, of the magistrates of Toulouse, and of the kings of Aragon, to awaken their genius, by the Courts of Love and the Floral Games, were vain.

The Troubadours themselves have attributed their decay to the degradation into which the Jongleurs, with whom they were generally confounded, had fallen. To make an occupation of amusing the rich and the powerful, and to sell laughter and entertainment, must always deteriorate the character. When gaiety and wit are repaid with a salary, the receiver is necessarily placed on a level with the lowest buffoons; and, in addressing the populace, such men, perhaps, have more success, in exciting admiration and in gaining rewards, than others of the most distinguished talents, whose productions are calculated to gratify real taste. The Jongleurs (*Joculatores*) used to take their stations in the cross-roads, clothed in grotesque habits, and attract a crowd around them, by exhibiting dancing apes, legerdemain tricks, and the most ridiculous antics and grimaces. In this manner, they prepared their audience for the verses which they recited; and they cared not what extravagancies they committed, provided they were well rewarded. The most distinguished Troubadours, when they presented themselves at the court of a prince, or the castle of a baron, were often introduced under this name of Jongleurs. Even when they experienced the reception due to their talents, and when the noblest ladies admitted them to familiar converse, or bestowed their affections upon them they were, yet, made to feel that they were considered as of a subordinate rank, and that their dissolute manners, their irritability, and their insatiable avarice, would not be borne with patience The jealousy, too, of the offended husbands, frequently compelled them to submit to outrage which degraded them. In a situation so unfavourable to that loftiness of spirit, which is the accompaniment of genius, it was not strange that the talents, even of the noblest characters, should not be developed.

All the Troubadours did not, however, make a trade of their art. A sufficient number of sovereigns and of powerful barons and knights were devoted to poetry, to preserve the nobility of its origin, even during the whole period of Provençal literature. Frederick, King of Sicily, who died in 1326, is the last of the Troubadours, whose works have been collected by M. de Sainte-Palaye, as the Count of Poitou was the first.

But the art of the Troubadour contained within itself a more immediate principle of decay, in the profound ignorance of its professors, and in the impossibility of their giving to their poetry a higher character than they themselves possessed. A few of them, only, were acquainted with the Latin language; and we may judge of their erudition, by the pretensions which they display in citing, not any poetical passages, but semi-barbarous phrases borrowed from the schoolmen. None of them were acquainted with the authors, whom we denominate classical. In the *Treasure* of Pierre de Corbian*, in which he makes a parade of his acquirements, and seems to think that he is reck-

* *Millot*, vol. iii. p. 227.

oning up the whole sum of human learning, he mentions only one of the Latin poets. This is Ovid, whom he calls a liar; nor can we collect that he had ever read him. In the extracts from two hundred Troubadours, I have scarcely found three or four passages, which contain any allusions to the mythology, or to the history of antiquity. They only, indeed, indicate such vague and uncertain information as an ignorant monk might display, in giving a summary of his acquirements. The Troubadours had no other models than the songs of the Arabians, which their earliest masters had studied, and which had perverted their taste. They had no idea of the elegance of the ancients, and, still less, of their invention; nor were they aware of the necessity of instilling into their poetry new ideas, and of connecting them with action. There is not, in all the poems which have been preserved, the least attempt at the epic; although the great revolutions, in the midst of which they lived, and the events of general interest which they witnessed, and in which they were frequently the actors, ought, naturally, to have given them the habit of relating facts in an animated manner, and of recording historical events in the language and with the spirit of a poet, who designs that his compositions shall be repeated from mouth to mouth. We are told, it is true, of a History of the Conquest of Jerusalem, by the Chevalier Béchada, a Limousin; but, as it is lost, it is impossible for us to determine whether it was not a mere chronicle in rhyme, of which many were written in the north of France. True merit and real talents, employed upon so national a subject, in which such vivid interest was felt by every cavalier, must surely have escaped the fate of Béchada's poem. The Troubadours had no idea of the theatre or of dramatic representations; although the two Nostradamus's, with their usual ignorance and inaccuracy, have given the names of tragedies and comedies to compositions, which were no more dramatic than the Divina Commedia of Dante. Thus, deprived of all the riches of antiquity, the Troubadours had few resources within themselves. The Germans, who have named all modern poetry *romantic,* have supposed all the literature of the Romance nations to have originated from Christianity, or, at least, to have been closely connected with it. The poetry of the Provençals, however, bears no traces of this source. It contains very few religious pieces; none, which display enthusiasm; nor any, where Christianity forms part of the sentiment or of the action. When, by chance, religion is introduced, if it be not, merely, some hymn to the Virgin, a poor imitation from the Latin church-service, it is only in some profane way. Thus, Bernard de Ventadour, when he compares his lady's kiss to the sweet delights of Paradise, adds, that her favours are a proof of what the Psalmist has said, "That a day, in her courts, is better than a hundred elsewhere." So, Arnaud de Marveil calls his lady "the perfect image of the Divinity, before whom all ranks are equal;" and says that "if God should grant him the enjoyment of his love, he should think that paradise was deprived of all its joy and gladness." Many revoked, in the face of the Church, the oaths by which they had bound themselves to their married mistresses, and were absolved from their adultery by the priest; while others caused masses to be said, and tapers and lamps to be burnt before the altar, to propitiate their ladies. Such was the light, in which religion was considered, by the poets of Provence. We see them fettered by the icy chains of superstition, but never animated by the fire of enthusiasm. Religion was a stranger to their hearts; but the dread which it inspired, remained like a weight upon their souls. Sometimes, in foolish security, they made sport of this fear; yet when it again assumed its empire over them, they trembled at its influence. Never did their faith furnish them with a single brilliant image or animated sentiment. A few pieces on the crusades, to which the reader has already been referred, may, perhaps, be excepted; but it is observable, that martial enthusiasm, the only enthusiasm which they display, is quite as conspicuous even in the war-songs of the same period, which have no reference to spiritual subjects.

It is not easy to account for the fact, but it is certain, that a romantic imagination was rarely discovered amongst the Troubadours; whilst the Trouvères, the poets and reciters of tales, in the countries on the north of the Loire, invented or perfected all the ancient romances of chivalry. The tales of the Troubadours have nothing romantic or warlike about them. They always relate to allegorical personages, Mercy, Loyalty, and Modesty, whose duty it is to speak, and not to act. In other poetical pieces of this kind, we are obliged to guess at the allegory, and to search for a key to the fiction; but here the moral stands perfectly naked, nor is it sufficiently interesting to prevent us from regretting that a thicker veil was not thrown over it.

Thus, the poetry of Provence had no resources which were not within itself; no classical allusions, no mythology, either native or borrowed, nor even a romantic imagination. It was a beautiful flower, springing up on a sterile soil; nor could any cultivation avail it, in the absence of its natural nourishment. The Greeks, it is true, who had no masters in their art, gave birth to their own inventions; but, in addition to the fact, that we cannot compare any other nation with the Greeks, so richly endowed as they were by nature, the culture of the latter was progressive. No foreign influence had driven them from their course. Their reason, their imagination, and their sensibility, were all developed at the same moment, and always preserved a happy harmony. Amongst the Provençals, on the other hand, the imagination had received a false direction, from their first mixture with the Arabians. Reason was entirely neglected, or perverted, by the study of school-theology, and of an unintelligible system of philosophy. Sentiment, abandoned to itself, was either weakened by monotony of expression, or perverted by the over-refined and affected language, which seemed to bear an affinity to that of the schools. Still, it is impossible to say, what might have been the influence of a single man of genius, upon the language and literature of Provence. Had Dante been born in the country of the Langue d'Oc; had he boldly united, in one great poem, all the high mythology of Catholicism, with the sentiments, the interests, and the passions of a knight, a statesman, and a crusader, he would have opened a mine of riches, unknown to his contemporaries. Numberless imitators would have followed in his steps, and, by his sole influence, the Provençal language might still have been in existence, the most cultivated as well as the most ancient language of southern Europe. But, in these regions, fanaticism kindled a flame, which repelled the advancing steps of the human intellect, and the crusade against the Albigenses, which will form the subject of the next chapter, decided the destiny of Provence.

CHAPTER VI.

The War against the Albigenses—The last Provençal Poets, in Languedoc and Catalonia.

The period now arrived, when the cruelties of civil war and a persecution of the most implacable description, spread desolation over the country, in which the Provençal poetry had so lately flourished. The deadly hatred of the combatants, inducing devastation and carnage, soon overwhelmed the people, amongst whom the Gay Science had been cultivated, and banished poetry from the land of its birth. The Troubadours, whose sole means of subsistence were found in the hospitality and liberality of the nobles, were now welcomed to desolated castles, whose masters had been ruined by war, and often driven to despair, by the massacre of their families. Those, who associated with the conquerors, gradually imbibed their ferocious prejudices and their fanaticism. Like them, they delighted in blood. Poetry had no longer any charms for them, and even the language of love appeared to them out of nature.

During the thirteenth century, the songs of th Troubadours are full of allusions to this fatal war the fury of which had stifled their genius, per haps, at the very period when it was about to b developed. The language and poetry of Provenc were extinguished in blood.

The excessive corruption of the clergy had, a we have already seen, furnished a subject for th satirical powers of all the Troubadours. Th cupidity, the dissimulation, and the baseness o that body, had rendered them odious both to th nobles and the people. The priests and monk incessantly employed themselves in despoilin the sick, the widowed, the fatherless, and indeed all, whom age, or weakness, or misfortune placed within their grasp; while they squandered in de- bauchery and drunkenness, the money which they extorted by the most shameful artifices. Thus, Raymond de Castelnau exclaims, " The clergy, in their covetousness, are aiming, every day, by their impositions, to shoe and to clothe them- selves well. The great prelates are so eager to advance their fortunes, that they extend their dioceses, without any show of reason. If you hold an honourable fief of them, they immediately wish to seize it ; and you cannot recover the pro- prietorship, unless you give them a sum of mo- ney, or enter into covenants more favourable to them.

" If God has willed the Black monks to be unrivalled in their good eating and in their amours, and the White monks in their lying bulls, and the Templars and Hospitallers in pride, and the Canons in usury; I hold Saint Peter and Saint Andrew to have been egregious fools, for suffering so many torments for the sake of God; since all these people, also, are to be saved."*

The gentry had imbibed such a contempt for the corrupted clergy, that they were unwilling to educate their children to the priesthood; and they granted the benefices, in their gift, to their servants and bailiffs. "I had rather have been a priest than have done so disgraceful a thing," became a proverbial expression.†

---

* Clerzia vol cascun jorn per engal
Ab cobeitat ben caussar e vestir,
Els gran Prelats volon tant enantir
Que ses razo alargan lor deital.
E si tenet del lor un onrat fieu,
Volran l'aver, mas nol cobraretz leu
Si non lor datz una soma d'argen
O no lor faitz pus estrey covinen.

Si monges ners vol Dieus que sian ses par,
Per trop manjar ni per femnas tenir,
Ni monges blancs per bolas a mentir,
Ni per erguelh temple ni espital,
Ni canorgues por prestar a renieu;
Ben tenc per fol sant Peyre sant Andrieu,
Que sofriron per Dieu tan de turmen
Sais i venon ais'els a salvamen.

† See the *Histoire de Languedoc*, par les PP. Vic et Vaisette, t. iii. p. 129. The word of a monk may be believed, when he

Whilst the respect for the Church had received so severe a shock, the Paulicians had introduced, from the East, a simpler faith and a greater purity of manners. The reformed Christian sect of the Paulicians had spread, during the seventh century, from Armenia, over all the provinces of the Greek empire. The persecution of Theodora, in 845, and of Basil the Macedonian, in 867 and 886, after having effected the destruction of more than a hundred thousand victims, compelled the remainder to seek refuge, some amongst the Mussulmans, and others amongst the Bulgarians. Once without the pale of persecution, their faith made the most rapid progress. The Bulgarians, who had established a considerable commerce between Germany and the Levant, by means of the Danube, spread their opinions over the north of Europe, and prepared the way for the Hussites

---

relates, in a very religious work, the corruption of the clergy and the contempt into which they had fallen. But the pious Benedictines, from whom we have borrowed these details, and many of those which follow, have other claims to our confidence. Few men have examined original documents and collected authorities, with the same zeal and indefatigable patience, and few have displayed so much impartiality, in their researches. Their attachment to learning seems to have corrected the prejudices of their order. It is true, we sometimes perceive that they possess knowledge which their habit does not permit them to communicate; but, with a small degree of critical acumen, we may collect, from their works alone, a very just idea of the history of the Albigenses.

of Bohemia; while those Paulicians, who had become subjects of the Mussulmans, insinuated themselves, through Spain, into the south of France and Italy. In Languedoc and Lombardy, the name of *Paterins* was given to them, on account of the sufferings to which they were exposed, wherever the pontifical authority extended itself; and they afterwards received the name of Albigenses, from the numbers who inhabited the diocese of Alby. According to the conference, reported by the Abbé Foncaude,* these sectarians, who were accused of sharing in the doctrines of the Manichæans, with respect to the two principles, differed from the Church of Rome, merely in denying the sovereignty of the Pope, the powers of the priesthood, the efficacy of prayers for the dead, and the existence of purgatory. Driven, by persecution, from the other parts of Europe, they enjoyed a wise toleration in the territories of the Count of Toulouse, the Viscount of Beziers, and amongst the Albigenses; and their numbers continually received accessions, by the harangues of Father Sicard Cellerier, one of their most eloquent pastors. At this period, the Provençals, who had been enriched by their commercial intercourse with the Moors and the Jews, and who had, of necessity, been thrown into contact with those people, respected the

* Hist. de Languedoc.

rights of conscience; whilst the inhabitants of the country to the north of the Loire, were completely subjected to the power of the priests and to the dominion of fanaticism. The Spaniards, more enlightened, still, than the Provençals, and not far removed from the period, when they had themselves been compelled to claim the freedom of opinion, under the Moorish yoke, were still more tolerant. They had not yet engaged in their tedious wars against the Church. A century before the Sicilian Vespers, the kings of Aragon were the declared protectors of all who were persecuted by the papal power; and, in emulation of the kings of Castile, they were, at one time, the mediators for the Albigenses, and at another, their defenders in the field.

Missionaries were despatched into Higher Languedoc, in 1147 and 1181, to convert these heretics; but with little success, as long as arms were not resorted to. Every day, the reformed opinions gained strength. Bertrand de Saissac, the tutor to the young Viscount of Beziers, himself adopted them. They had spread even beyond Languedoc, and had gained many powerful partizans in the Nivernois. At length Innocent III. resolving to destroy these sectarians, whom he had exterminated in Italy, despatched, in the year 1198, two Cistercian monks, with the authority of Legates *a latere*, to discover them, and to bring them to justice. The monks, ambitious of extending the unprecedented powers with which they had been intrusted, not contented with attacking merely the heretics, whom they punished with exile and with confiscation of their goods, quarrelled with all the regular clergy, who had attempted to protect their country from such violent proceedings. They suspended the Archbishop of Narbonne, and the Bishop of Beziers. They degraded the Bishops of Toulouse and of Viviers, and raised to the See of Toulouse, Folquet de Marseille, a Troubadour, who had gained some fame by his amatory verses, but who, disgusted with the world, had retired to the cloister, where he had fostered the passions of fanaticism and persecution.* Pierre de Castelnau, the most eager of the Pontifical Legates, astonished at his slow success in the conversion of the heretics, accused Raymond VI. Count of Toulouse, of favouring them; because that prince, being of a mild and timid disposition, refused to lend himself to those sanguinary proceedings against them, which had been suggested to him. The anger of the priest, at last, induced him to excommunicate the Count in 1207, and to place his states under an interdict. In a conference, which took place a year later, he again treated him with the most violent outrage; and it was, doubtless, upon this occasion, that he quarrelled with one of the Count's gentlemen, who followed

* As to Folquet, see *Millot*, vol. i. p. 179, &c.

him to the banks of the Rhone, on his return, and killed him on the 15th of January, 1208. The murder of this monk, himself polluted with blood, was the completion of the misfortunes of Languedoc. Innocent III. addressed a letter to the King of France, and to all the princes and most powerful barons, as well as to the metropolitans and the bishops, exhorting them to avenge the blood which had been shed, and to extirpate the heresy. All the indulgences and pardons, which were usually granted to the crusaders, were promised to those who exterminated these unbelievers, a thousand times more detestable than the Turks and the Saracens. More than three hundred thousand men appeared in arms, to accomplish this butchery; and the first nobles of France, the most virtuous, and, perhaps, the mildest of her aristocracy, believed that they were rendering an acceptable service to God, in thus arming themselves against their brethren. Raymond VI. terrified at this storm, submitted to every thing that was required of him. He delivered up his fortresses, and even marched to the crusade, against the most faithful of his own subjects; and yet, notwithstanding this disgraceful weakness, he did not escape the hatred or the vengeance of the clergy. But Raymond Roger, Viscount of Beziers, his youthful and generous nephew, without sharing himself in the heretical opinions, would not consent to the atrocities, which were about to be committed in his states. He encouraged his subjects to defend themselves; and shutting himself up in Carcassone, and delivering Beziers to the care of his lieutenants, he awaited, with firmness, the attack of the crusaders.

I am unwilling to detail the progress of this frightful war, which yet possesses a strange interest. It is only connected with the subject of the present work, inasmuch as it caused the destruction of Provençal poetry. Beziers was taken by assault, on the 22d of July, 1209; and fifteen thousand inhabitants, according to the narrative which the abbot of the Cistercians transmitted to the Pope*, or sixty thousand, according to other contemporary writers, were put to the sword. The city itself, after a general massacre, not only of its inhabitants, but likewise of the neighbouring peasantry, who had thrown themselves into it, was reduced to ashes. An old Provençal historian has augmented, by the simplicity of his language, the horror of this picture.†

---

* It was the same Arnold, abbot of the Cistercians, whose narrative is here cited, who, when he was asked, before the city was taken, how he could separate the heretics from the catholics replied, "*Kill them all; God will know who belong to him.*"

† Dins la villa de Beziers son intrats, ou fouc fait lo plus grand murtre de gens que jamas fossa fait en tout lo monde; car aqui non era sparniat vieil ni jove; non pas los enfan que

"They entered the city of Beziers, where they murdered more people than was ever known in the world. For they spared neither young nor old, nor infants at the breast. They killed and murdered all of them; which being seen by the said people of the city, they that were able did retreat into the great church of St. Nazarius, both men and women. The chaplains thereof, when they retreated, caused the bells to ring, until every body was dead. But neither the sound of the bells, nor the chaplains in their priestly habits, nor the clerks, could hinder all from being put to the sword; one only escaped, for all the rest were slain, and died. Nothing so pitiable was ever heard of or done; and when the city had been pillaged, it was set on fire, so that it was all pil-

---

popavan: los toavan et murtrisian, la quella causa vesen por los dits de la villa, se retireguen los que poudian dins la grant gleysa de san Nazary, tant homes que femes. La ont los capelas de aquella se retirereguen, fasen tirar las campanas, quand tout lo monde fossa mort. Mais non y aguet son ni campana, ni capela revestit, ni clerc, que tout non passis per lo trinchet de l'espaia, que ung tant solament non scapet, que non fossen morts et tuats; que fouc la plus grant pietat que jamay despey se sie ausida et facha; et la villa piliada, meteguen lo foc per tota la villa, talamen que touta es pillada et arsa, ainsin que encaras de presan, et que non y demoret causa viventa al mondo, que fouc una cruela vengança, vist que lo dit Visconte non era Eretge, ni de lor cepte. (*Preuves de l'Histoire de Languedoc*, t. iii. p. 11.)

This prose, which is properly the Languedoc dialect, is much more intelligible than the verses of the Troubadours.

laged and burned, even as it appears at this day. No living thing was left, which was a cruel vengeance, seeing that the said Viscount was neither a heretic nor of their sect."

This fragment has been selected, for the purpose of shewing that the Provençal language, at that time, could boast not only of poets, but, also, of prose writers. It was a formed language, like the Italian, and, like that tongue, its merit was its simplicity. The anonymous historian, from whom the above extract is borrowed, reminds us of the Florentine historian, Villani, by his candour and his powers of description. The language might, perhaps, have become more pure and fixed, and the prose writers might have produced a revolution in their literature, had not these massacres and the subsequent servitude of Provence, destroyed the national character.

The courage of the Viscount of Beziers did not fail, even under these horrible circumstances; and the brave inhabitants of Carcassonne renewed their oath of attachment to him, and of fidelity to one another. In several sallies, they had the advantage; and at length Peter II. of Aragon offered himself as mediator, soliciting the forbearance of the crusaders to the viscount, who was his friend and relation. All the favour which could be procured from the priests, who presided over the army, was an offer to allow thirteen of the inhabitants, including the viscount, to leave the city. The remainder were reserved for a butchery similar to that of Beziers. The answer of the viscount was, that he would consent to be flayed alive, before he would abandon a single one of his fellow-citizens; and he persisted in defending himself with unconquerable valour. He was, at last, betrayed by a pretended negotiation, and made prisoner, in contempt of the safe conduct by which he was allowed liberty to treat; and being delivered to the Count de Montfort, he was, ultimately, poisoned in prison. The inhabitants of Carcassonne, according to the anonymous chronicler before cited, made their escape, in the night, over the fortifications. According to others, they were permitted to leave the city in their shirts, with the exception of four hundred who were burnt, and fifty who were hanged. The legate was desirous of immediately creating a new Viscount of Beziers, but the Duke of Burgundy, the Count of Nevers, and the Count de Saint Paul, ashamed of the treachery and crimes to which their success was owing, refused the odious gift. Simon de Montfort alone, the most ferocious, the most ambitious, and the most perfidious of all the crusaders, consented to bear the title. He immediately did homage to the Pope, procured the rightful viscount to be delivered to him, that he might be put out of the way, and created a ground of quarrel with Raymond VI., Count of Toulouse, whom, in his turn, he wished to despoil of his territories. But we shall not follow this conqueror into the frightful wars, with which he devastated the whole of the south of France. They, who escaped from the sacking of the towns, were sacrificed by the faggot. From 1209 to 1229 nothing was seen but massacres and tortures. Religion was overthrown, knowledge extinguished, and humanity trodden under foot. In the midst of these misfortunes, the ancient house of Toulouse became extinct, on the death of Raymond VII., in 1249; and that county, formerly a sovereignty, was united to the crown of France by Saint Louis. A few years before, in 1245, the family of Provence had failed, in the person of Raymond Berenger IV.; and Charles of Anjou, the ferocious conqueror of the kingdom of Naples, had claimed that territory as his inheritance. Thus, the sovereign families disappeared in the south of France; and the Provençals, and all the people who spoke the Langue d'Oc, became subject to a rival nation, to which they had always entertained the most violent aversion. In their servitude, a few plaintive songs of grief were heard; but the muses fled from a soil polluted with carnage.

A few Troubadours were found amongst the ranks of the persecutors, the most celebrated of whom, was the ferocious Folquet, Bishop of Toulouse, who rendered himself more odious by his infamous treacheries than even by the punishments which he inflicted. Betraying alike his prince and his flock, he entered without hesitation int all the intrigues of Simon de Montfort, for de spoiling Raymond VI. of his estates. He orga nized, even in Toulouse, a band of assassins, wh were called the White Company, at the head o whom he marched, for the purpose of massacrin all who were suspected of favouring heretica opinions. This band was united to the army o Simon de Montfort, when, on two different occasions, he besieged Toulouse. At the second siege all the crusaders and the allies of De Montfor besought him to be merciful; but Folquet alone advised him to despoil the citizens of their goods, and to throw the most distinguished of them int prison. When he entered Toulouse, he announced to the inhabitants that he had obtained their pardon, and invited them to throw themselves at the feet of De Montfort. The citizens rushed out o the gates in crowds; but, as they entered the camp, they were loaded with chains, and Folquet took advantage of their absence to deliver up the city to pillage. A sufficient number of the armed inhabitants yet remained to offer resistance. The combat again commenced, and its result was doubtful. Folquet presented himself before the enraged inhabitants, and solemnly engaged to set all the prisoners at liberty; an engagement, which he guaranteed by his own oath and that of the Abbot of the Cistercians. But, at the same time, he demanded that the citizens should deliver up to him their arms and fortifications. The inhabitants were weak enough to rely once more on the oath of their bishop, but no sooner were their arms surrendered, than Folquet, by his pontifical authority, absolved Simon de Montfort from the oath which he had taken. The prisoners were thrown into dungeons, where nearly the whole of them perished, and the city, under pain of being razed, was subjected to a contribution of thirty thousand marks of silver. Folquet died in 1231, and his crimes were thought to have secured him a reception in heaven. He is one of the most conspicuous saints of the Cistercians, and the title of *Bienheureux* was conferred upon him. Petrarch mentions him with distinction in his Triumph of Love, and Dante sees him in Paradise amongst the souls of the elect. As a Troubadour, we have no remains of this fanatic, except some love-verses addressed to Azalais de Roquemartine, the wife of the Viscount of Marseilles, whom he had attempted to seduce.

Izarn, a Dominican missionary and inquisitor, preserved his character, with greater consistency, in his poetry. We find him, in about eight hundred Alexandrine verses, sustaining a dispute with one of the Albigenses, whom he is desirous of converting.* His style of reasoning is, to treat his

---

* The following is the commencement of this poem:

Aiso fou las novas del heretic.

Dignas me tu heretic, parlap me un petit,
Que tu non parlaras gaire, que ja t'sia grazit,

adversary in the most insulting manner; to present to him, all at once, the most unintelligible dogmas; to exact his submission to them; and to menace him, at the end of every sentence, with death, torture, and hell.*

As you declare you won't believe, 'tis fit that you should burn,
And as your fellows have been burnt, that you should blaze in turn;
And as you've disobey'd the will of God and of St. Paul,
Which ne'er was found within your heart, nor pass'd your teeth at all,
The fire is lit, the pitch is hot, and ready is the stake,
That through these tortures, for your sins, your passage you may take.

Could the horrors of the Inquisition be forgotten, this poem alone would be sufficient to recall them.

Si per forza not ve, segon i aveuz auzit,
Segon lo mien veiaire, ben at Dieu escarnit,
Tau fe e ton baptisme renegat e guerpit,
Car crezes que Diables t' a format et bastit,
E tan mal a obrat, e tan mal a ordit
Por dar salvatio; falsamen as mentit,
Et de malvais escola as apris e auzit
E ton crestianisme as falsat e delit.

* E s' aquest no vols creyre vec t' el foc arzirat
Che art tos companhos. . . . .
Con es de Dieu e San Paul non c'est obediens
Ni 't pot entrar en cor, ni passar per las dens,
Per qu' el foc s'aparelha e la peis el turmens
Per ou deu espassar. . . . .

But the greater part of the Troubadours beheld, with equal detestation, both the crusade and the domination of the French. Tomiez and Palazis, two gentlemen of Tarascon, invoked, in their *sirventes*, the succour of the King of Aragon, in favour of the Count of Toulouse. They denounced eternal infamy on the Prince of Orange, who had abandoned the Count of Toulouse, his immediate lord; and they exhorted the Provençals, that it was better to defend themselves in the field than to suffer death in the dungeon. A martial ballad, the burthen of which was "Lords! be stout, and trust in succour!" transports us, as it were, into the field of battle, amongst the unfortunate Provençals, who were defending themselves against this infamous crusade.* Paulet de Marseilles does not bewail the crusade, which was then terminated, but the subjection of Provence to Charles of Anjou. The poet deplores the dishonour which that country had sustained, in taking part in the war of Naples, and thus staining itself with the judicial murder of Conradin, and the imprisonment of Henry of Castile. In a very curious pastoral, he expresses the universal hatred of the people for their new masters; his attachment to the Spaniards, and his persuasion that the King of Aragon was alone entitled to the sovereignty of Provence.† Boniface III., of Cas-

* *Millot*, iii. 45, 49, &c. [A translation of the whole of this curious piece will be found at the end of the chapter.—*Tr.*]

† *Millot*, iii. 141, &c.

tellan, seems to feel, still more vividly, the affront put upon the Provençals by this foreign usurpation; while, at the same time, he accuses them of having merited, by their cowardice, the opprobrium of being subjected to a rival nation. He attempts, by every mode, to rouse them from this languor; and he excites to vengeance James I. of Aragon, whose father, Peter II., had been slain in 1213, at the battle of Muret, whilst fighting in defence of the Count of Toulouse and the Albigenses. Castellan at length succeeded in rousing Marseilles to revolt, and placed himself at the head of the insurgents; but Charles of Anjou having menaced the city with a siege, Castellan was delivered up. He was beheaded, and his goods were confiscated. The great satirist of the Provençals, Pierre Cardinal, whose verses display the most impetuous passions, seems to have been struck with horror at the conduct of the Crusaders. Sometimes he paints the desolation of the country, which was the theatre of the war; at other times, he attempts to inspire the Count of Toulouse with courage. "Neither the Archbishop of Narbonne, nor the King of France, have the power to change one so wicked, into a man of honour (speaking of Simon de Montfort.) They may bestow gold and silver, and garments, and wines, and viands, upon him; but, for goodness, God alone can give it. Would you know what share he will have in the spoils of this war?—the cries, the terror, the frightful spectacles, which he has beheld, the misfortunes and thé evils which he has occasioned, these will form the equipage with which he will return from the battle."* De Montfort perished in an action before Toulouse, on the 25th June, 1218, though not without having lived to enjoy, for a considerable time, the bloody spoils of Raymond VI.

During the period at which the country of the Langue d'Oc was in its most flourishing state, and the Counts of Provence and Toulouse, rivalling one another in riches and power, invited the most distinguished poets to their courts, all the neigh-

---

* L' arsivesque de Narbona
Nil Rey non an tan de seu
Que de malvaiza persona
Puescan far home valen;
Dar li podon aur o arjen
E draps, e vi e anona,
Mais lo bel essenhamen
Ha sel a cui Dieus lo dona
. . . .
Tals a sus el cap corona
E porta blanc vestimen
Quel' volontatz es felona,
Com de lops e de serpen;
E qui tols ni trai ni men
Ni aussiz ni empoizona (†)
Ad aquo es ben parven
Quals voler hi abotona.

(†) Alluding to the death of the Viscount de Béziers.

bouring princes and people attempted to make themselves familiar with a language, which seemed to be appropriated to love and gallantry. The dialects of the other countries were, hitherto, by no means fixed, and were regarded as vulgar when compared with the pure Provençal. All the north of Italy received with eagerness the lessons of the Troubadours. Azzo VII. of Este invited them to the court of Ferrara, and Gerard de Camino, to Treviso; while the Marquis of Montferrat introduced them into his kingdom of Thessalonica, in Greece. The crusade against the Albigenses, however, entirely put an end to the influence of the Provençals. The country which had given birth to so many elegant poets was now only a scene of carnage and torture For a long period after the first war, the massacres and persecutions, as well as the resistance of the unfortunate victims, continued even down to the reign of Louis XIV., when the war of the Camisards may be said to be the last scene of the fatal tragedy of the Albigenses. A language which appeared only to serve the purpose of repeating funereal lamentations, was heard with a kind of horror; while the Italians, perhaps, believed that it was exclusively applied to spreading the venomous doctrines of heresy. Charles of Anjou, moreover, in the middle of this century possessed himself of the kingdom of Naples, carrying with him in his train the principal nobility of Provence; and the latter, consequently, became familiar with the Italian language, which, at that period, was assuming a more polished shape. This ferocious monarch would have contributed little to the advancement of poetry, whether he favoured the language of his wife, the Provençal, or that of his new subjects, the Italians; for his talent was rather to destroy than to create, and he sacrificed the prosperity of the beautiful country which his wife had brought him as her dowry, to his passion for war and his unmeasured ambition. He loaded the people with excessive taxes, destroyed the liberty and privileges of his barons, dragged into Italy all his subjects who were capable of bearing arms, and desolated Provence,* for the purpose of carrying

* This terrific prince was, however, a poet, for at this period, to which we have given the title of barbarous, all the sovereigns and the powerful nobles were compelled to sacrifice to the muses. In the manuscripts in the Royal Library, there exists a love-song by him in the Langue d'Oil, which has nothing very remarkable about it. The following lines form the conclusion.

Un seul confort me tient en bon espoir,
Et c'est de ce qu'oncques ne la guerpi,
Servie l'ai tojours à mon pooir
N'oncques vers autr ai pensé fors qu'à li;
Et à tout ce, me met en non châloir;
Et si, sai bien ne l'ai pas desservi.
Si me convient attendre son voloir
Et atendrai come loyal ami.'

Pur li quens d'Anjou, p. 148.

desolation into the heart of new territories. In his reign, the Courts of Love were abolished, which had so long excited the emulation of poets, by granting the most brilliant rewards to talent; and which had largely contributed to the refinement of manners, by inflicting, with the assistance of public opinion, a punishment upon those who trespassed against the laws of delicacy. Not only temporary Courts of Love were erected in all the manors of the greater barons, after every fête and tourney, but some of them appear to have received a more solemn form, and a more durable existence. Thus, mention is made of the Court of Love of Pierrefeu, in which Stephanette des Baux, daughter of the Count of Provence, presided, and which was composed of ten of the most considerable ladies of the country; of the Court of Love of Romanin, presided over by the lady of that name; and of the Courts of Aix and of Avignon, the latter of which was established under the immediate protection of the Pope. These four courts appear to have been permanent bodies, which assembled at fixed periods, and acquired a high reputation for delicacy and gallantry; and to them were submitted such love-causes as the inferior courts did not dare to decide. The *Arrêts d'Amour* were religiously preserved; and Martial d'Auvergne, in 1480, made a compilation of fifty-one of these *ar-*

rêts, which were afterwards translated into Spanish by Diego Grazian *.

But all this solemnity, this studious attention to gallantry and poetry, ceased in the absence of the sovereign, who adopted a foreign language, and drew to the court of Naples the knights and ladies, who used to combat at the tourneys and sit in the Courts of Love. The successors of Charles I., though more literary in their habits, were more entirely Italian. Charles II., and especially Robert, patronized the literature of Italy. The latter was the friend and protector of Petrarch, who elected him as judge before he received the poetical crown. Some Provençal poems, addressed to him, still remain. Crescimbeni makes mention, amongst others, of a sonnet, in his honour, by Guillaume des Amalrics †; but this little poem, which is composed in the Italian style,

---

* [If we are to take the *arrêts* of Martial D'Auvergne as real specimens of the proceedings in the Courts of Love, they certainly could not have been of that grave and solemn cast, which M. De Sismondi and other writers would lead us to believe. Nor do they give us, by any means, a favourable idea of the *delicacy* of the fair judges. The most ridiculous questions are propounded and argued in the gravest manner, and sometimes fictitious personages, as Love and Death, are introduced. If, indeed, these *arrêts* be the original judgments of the Courts of Love, it proves that all their proceedings were mere jests and *badinage*; but probably the work was intended by the author as a satire upon the real courts.—*Tr.*]

† *Vite de' Poeti Provenzali*, p. 131.

gives no idea of the ancient poetry of Provence. Joanna I. of Naples, the grandaughter of Robert, appears, during her residence in Provence, to have made an attempt to reanimate the former ardour of the Troubadours, and to infuse new life into the Provençal poetry. The beautiful Joanna, whose heart was proved to be so tender and passionate, was, certainly, the fittest of all the princesses of Europe to preside in the Courts of Love, and to discuss questions of sentiment. Her stay in Provence, however, was not of long duration, and, during all that period, she suffered misfortunes and oppression; while her return to Naples, in 1348, separated her again from the poets whom she had patronized. Joanna, on being dethroned, thirty years afterwards, adopted a French prince, Louis I. of Anjou, to whom, however, she could only assure the possession of Provence; the kingdom of Naples passing to the house of Duraz. But though Provence, after a separation of a century and a half, again possessed her sovereign in her bosom, literature experienced no protection from him. Louis spoke the Langue d'Oui, or the dialect of the north of France, and had no taste for the poetry of the Langue d'Oc; and, moreover, he was engaged, as were afterwards his son Louis II. and his grandson Louis III. in a series of unfortunate wars in Italy. His other grandson, René, who in his turn assumed, in the fifteenth century, the title of King of Naples and Count of Provence, endeavoured, it is true, with great earnestness, to revive the poetry of Provence. The effort, however, was too late; the race of the Troubadours was extinct; and the invasions of the English, who desolated France, did not dispose the minds of the people to renew the cultivation of the Gay Science. It is, however, to the zeal of this king that we owe the Lives of the Troubadours, which were collected for him by the Monk of the Isles of Gold.

If the establishment of the sovereign of Provence in Italy was so deadly a blow to the Provençal language, the establishment of an Italian sovereign in Provence was no less fatal to it. At the commencement of the fourteenth century, the court of Rome was transferred to Avignon. The Popes, it is true, who, for seventy years, filled the pontifical chair while it was fixed at that place, were all of them Frenchmen by birth, and inhabitants of the country where the Langue d'Oc was spoken. But, like the sovereigns of Rome, and of a great part of Italy, their courts were composed of Italians; and the Tuscan language became so familiar in the city which they inhabited, that Petrarch, the first poet of the age, who lived at Avignon, and loved a Provençal lady, never employed any other language than the Italian to express his attachment.

Whilst the native poetry, and even the language of Provence, properly so called, were every day declining, reiterated efforts were made, in the county of Toulouse, to re-illume the ancient flame. The house of Saint-Giles, the ancient counts, was extinct, and most of the great feudatories had either perished, or been ruined by the crusades. The castles were no longer the asylum of pleasures and chivalric festivals, although some of the towns were recovering from the calamities of war. Toulouse could again boast of her numerous population, her riches, her elegance, and her taste for letters and poetry.

In southern France, from the eleventh to the thirteenth century, the nobility gave to the age its character and spirit. In the two centuries which succeeded, the inhabitants of the towns assumed a more important rank. Their privileges had been augmented by the sovereign. They were allowed to raise fortifications, to choose their own magistrates, and to possess a militia. The crown was thus enabled either to oppose the powerful barons, whom it wished to humble; or to defend itself in the wars between France and England; or, lastly, to raise, from this source, increased taxes, since the principal part of the revenues of the state were derived from the towns. The inhabitants speedily imbibed republican sentiments; the principles of equality became general; and a respect for property, and an enlightened protection of industry and activity, were the consequences. Zeal for the public good, and a great degree of the *esprit de corps*, united the citizens in their patriotic bonds. The state was much better governed; but the poetical spirit had declined. It is not under the operation of the wisest laws, and in times of good order and prosperity, that the imagination of a people is most powerfully developed. Idleness is much better suited to the poet than activity; and that vigilant and paternal administration which forms good fathers, good merchants, good artisans, and honest citizens, was much less calculated to elicit the genius of the Troubadours, than a life spent in wandering from castle to castle; in alternate intercourse with the nobles and the people, the ladies and the shepherds; and amid the enjoyments of luxury, rendered more exquisite by poverty.

The good citizens of Toulouse, or of Marseilles, had their business to superintend and their livelihood to earn; and if a man devoted himself, from his youth, to singing at festivals, or meditating in groves, he was looked upon by his fellow citizens either as a fool, or as one who wished to live on the contributions of others. No esteem was felt for a man, who, when he was capable of becoming independent by his own labour, chose to owe his subsistence to the bounty of the great. Reason and good sense are both the accompaniments of prose; and the most brilliant faculties of the human mind, are not always those which are most requisite to our happiness.

Still the *Capitouls de Toulouse*, the name by which the chief-magistrates of that city were distinguished, were desirous, for the honour of their country, of preserving the brilliant reputation which it had formerly enjoyed for poetical studies, and which was now about to expire. They were not, perhaps, themselves, very sensible of the charms of verse and harmony; but they were unwilling that it should be said, that under their administration, the flame, which had shed such lustre on the reigns of the Counts of Toulouse, was extinguished. A few versifiers of little note had assumed, at Toulouse, the name of Troubadours, and were accustomed, half-yearly, to assemble together in the gardens of the Augustine monks, where they read their compositions to one another. In 1323, these persons resolved to form themselves into a species of academy *del Gai Saber*, and they gave it the title of *La Sobregaya Companhia dels sept Trobadors de Tolosa*. This "most gay society" was eagerly joined by the *Capitouls*, or venerable magistrates, of Toulouse, who wished, by some public festival, to reanimate the spirit of poetry.*

---

* If the celebrated *Clémence Isaure*, whose eulogy was pronounced every year in the assembly of the Floral Games, and whose statue, crowned with flowers, ornamented their festivals

A circular letter was addressed to all the cities of the Langue d'Oc, to give notice that, on the 1st of May, 1324, a golden violet would be decreed, as a prize, to the author of the best poem in the Provençal language. The circular is written both in prose and verse; in the name as well of "the very gay company of Troubadours," as of "the very grave assembly of Capitouls." The gravity of the latter is manifested by their wonderful display of learning, and by the number of their quotations; for when the Gay Science was transported from the castles into the cities, it was united to a knowledge of antiquity, and of those studies which were again beginning to be cultivated. Harmony and sentiment alone were not now all-sufficient. On the other hand, the Troubadours cited the scriptures, in defence of their recreations. "Is it not," said they, "pleasing to God, our Creator, and our Sovereign Lord and Master, that man should render homage to him in joy and gladness of heart, as the Psalmist has borne testimony when he says, 'Sing and be glad in

---

be not merely an imaginary being, she appears to have been the soul of these little meetings, before either the magistrates had noticed them or the public were invited to attend them. But neither the circulars of the *Sobregaya Companhia*, nor the registers of the magistrates, make any mention of her; and, notwithstanding all the zeal with which, at a subsequent period, the glory of founding the Floral Games has been attributed to her, her existence is still problematical.

the Lord." The crowds which collected on the first of May, were prodigious. The magistrates the neighbouring nobility, and the common people, all assembled in the garden of the Augustines, to hear the songs publicly read, which were intended to dispute the prize. The violet was adjudged to Arnaud Vidal of Castelnaudary, for his song in honour of the Holy Virgin, and the successful candidate was immediately declared a Doctor in the Gay Science. Such was the origin of the Floral Games. In 1355, the Capitouls announced that, instead of one prize, they would give three. The violet of gold was reserved for the best song. An eglantine of silver, not the flower of the rose, but of the Spanish jasmine, was promised to the author of the best *sirvente*, or of the most beautiful pastoral; and lastly, the *flor de gaug*, or joy-flower, the yellow and odoriferous flower of the thorny acacia, was to be bestowed upon the writer of the best ballad. These flowers were more than a foot high, and were carried on a pedestal of silver gilt, upon which were engraved the arms of the city. It seems that in copying these flowers always from the same model, the artists forgot what they originally represented: the eglantine became a columbine, and the joy-flower, a marigold. The Academy of the Floral Games has survived to the present day, although it seldom crowns any but French poets. Its secretary is always a doctor of laws, and its rules are denominated the Laws of Love. The name of Troubadour is still heard there, and the ancient forms of Provençal poetry, the song, the *sirvente*, and the ballad, are preserved with reverence. No man of real talent, however, has signalized himself amongst the fraternity; and as for the Troubadours, properly so called, the chanters of love and of chivalry, who bore from castle to castle, and from tourney to tourney, their own verses and the fame of their ladies, the race was extinct before the commencement of the Floral Games.

In another quarter, however, a flourishing kingdom was daily making rapid steps towards power, prosperity, and military glory. The kingdom of Aragon had preserved the Provençal language, and placed her fame in the cultivation of that literature. The employment of that tongue, in all the acts of government, was considered, nearly to our own times, as one of the most precious privileges which that country possessed. Marriage, succession, and conquest, had united many rich provinces under the dominion of the kings of Aragon; originally, merely the chiefs of a few Christian refugees, who had escaped into the mountains to avoid the Moors. Petronille, in 1137, carried the crown of Aragon to Raymond Berenger V., then sovereign of Provence, of Catalonia, of Cerdagne, and of Roussillon. In 1220, their descendants conquered the islands of Majorca, Minorca, and Ivica; and, in 1238, the kingdom of Valencia. Sicily fell under their dominion in 1282, and, in 1323, they conquered Sardinia. At the period when all these kingdoms were united under one crown, the Catalans were the hardiest navigators of the Mediterranean. Their commercial relations were very extended. They had frequent intercourse with the Greek empire, and were the constant rivals of the Genoese, and the no less faithful friends of the Venetians. Their reputation in arms was as brilliant as in the arts of peace. Not content with fighting the battles of their own country, they sought opportunities of practising their military skill in foreign service, and exercised their valour in combats, in which they had no sort of interest. The redoubtable soldiery of the Almogavares, issuing out of Aragon, carried terror into Italy and Greece. They vanquished the Turks and humbled Constantinople; conquering Athens and Thebes, and destroying, in 1312, in the battle of the Cephisus, the remnant of the French cavaliers who had formerly overthrown the Greek empire. The Aragonese succeeded in rendering their liberties secure and respected by their chiefs. Even the kings themselves were under the dominion of a supreme judge, called the *Justicia*, who girt on the sword in their support, if they were faithful, and against them, if they abandoned their duty.

The four members of the Cortes, by virtue of the privilege of union, similar to that of the Confederation of Poland, had the power of legally opposing force and resistance to any usurped authority. Their religious freedom was equal to their civil immunities; and, to preserve it, the Aragonese did not scruple to brave, for the space of two centuries, the Papal excommunications. This bold and troubled life, this constant success in every enterprise, this national glory, which was continually encreasing, were much better fitted to inflame the imagination, and to sustain a poetical spirit, than the prudent, but confined and citizen-like life of the good people of Toulouse. Many celebrated Troubadours issued from the kingdoms of Aragon and Catalonia, during the twelfth and thirteenth centuries; and on the extinction of the Troubadours, the Aragonese displayed a new kind of talent. The Provençal, or rather the Catalan, literature did not die with the poets of Provence.

One of the most celebrated of those who cultivated the art of poetry, after the disappearance of the Troubadours, was Don Henri d'Aragon, Marquis of Villena, who died in 1434, at an advanced age. His marquisate, the most ancient in Spain, was situated on the confines of the kingdoms of Castile and Valencia; and, in fact, Villena belonged to both the monarchies. In both, he filled the most important offices, and governed them alternately during the minorities of their princes; and in both, after having been the favourite of the kings, he was persecuted and despoiled of his property. During his administration, he made some attempts to awaken a taste for letters, and to unite the study of ancient literature to the cultivation of Romance poetry. He persuaded John I., of Aragon, to establish, in his states, an academy, similar to the Floral Games of Toulouse, in order to reanimate the ardour of the Troubadours, who were now rapidly declining. The Academy of Toulouse dispatched, in the year 1390, two *Doctors of Love* to Barcelona, to found in that city a Branch Academy. All the rules, the laws, and the judgments of Love were adopted, and the Floral Games commenced at Barcelona; but the civil war soon afterwards interrupted them. Henri de Villena, on the establishment of peace, attempted to reopen his favourite academy at Tortosa. In the midst of all the occupations in which his turbulent political career engaged him, he found time to write a treatise on poetry for this academy, which he entitled *De la Gaya Ciencia*, and in which he explained, with more erudition than taste, the laws which the Troubadours had observed in the composition of their verses, and which the Italians, in their application of them, were now beginning to refine. Notwithstanding all his exertions, his academy was of short duration, and expired, probably, with himself. Villena likewise composed, about the year 1412, a still more curious work. It was a comedy; probably the only one ever written in the Provençal language, and one of the first which we find in modern literature. It was composed on occasion of the marriage of the King of Aragon, Ferdinand I. The characters were all allegorical, such as Truth, Justice, Peace, and Mercy; and the work, no doubt, possessed very little interest. It is, however, not the less an object of curiosity, as having prepared the way, together with the French mysteries and moralities, for that career which more modern poets have run with so much glory.

Ausias March, of Valencia, who died about 1450, is entitled to the second place amongst the Catalan Poets. He has been called the Petrarch of Catalonia, and is said to have equalled the lover of Laura in elegance, in brilliancy of expression, and in harmony; and while, like him, he contributed to the formation of his language, which he carried to a high degree of polish and perfection, he possessed more real feeling, and did not suffer himself to be seduced by a passion for *concetti* and false brilliancy. By a strange coincidence of circumstances, we are also told, that his poetry, like Petrarch's, forms two classes; the pieces composed during the life of his mistress, and those which were written on her death. The lady, whose name was Theresa de Momboy, was of a noble family in Valencia. Like Petrarch, also, Ausias March beheld his mistress, for the first time, during the celebration of service, in a church, on Good-Friday; unless we must suppose that this was a fictitious circumstance, adopted by the poet in imitation of his great master. His Theresa, however, did not resemble Laura in one point, for she was unfaithful to her lover; from which we must conclude that she was at one period attached to him.

Although Ausias March is one of the few Catalan poets whose works I have been able to procure, yet a rapid and imperfect perusal of poems, written in a foreign language, has scarcely qualified me to pass any judgment upon his compositions. Yet the similarity between Petrarch and this poet appears to me very surprising. Ausias March evidently possesses more of the spirit of French literature than of the Romance taste. He seems to be infinitely less studious, than the Italians generally are, of employing those real or fictitious ornaments of poetry, comparisons and *concetti*. From thought and philosophy, on the contrary, he derives his principal beauties. Instead of colouring all his ideas, so as to make them harmonize with the senses, he generalises them, he reasons upon them, and often loses himself in abstraction. Although his language differs from the French more than that of the Troubadours, its construction is much more clear. In his verse, he has preserved, with great correctness, the forms and the metres of the ancient poets. The collection of his works, which is divided into three parts, *Poems on Love*, *Poems on Death*, and *Moral Poems*, contains merely songs, which are usually in seven stanzas, followed by an envoy, which he calls a *tornada*. It is due to the high reputation of Ausias March, which has been too long forgotten, to his admitted superiority over all the writers of the Provençal language, and to the extreme rarity of his works, to present a few fragments of them to the reader. In the second of his Love songs, he tells us that his heart vacillated a long time between two fair ladies.

As he who seeks for viands to appease
His hunger, and beholds, on some fair tree,
Two ruddy apples bloom deliciously,
On both of which he eagerly would seize,
Is forced, ere he the luscious dainty prove,
To choose or this or that; even so am I
Smit with the love of two fair dames, and sigh
That I must choose, ere I can taste of love.*

* Axi com cell qui desija vianda
Per apagar sa perillosa fam,
E veu dos poms de fruyt en un bell ram
E son desig egualment los demanda,
Nol complira fins part haja legida
Si que l'desig vers l'un fruyt se decant;
Axi m'a pres dues dones amant,
Mas elegesch per haver d'amor vida.

As when the sea groans heavily and cries,
When two contending winds sweep o'er its breast,
One from the East, the other from the West,
Till the one yielding to the other, dies.
Even so two mighty passions, angrily,
Have long contended in my breast, until
Obeying the high dictates of my will,
I followed one—that one was, love to thee!

There is, generally, much nature in the expression of Ausias March; and this, instead of injuring the vigour of the sentiment, adds to its vivacity, even more than the most brilliant metaphors could have done. The following stanza appears to be an illustration of this remark.

Abandoning the Troubadours' false verse,
Who trespass o'er the modest bounds of truth,
I must repress the wishes of my youth,
Since words are vain thy virtues to rehearse.*

Si com la mar se plang greument e crida
Com dos forts vents la baten egualment,
Hu de Levant e l'altre de Ponent,
E dura tant fins l'um vent la jequida
Sa força gran per lo mas poderos:
Dos grans dezigs han combatut ma pensa,
Mas lo voler vers un seguir dispensa;
Yo l'vos publich, amar dretament vos.

* Leixant a part le stil dels trobados
Qui per escalf trespasen veritat,
E sostrahent mon voler affectat
Perque nom trob dire l' que trobe en vos,

All I could say to those, who know thee not,
Were little worth ; they could not credit me ;
And those that knowing thee, live not for thee,
Did *they* believe, how sad would be their lot.

In the elegies (*Obres de Mort*) of this poet, here is a tranquillity and reflection, a sort of philosophical grief, which, though it, perhaps, is not quite just, gives an idea of deep feeling.

The hands, which never spare, have snatch'd thee hence,
Cutting the frail thread of thy tender life,
And bearing thee from out this scene of strife,
Obedient still to fate's dark ordinance.
All that I see and feel now turns to pain,
When I remember thee I loved so well ;
Yet, from the griefs that in my bosom swell,
I seem to snatch some taste of bliss again ;
Thus, fed by tender joy, my grief shall last :
Unfed, the deepest sorrow soon is past.*

Tot mon parlar als que no us havran vista
Res noy valvra, car fe noy donaran ;
E los vehents que dins vos no vevran
En crevre mi lur alma sera triste.

* Aquelles mans que james perdonaren
Han ja romput lo fill tenint la vida
De vos, qui son de aquest mon exida
Segons los fats en secret ordenaren.
Tot quant yo veig e sent dolor me torna
Dant me recort de vos que tant amava.
En ma dolor, si prim e bes cercava
Si trobara que 'n delit se contorna.
Donchs durara, puix té qui la sosting,
Car sens delit dolor cresch nos retinga.

Within a gentle heart love never dies;
He fades in breasts which guilty thoughts distress,
And fails the sooner for his own excess;
But lives, when rich in virtuous qualities.
When the eye sees not and the touch is gone,
And all the pleasures Beauty yields are o'er,
Howe'er the conscious sufferer may deplore,
We know that soon such sensual griefs are flown.
Virtuous and holy love links mind to mind;
And such is ours, which death cannot unbind.

We are astonished at finding the poet, whose boast it was that he had never loved his mistress Theresa, with a dishonourable passion, expressing doubts as to her salvation, certainly incompatible with that admiration for a beloved object which sanctifies all her acts in our eyes. In one of his elegies, he says:

The heavy grief, which words can never tell,
Of him who dies, and knows not if the hand
Of God will place him on the heavenly strand,
Or bury him beneath the vaults of hell—

En cor gentil amor per mort no passa,
Mas en aquell qui sol lo vici tira;
La quantitat d' amor durar no mira,
La qualitat d' amor bona no 's lassa.
Quant l' ull no veu e lo toch no pratica
Mor lo voler que tot por el se guanya,
Qui 'n tal punt es dolor sent molt e stranya
Mas dura poch qui 'n passau testifica.
Amor honest los sancts amant fa colre
D' aquest vos am, et mort nol me pot tolre.

Such grief my spirit feels, unknowing what
Of good or ill, God has ordained to thee;
Thy bliss is mine, and mine thy misery:
Whate'er betide thee, still I share thy lot.*

When once the mind is struck with the terrific idea, that salvation or condemnation must depend on the last moments of life, the frightful belief destroys all our trust in virtue; and Ausias March, in the wanderings of his brain, abandoned the mistress, whom he had worshipped as an angel upon earth, to the ministers of celestial vengeance. Sometimes, he seems determined to share her lot, though she should be devoted to eternal torments:

On thee my joy and sorrow both depend,
And with thy lot God wills that mine should blend.†

It is not merely in these melancholy presentiments that the passion of Ausias March assumes a religious cast. On all occasions, it displays a spirit

---

* La gran dolor que lengua no pot dir
Del qui s' veu mort e no sab hon ira,
No sab son Deu si per a si l' volra
O si n' infern lo volra sebellir.
Semblant dolor lo meu esperit sent,
No sabent que de vos Deus ha ordenat;
Car vostre mal o be a mi es dat,
Del que havreu, yo n' saré soffirent.

† Goig o tristor per tu he yo complir,
En tu esta quant Deu me volra dar.

of exalted piety, and acquires, from that circumstance, a more touching character. The death of his beloved friend, far from weakening his attachment, seems only to have superadded to it a nobler feeling of religion.

As when rich gold, fresh gather'd from the mine,
  Is mix'd with metals valueless and base,
  Till, purged within the fire some little space,
The alloy flies off, and leaves it pure and fine;
So death has banish'd every grosser stain
  Which mark'd my passion; and my earthly love
  Has changed into such hope of bliss above,
That nothing but the holiest thoughts remain.*

While the poet is reasoning, with apparent coldness and philosophic subtlety, on the circumstance upon which his life depends, his grief sometimes bursts from him with violence, and prompts him to the most passionate expressions.

O God! why will not then this bitter draught
  Destroy the wretch who saw his mistress die?
  How sweet would be my mortal agony,
Remembering her for whom the cup was quaff'd!

---

* Axi com l' or quant de la mena l' trahen
Esta mesclat de altres metalls sutzens,
E mes al foch en fum s' en va la liga
Leyxant l' or pur, no podent se corrompre,
Axi la mort mon voler gros termena;
Aquell fermat, en la part contra sembla
D' aquella, que la mort al mon la tolta,
L' honest voler en mi reman sen mezcla.

Pity! why sleep'st thou, when I waste in grief?
 Why break'st thou not the heart which torments sear?
 Thou must be powerless, if thou dost not hear,
Or cruel, if thou wilt not grant relief.*

Although the works of many other poets of Valencia are said to have been printed, I have never met with them in a separate form. I am only acquainted with them, as they exist in the ancient Spanish *cancioneri*. We there find specimens of Vicent Ferradis, Miquel Perez, Fenollar, Castelvy, and Vinyoles; and these enable us to perceive that true taste was little cultivated at that period. Ausias March, indeed, appears to have been inspired with real feeling; but the rest courted ingenuity and wit, and often false wit. Of this description, is a little poem, which is reprinted in all the *cancioneri*, by Vicent Ferradis, on the name of Jesus, in which, we are told, the deepest piety may be found mingled with the most beautiful poetry. We may judge of this production by the following stanza, which contains an anagram on the letters I. H. S. Jesus Hominum Salvator.

---

* O Deu perque no romp la 'marga fel
Aquell qui veu a son amich perir!
Quant mes puix vols tan dolça mort soffrir,
Gran sabor ha, puix se pren per tal zel.
Tu pietat com dorms en aquell cas?
Quel cor de carn fer esclatar no sals?
No tens poder quen tal temps lo acabs
Qual tant cruel qu' en tal cas not lloas.

Triumphant name! presenting visibly
  The glorious picture of the crucifixion!
Lo! in the midst, the H, which legibly
  Points out the God who died 'neath this infliction!
The aspirate marks his nature all divine;
  The I and S, the thieves on either hand,
Who with their Saviour do their breath resign;
  The stops denote the two, who sadly stand,
John and the Virgin Mary, at the feet
Of the Redeemer, making his death sweet.*

In very few of the productions of the poets of Valencia, do we find any remains of the old simplicity and sensibility. There is, however, something approaching to them, in the following stanza of Mossen Vinyoles.

Where is the day, the moment, and the hour,
  Whereon I lost my much-loved liberty?
  Where are the snares which so inveigled me?
Where are the ills for which these salt tears shower?†

---

* Nom trihumfal queus presenta visible
Del crucifix la bella circunstancia,
En mig la *h* que nos letra legible
L' inmens ja mort, tractat vilment y orrible.
La title d' alt de divinal sustancia.
La *j* y la *s* los ladres presenten
A les dos parts per fer li companyia,
Y pels costatz dos punts pue s' aposenten,
Denoten clar los dos que l' turment lenten
Del redemptor, Johan y la Maria.

† On es lo jorn, on es lo punt y l'ora
On yo perdy los bens de libertat?
On es lo lac qu' axim me cativat?
On es lo mal per qui ma lengua plora?

Where is the good I sought with so much pride?
  Where is the bond of habit's firm connexion?
  Where is the boundless love, the fond affection,
Which made me doubt of every thing beside?

It is almost from a sense of duty that I have selected and translated a few specimens of these amatory poems; passionate feelings, breathing in a forgotten language; tender attachments and fond regrets, confided to the custody of poetry, which posterity regards not. These old Catalonian poems have always seemed to me like inscriptions upon tombs.

Whilst Ausias March is considered, by the Catalans, as the Petrarch of the Provençal language, John Martorell is said to be its Boccacio. It is to him that their light style of prose composition is attributed. To him, it owes its pliancy and nature, and its adaptation to the purpose of graceful narration. His work enjoys, even beyond his own country, a considerable reputation. It is a romance entitled, *Tirante the White,* and it is mentioned by Cervantes, with great praise, in his catalogue of Don Quixote's library, and called by him "a treasure of contentment, a mine of delight, and, with regard to style, the best book

---

On es lo be que m' fa tant desigar?
On es l' engan de tanta conexença?
On es lo grat amor y benvolença
Que del pus cert me fa desesperar?

in the world." John Martorell appears to have given it to the public about the year 1435, and it was one of the first books which was printed, on the introduction of that art into Spain. The first Catalan edition is that of Valencia, 1480, in folio. It was translated into various languages, and the French version is to be found in almost every library.

It is difficult to separate a work of chivalry, like this, from its class, and to judge of it independently of other compositions of the same kind. Martorell is posterior to many other Romance writers; to the authors of the romances of the *Round Table*, and of those of *Charlemagne*. In *Tirante the White*, we find less of fairy-land, and fewer supernatural wonders, than in its predecessors. The action is more grave, the tenor of the story more consistent; and, although the hero, from the rank of a simple knight, becomes Emperor of Constantinople, we can follow and comprehend his elevation, as well as his achievements. On the other hand, there is, perhaps, less poetry; and fewer instances occur of a brilliant imagination than in the *Amadis*, the *Tristan*, and the *Lancelot*. Martorell occupies, in fact, the middle place between the ancient and the modern Romance writers. Other poets and Romance writers succeeded him; and the Catalans mention with praise, Mossen Jaume Royg of Valencia, who wrote a long poem on coquetry, in a very bitter style*; the two Jordi†; Febrer, the historian of Valencia; and, lastly, Vincent Garzias, the rector of Balfogona, who died at the commencement of the seventeenth century, and who was the last poet of Catalonia, or Valencia, who wrote in the Provençal language. The increasing prosperity of the Kings of Aragon was fatal both to the language and to the liberties of their subjects. Ferdinand the Catholic married Isabella of Castile; and that princess, on mounting the throne of Castile, in 1474, virtually divided her crown with her husband. The monarchy of Castile was more powerful than that of Aragon; its capital was more brilliant, and its revenues were more considerable. The courtiers were drawn to Madrid by their interest, and all the nobility of Spain conceived it necessary to learn the language of Castile. Even the Catalans, and the Aragonese, who, for so long a period, had placed the highest value

---

* [A specimen of this poet's compositions may be found in the article on the Poetical Literature of Spain, before alluded to. *Retrospective Review*, vol. iv. p. 54.—*Tr.*]

† [It should be observed, that Mossen Jordi de Sant Jordi, is contended, by the Catalonians, to have flourished as early as the thirteenth century; two centuries before Ausias March, and in the most splendid æra of the Provençal Troubadours. The question turns chiefly on the circumstance of some of his verses coinciding almost literally with part of one of Petrarch's sonnets, and it is yet to be decided who is the original.—See the whole piece, and some further particulars, in the *Retrospective Review*, vol. iv. p. 46.—*Tr.*]

on their language, and who, by a fundamental law had required, in the reign of James I. (1266 1276), that it should be substituted for the Lati in all public proceedings, now abandoned it, and suffered it to perish, from motives of personal aggrandisement. It was from those provinces that in the reigns of Charles V. and Philip, Boscan and Argensola issued, who caused a revolution in Spanish poetry. But when the Catalans, unable to offer further resistance to the despotic dominion of the House of Austria, and resolving to cast off that odious yoke, delivered themselves up to France, by the treaty of Péronne, they petitioned for the restoration of their ancient and noble language, begging that it alone might be employed in all the acts of government and public transactions. They regretted their language as well as their laws, their liberties, their prosperity, and their ancient virtue, all of which had passed away. The most powerful bond which attaches a people to their manners, their customs, and their sweetest associations, is the language of their fathers. The deepest humiliation to which they can be subjected, is to be compelled to forget it, and to learn a new tongue.

There certainly is, even to a foreigner, something peculiarly melancholy in the decay and destruction of a beautiful language. That of the Troubadours, so long esteemed for its sonorous and harmonious character, which had awakened the enthusiasm, the imagination, and the genius, of so large a portion of Europe, and which had extended itself not only over France, Italy, and Spain, but even to the courts of England and of Germany, no longer meets the ears of men who are worthy of listening to the sound. It is still spoken in the South of France; but so broken up into dialects, that the people of Gascony, of Provence, and of Languedoc, no longer suspect that they are speaking the same tongue. It is the basis of the Piedmontese; it is spoken in Spain from Figuieras to the kingdom of Murcia; and it is the language of Sardinia and the Balearic Isles. But, in all these various countries, every man of education abandons it for the Castilian, the Italian, or the French; and to speak in the language which boasts of poets, who have been the glory of their country, and to whom we are indebted for modern poetry, is avoided as ridiculous and vulgar.

In finishing our inquiries into the language and the literature of the Troubadours, let us not judge them too severely, on account of the slight impression, and the few brilliant recollections which they leave on our memory. We ought not to forget, that the age in which they lived was degraded by ignorance and by almost universal barbarism. It is impossible, in analyzing their works, not to compare them continually with the French poets in the reign of Louis XIV., with the

Italians during the age of Leo X., with the English of Queen Anne's time, and with the German poets of the present day. Yet this comparison is certainly unjust. Whilst the Troubadours must decidedly yield to the great masters of our modern literature, they are, nevertheless, much superior to the versifiers of their time in France, Italy England, and Germany. A fatality seems to have attended their language; destroying the sovereign houses which spoke it, dispersing the nobility who gloried in its use, and ruining the people by ferocious persecutions. The Provençal, abandoned in its native country by those who were best able to cultivate it, at the precise point of time when it was about to add to its poets historians, critics, and distinguished prose-writers; discountenanced in the territories which had been newly gained from the Arabians, and confined between the proud Castilian and the sea, perished, at last, in the kingdom of Valencia, at the very period when the inhabitants of those provinces, once so free and haughty, were deprived of their liberties. This school of poetry the only light amid the darkness of universal barbarism, and the bond which, combining noble minds in the cultivation of high sentiments formed so long the common link of union amongst different nations, has lost, in our eyes, all its charms and its power. We can no longer be deceived by the hopes which it held orth. The songs which seem to contain the germ of so many noble works, and to which that expectation gave so much interest, appear cold and ifeless, when we reflect how unproductive they ave been.

NOTE.

In p. 228, is mentioned a warlike song to rouse the persecuted Provençals to resist the plundering invasion which St. ouis was directing against them, under the pretence of a zeal or religion and social order. A friend furnishes us with a transation of this piece, which is now very curious, as shewing the ght in which some of his contemporaries viewed the hypocrisy nd cruelty of this St. Louis, whose God is, in the year 1823, ivoked in support of similar projects.

I'll make a song, shall body forth
My full and free complaint,
To see the heavy hours pass on,
And witness to the feint
Of coward souls, whose vows were made
In falsehood, and are yet unpaid;
Yet, noble Sirs, we will not fear,
Strong in the hope of succours near.

Yes! full and ample help for us
Shall come, so trusts my heart;
God fights for us, and these our foes,
The French, must soon depart.
For, on the souls that fear not God,
Soon, soon shall fall the vengeful rod:
Then, noble Sirs, we will not fear,
Strong in the hope of succours near.

And hither they believe to come,
(The treacherous, base Crusaders!)
But, ev'n as quickly as they come,
We'll chase those fierce invaders;
Without a shelter, they shall fly
Before our valiant chivalry:
Then, noble Sirs, we will not fear,
Strong in the hope of succours near.

And ev'n if Frederic, on the throne
Of powerful Germany,
Submits the cruel ravages
Of Louis' hosts to see;
Yet, in the breast of England's King,
Wrath, deep and vengeful, shall upspring:
Then, noble Sirs, we will not fear,
Strong in the hope of succours near.

Not much those meek and holy men,
The traitorous Bishops, mourn,
Though from our hands the sepulchre
Of our dear Lord be torn;
More tender far, their anxious care
For the rich plunder of Belcaire:
But, noble Sirs, we will not fear,
Strong in the hope of succours near.

And look at our proud Cardinal,
Whose hours in peace are past;
Look at his splendid dwelling-place,
(Pray Heaven it may not last!)
He heeds not, while he lives in state,
What ills on Damietta wait:
But, noble Sirs, we will not fear,
Strong in the hope of succours near.

I cannot think that Avignon
Will lose its holy zeal
In this our cause, so ardently
Its citizens can feel.
Then, shame to him who will not bear,
In this our glorious cause, his share!—
And, noble Sirs, we will not fear,
Strong in the hope of succours near.

CHAPTER VII.

On the Romance-Wallon, or Langue d'Oïl, and on the Romances of Chivalry.

It is not the design of this work to treat of the language and literature of France. On that subject, many agreeable and profound works have been written, which are in the hands of every one; and it would be an useless task to repeat, in a curtailed and imperfect manner, all that has been said on this subject, with so much justice and liveliness, by Marmontel, La Harpe, and others. The elder period of French literature has, however, something of a foreign character. Our poets, the heirs of the Trouvères, did not accept the inheritance which devolved upon them; and the language of the twelfth and thirteenth centuries sufficiently varies from our own, to render many of the literary remains of that period inaccessible to most of my readers. It is, moreover, almost impossible to speak of the Troubadours, without giving some account of the Trouvères; or to enquire into the origin and progress of the Romance-Provençal, without, at the same time, discoursing of the Romance-Wallon.

It is not necessary to refer so far back as the Celtic, for the first origin of French literature. That language, which had been long forgotten, could have had little influence upon the characters of those, whose ancestors had spoken it. When the Franks conquered Gaul, it is probable that the Celtic was only to be found in some of the districts of Brittany; where, indeed, it has remained to the present day. That mother-tongue, which appears to have been common to France, to Spain, and to the British Isles, has so completely disappeared, that we are no longer able to ascertain its peculiar character. Although it is regarded as the mother of the *Bas-Breton*, of the Gaelic of Scotland, of the Welsh, and of the dialect of Cornwall, yet the analogy which exists between those languages can with difficulty be defined; nor is their common derivation discoverable. In all the provinces of Gaul, the Latin had taken place of the Celtic, and had become, amongst the people at large, a sort of native tongue. The massacres which accompanied the wars of Julius Cæsar, the subjection of the vanquished, and the ambition of those Gauls who procured the privileges of Roman citizens, all concurred to produce a change in the manners, the spirit, and the language, of the provinces situated between the Alps, the Pyrenees, and the Rhine. From that country, accomplished Latin scholars and celebrated teachers of rhetoric and grammar, proceeded; while the people at large acquired a taste for Roman spectacles, and ornamented their principal cities with magnificent theatres. Four hundred and fifty years of submission to the Roman yoke, caused an intimate union between the Gauls and the inhabitants of Italy.

The Franks, who spoke a Northern or German dialect, introduced a new idiom amongst the Gauls. This intermixture soon corrupted the Latin, which suffered still more from ignorance and barbarism; and the Gauls, who called themselves Romans, because they imagined they spoke the language of Rome, abandoned all the refinements of syntax for the simplicity and rudeness of a barbarian tongue. In writing, an attempt was still made to keep alive the Latin; but in conversation, every one gradually yielded to the prevailing habit, and dropped the use of letters and terminations, which were regarded as superfluous. Even at the present day, we exclude, in the pronunciation of the French language, a fourth part of the letters which we use in writing. After the lapse of some time, a distinction was drawn between the language of the Roman subjects and that of the Latin writers; and the Romance language, founded on the first, and the Latin language perpetuated by the latter, were recognized as distinct. But the former, which occupied several centuries in its formation, had no name as long as the conquerors preserved the use of the German. At the commencement of the second race of monarchs, German was still the language of Charlemagne and his court. That hero spoke, say the historians of the time, the language of his ancestors, *patrium sermonem;* and many French writers have fallen into a strange error, in supposing that the *Francisque* signified the old French. But, whilst the German was employed in conversation, and in martial and historical poems, Latin was the written language, and the Romance, still in its state of barbarism, was the dialect of the people.

In the reign of Charlemagne, too, the great difference between the language of the common people and the Latin, compelled the church to preach in the vulgar tongue. A Council, held at Tours, in 813, directed the bishops to translate their homilies into the two languages of the people, the rustic Romance and the *Theotisque,* or German. This decree was confirmed by the Council of Arles, in 851. The subjects of Charlemagne were composed of two very different races; the Germans who inhabited along and beyond the Rhine, and the Walloons, who called themselves Romans, and who alone, of all the people of the South, were under the dominion of the Franks. The name of *Waelchs,* or Walloons, which was given them by the Germans, was the same as that of *Galli* or *Galatai,* which they received from the Latins and Greeks, and of *Keltai*, or Celts, the name which, according to Cæsar, they themselves acknowledged.* The language which they spoke, was called after them the *Romance-Wallon*, or rustic Romance and it was pretty much the same throughout all France, except that, as it extended southward, a nearer approach to the Latin was perceptible; whilst, on the North, the German prevailed. In the partition, made in 842, amongst the children of Louis the Debonnaire, the common language was made use of, for the first time, in a public proceeding, as the people were a party to the transaction in taking the oath of allegiance to the King. The oath of Charles the Bald, and that of his subjects, are two of the most ancient remaining monuments of the Romance language. The language employed in them resembles the Provençal as much as that which was afterwards called the Romance-Wallon.

The coronation of Bozon, King of Arles, in 879, divided France into two portions, which continued rival and independent states, during four centuries. These provinces seemed destined to be constantly inhabited by different races of men

* All these names differed only in the pronunciation; but the Bas-Bretons, a remnant of the Celts, preserved in their language another celebrated name, of a different origin, and which was perhaps, with them, an honourable title. They called themselves *Cimbri*.

æsar has remarked, that in his time the Aquitani iffered from the Celtæ in language, manners, and aws. In the country of the former, the Visigoths nd the Burgundians established themselves, and he Franks, in the territories of the latter; while he division of the two monarchies, which took lace at the end of the Carlovingian race, only, erhaps, confirmed the ancient distinction beween the people. Their language, though formed rom the same elements, grew every day more issimilar. The people of the South called themelves *Romans-provençaux;* while the northern ribes added to the name of Romans, which they ad assumed, that of *Waelchs,* or Wallons, which hey had received from the neighbouring people. he Provençal was called the Langue d'Oc, and he Wallon the Langue d'Oil, or d'Oui, from the ffirmative word of each language, as the Italian as then called the *Langue de si,* and the German he *Langue de ya.*

Normandy, a province of France, was invaded, the tenth century, by a new northern tribe, ho, under the command of Rollo, or Raoul, the ane, incorporated themselves with the ancient habitants. This mixture introduced into the omance new German words and idioms. Yet he active spirit which led the conquerors to this rovince, their good laws, their wise administraon, and their adoption of the language of the onquered, were the means of giving the Romance-

Wallon, a more fixed form, and a greater polish in Normandy, than in any other province of France Rollo acquired the Dukedom in 912; and a century and a half later, one of his descendants, William the Conqueror, was himself so much attache to the Romance-Wallon, and encouraged it s greatly amongst his subjects, that he introduce it into England, and forced it upon the people b rigorous enactments, instead of their ancient lan guage, which nearly resembled that of his ow ancestors.

It was from Normandy that the first writer and the first poets in the French language sprung The laws which William the Conqueror, wh died in 1087, imposed upon his English subjects are the most ancient work in the Romance-Wal lon, which has come down to us. After this le gal memorial, the two first literary works, whic prove that the Langue d'Oui was beginning to b cultivated, are the *Book of the Britons*, or *Brutu* a fabulous history of the Kings of England, writte in verse, in 1155, and the Romance of the *Knigh of the Lion*, written at the same period, both them in Normandy, or at least by Normans.* I

* There are many copies of the Romance of Brutus. Th which I have examined, is in the Royal Library. It commenc with the following lines:

Qui velt oïr, qui velt savoir
De roi en roi et d'hoir en hoir

Rou des Normands, or *Le Livre de Raoul*, composed by Gasse in 1160, and which gives a history of the establishment of that people in Normandy, must be placed in the third rank. The period was not now far distant, when the romances of chivalry were to make their appearance in the same language. The first of these was *Tristan de Léonois*, written in prose, about the year 1190. A few years afterwards, appeared the romances of *Saint Gréaal* and *Lancelot*; and these, likewise, proceeded either from Normandy, or from the court of England. Before the year 1200, an anonymous translation of the Life of Charlemagne was made; and previously to 1213, Geoffrey de Ville-

---

Qui cil furent, et dont ils vinrent
Qui Engleterre primes tinrent,
Queus rois y a en ordre eu
Qui ainçois et qui puis y fu,
Maistre Gasse l'a translaté
Qui en conte la vérité,
Si que li livres la devisent.

The romancer takes up his history sufficiently early. He thus begins:

Por la veniance de Paris
Qui de Gresse ravit Hélène.

In these and the subsequent extracts, I have not confined myself scrupulously to the ancient orthography. Although it may be essential to the study of the language, it is not so to an acquaintance with the spirit of the ancient poetry. By changing a few letters, I have probably saved the reader much useless difficulty.

hardouin had written, in the French language, a History of the Conquest of Constantinople.

Amongst the different works which appeared at this period, the poem of *Alexander* is that which has enjoyed the greatest share of reputation. It was, probably, given to the world about the year 1210, in the reign of Philip Augustus; as there are many flattering allusions to incidents which occurred at the court of that prince. It is not the work of one individual only, but contains a series of romances and marvellous histories, which are said to be the result of the labours of nine celebrated poets of the time. Those best known at the present day are, Lambert li Cors, or the Little; Alexander de Bernay, who continued Lambert; and Thomas of Kent. Alexander, perhaps the only hero of Greece, who was known in the middle ages, is introduced, not surrounded by the pomp of antiquity, but by the splendours of chivalry. Of the different parts of this poem, one is called *Li Roumans de tote Chevalerie,* because Alexander is represented in it, as the greatest and noblest of cavaliers. Another bears the title of *Le Vœu du Paon,* or The Vow of the Peacock, from its containing a description of the taking of the oath of chivalry, as it was practised at the court of the Macedonian hero. The high renown of this poem, which was universally read, and translated into several languages, has given the name of Alexandrine verse to the measure in which it is written; a measure, which the French have denominated the heroic.*

Thus, in the twelfth century, the Romance-Wallon became a literary language, subsequent, by at least a hundred years, to the Romance-provençal. The wars against the Albigenses, which at this period caused an intercourse between the two nations into which France was divided, contributed, probably, to inspire a taste for poetry in that province, which was the most tardy in emerging from a state of barbarism, and which could boast, only towards the year 1220, a poetical literature consisting of lyrical pieces, of songs, virelays,

* The poems mentioned above, are written in verses of eight yllables, rhymed two and two, and preserving the distinction f masculine and feminine verses, but without regarding the rule, which the French poets of the present day observe, of using hem alternately. Nearly all the Fabliaux are written in the ame measure. The Alexandrine of twelve syllables, with the æsura in the middle, divides itself generally, to the ear, into o lines of equal length. Formerly it was even more monotoous and laboured than at present, for the poets used frequently o leave a mute syllable in the middle of the verse, at the end of he cæsura. The Italians, in their Leonine verses, and the panish, in their verses *de arte mayor*, have the same monotonous efect. It may be observed in the commencement of the poem f *Alexander*.

> Qui vers de riche estoire veut entendre et oïr,
> Pour prendre bon exemple de prouesse cueillir,
> La vie d'Alexandre, si com je l'ai trovée
> En plusieurs leus écrite et de boche contée . . . . &c.

ballads, and *sirventes*. The reciters of tales, and the poets, giving the name of Troubadour a French termination, called themselves Trouvères.*

With the exception of the difference of language, it may be thought that the Troubadour and the Trouvère, whose merit was pretty nearly equal; who were equally ignorant or well-informed; who both of them spent their lives at courts, at which they composed their poems, and where they mingled with knights and ladies; and who were both accompanied by their Jongleurs and minstrels, should have preserved the same resemblance in their productions. Nothing, however, can be more dissimilar than their poems. All that remains of the poetry of the Troubadours is of a lyrical character, while that of the Trouvères is decidedly epic. The Provençals, it is true, have appealed against the judgment which has been passed upon their poets, to whom the partizans of the Trouvères have denied all the merit of invention. The former maintain that, it is evident that this charge is false, from the long catalogue of the tales, romances, and fables, with which it was the duty of the Jongleurs to be acquainted, in order to entertain the great, and which have since either been lost or are preserved in the

* We have elsewhere remarked, that in Provençal, *Trobaire* is the nominative of Troubadors.

Langue d'Oil. They further insist, that, amongst the poems of the Trouvères, many are to be found of Provençal origin, which appears from the scene being laid in Provence; and they maintain that the Trouvères contented themselves with translating the romances and *fabliaux*, of which they were not the inventors. It seems, however, exceedingly unaccountable, that the *songs* only of the Provençals, and the *tales* of the French, should have been preserved, if the genius of the two nations, in this respect, were not essentially distinct.*

The biography of the Troubadours has been frequently given to the public. The lives which were published by Nostradamus, and the accounts collected by M. de Sainte-Palaye, and afterwards made known to the public by

---

* [This must be taken with much qualification. A mere reference to the pages of Laborde's Essay on Music, will show that there are yet remaining, in manuscript, an immense number of lyric pieces of the Northern school. It is hardly safe to found any very positive opinions on the absence of tales and romances from the manuscript collections of the Troubadours yet preserved to us. It had often been a subject of wonder, that, notwithstanding the prevalence of Troubadour poetry in Catalonia, no remains of it were known to be preserved there. Yet a recent visit to the archives of its churches, has shown that an immense quantity is yet in existence, though unpublished. Had it not been for the literary zeal of one individual, the historian might now have asserted, without fear of contradiction, that the *Minnesingers* wrote no lyrical poetry.—*Tr.*]

Millot, are, for the most part, highly romantic. They contain the history of their intrigues with noble ladies, of their sufferings, and of their chivalric achievements. The lives of the Trouvères are much more obscure. Scarcely have the names of any survived, nor is the history of the most celebrated individuals known. If a few anecdotes have been preserved, they possess little either of interest or of adventure.

The Trouvères have left us many romances of chivalry, and *fabliaux*; and upon the former, the twelfth and thirteenth centuries must rest their claims to glory. The spirit of chivalry, which burst forth in these romances; the heroism of honour and love; the devotion of the powerful to the weak; the noble purity of character, triumphing over all opposition, which is held forth as a model in these works; and the supernatural fictions, so novel and so dissimilar to every thing which either antiquity or later times had produced, display a force and a brilliancy of imagination, which, as nothing had prepared the way for them, seem quite inexplicable.

After searching, on all sides, for the inventors of that chivalric spirit which burns in the romances of the middle ages, we are astonished to observe how sudden was that burst of genius. We in vain attempt to discover, in the manners or in the traditions of the Germans, the birth of chivalry. That people, although they respected women and admitted them to their counsels and their worship, had still more deference than tenderness for the sex. Gallantry was unknown to them; and their brave, loyal, but rude manners, could never have contributed to the developement of the sentiment and heroism of chivalry. Their imagination was gloomy, and their supernatural world was peopled with malicious beings. The most ancient poem of Germany, that of the Niebelungen, in the form in which we at present find it, is posterior to the first French romances, and may have been modified by them. But the manners it describes are not those of chivalry. Love acts no part in it; for the warriors are actuated by far different interests and far different passions from that of gallantry. Women are seldom introduced, and then not as objects of devotion; while the men are not softened down and civilized by their union with them. The inventors of the romances of chivalry, on the contrary, have united in painting their heroes, as endowed with the most brilliant qualities of all the nations with which they had come in contact; with the fidelity of the Germans, the gallantry of the French, and the rich imagination of the Arabians.

It is to the last source, according to others, that we are to look for the primary origin of the romance of chivalry. At the first view, this opinion appears to be natural, and to be supported by many facts. Some very ancient romances represent the system of chivalry as having beei established amongst the Moors, as well a: amongst the Christians, and introduce Moorisl knights; whilst all the reciters of tales, the histo rians, and the poets of Spain, represent the man ners of the Moors as those of chivalry. Thu Ferragus, Ferraù, or Fier-à-bras, the bravest an(the most loyal of the Moorish knights, figures in th(Chronicle of Turpin, which preceded all the ro mances of chivalry. The same chronicle affirms that Charlemagne was dubbed a knight by Galafron Emir (Admirantus,) or Saracen prince of Coleto in Provence. So, Bernard Carpio, the most an cient hero of Christian Spain, signalized himsell chiefly in the Moorish army, by his chivalrou deeds. The History of the civil wars of Grenad: is a chivalric romance; and, in the Diana of Monte mayor, the only chivalric adventure which i contained in that pastoral composition, is lai(amongst the Moors. It is the history of Abin darraes, one of the Abencerrages of Grenada, an(the beautiful Xarifa. The ancient Spanish rc mances, and their oldest poem, the Cid, attribut the same manners to the Arabians, as early a the twelfth century. All that portion of Spair which was occupied by the Moors, was coverec with strong castles, built on all the heights; an every petty prince, every lord, and even every *cheil* exercised an independent power. There certainl existed, in Spain, at least, a sort of Arabia feudalism, and a spirit of liberty, very different from that of Islamism. The notions on the point of honour, which not only possessed a great influence over the system of chivalry, but even over our modern manners, rather belonged to the Arabians than to the German tribes. To them, we owe that spirit of vengeance which has been so religiously observed, and that fastidious sensibility to insults and affronts, which has induced men to sacrifice not only their own lives but those of their families, to wash out a stain upon their honour; and which produced the revolt of the Alpuxarra of Grenada in the year 1568, and the destruction of fifty thousand Moors, to avenge a blow given by D. Juan de Mendoza to D. Juan de Malec, the descendant of the Aben-Humeyas.

Devotion to the female sex appears to be still peculiar to those nations, whose blood has felt the ardent influence of a burning sun. They love with a passion and an excess, of which neither our ordinary life nor even our romances present any idea. They regard the habitations of their wives as a sanctuary, and a reflection upon them as a blasphemy. The honour of a man is deposited in the hands of her whom he loves. The period, when chivalry took its rise, is precisely that, when the moral feelings of the Arabians attained their highest pitch of delicacy and refinement. Virtue was then the object of their enthusiasm; and the purity of the language, and of the ideas of their authors, ought to make us ashamed of the corruption of our own. As a farther proof, of all the nations of Europe, the Spanish are the most chivalric; and they alone were the immediate scholars of the Arabians.

But, if chivalry be of Arabic origin, whence comes it, that we have so few traces of it in their writings? Whence comes it, that we are not indebted to the Spanish and the Provençals, for our first romances? and how does it happen, that the scene, in the earliest works of that kind, is laid in France or England; countries, over which the Arabians had, certainly, never any influence?

The romances of chivalry are divided into three distinct classes. They relate to three different epochs, in the early part of the middle ages; and they represent three communities, three bands of fabulous heroes, who never had communication with each other. The origin and peculiar character of these three romantic mythologies, may perhaps, throw considerable light on the first invention of chivalry.

In the romances of chivalry of the first class the exploits of Arthur, son of Pendragon, the last British king who defended England against the invasions of the Anglo-Saxons, are celebrated. At the court of this king and his wife Genevra we find the enchanter, Merlin; and to it belonged the institution of the Round Table, and the knights, Sir Tristan of Leonois,* Lancelot of the Lake, and many others. The origin of this history may be traced in the Romance of Brutus, by Gasse, the text of which contains the date of 1155. In this fabulous chronicle, both King Arthur, and the Round Table, and the prophet Merlin, are to be found.† But it was the later romances which perfected this idea, and peopled the court of King Arthur with living beings, who were then as well known as the courtiers

---

[* The Lyonnese, a part of Cornwall, no longer visible above water.—*Tr.*]

† The author of the Romance of Brutus, who grounds himself upon the authority of more ancient histories, or rather versifies all kinds of traditions, and every historical and poetical rumour which was afloat at the time, represents Arthur and his twelve peers as treating with the Emperor of the Romans:

Artus fut assis à un dois,
Environ lui contes et rois,
Et sont doze hommes blancs venus,
Bien atornés et bien vestus,
Deux et deux en ces palais vindrent
Et deux et deux les mains se tindrent,
Douze estoient, et douze Romains ;
D'olive portent en lors mains,
Petit pas ordinairement,
Et vindrent moult avenamment.
Parmi la sale trespassèrent,
Al roi vindrent ; le saluèrent,
De Rome, se disant, venoient, etc.

Manusc. de la Biblioth. du Roi. Cangé 27.

of Louis XIV. are to us. The Romance of Merlin, who was said to be the son of the devil and a Breton lady, who lived in the reign of Vortiger, makes us acquainted with the wars of Uther and Pendragon against the Saxons, the birth and youth of Arthur, the miracles with which the prophet of chivalry sanctified the establishment of the Round Table, and the prophecies which he left behind him, and to which all the subsequent Romance writers have had recourse. The Romance of Saint-Gréaal, which is written in verse, by Christian de Troyes, in the twelfth century, is a mixture of Breton chivalry and sacred history. The cup out of which the Messiah drank, during his crucifixion, was known to the Romance writers under the name of Saint-Gréaal. They suppose it to have been carried into England, where it came into the possession of the knights of the Round Table. Lancelot of the Lake, Galaar, his son, Percival of Wales, and Boort, of whom the history of each is given.* King Arthur, Gawain

* The original Romance of Saint-Gréaal may be found in the Royal Library, No. 7523. It is a very large manuscript volume, in 4to. written in double columns, and containing nearly the whole history of the Knights of the Round Table. It was afterwards translated into prose, and printed *lit. Goth. Paris,* 1516, *fo.* Christian de Troyes, who originally composed it in verse, may fairly be ranked amongst the best poets of the earlier ages of his language. There is both harmony in the verses, and sensibility in the narrative. At the commencement of the Romance, we

his nephew, Perlevaux, nephew of King Pecheur, Meliot de Logres, and Meliaus of Denmark, are the heroes of this illustrious court, whose adven-

---

find a mother, who, after having lost her husband and her two elder sons in battle, attempting to prevent her third child from taking up arms, and entering upon the career of glory, detains him in a solitary castle, never allowing him to hear even the name of knight. The young gentleman, however, during one of his visits to the neighbouring peasantry, accidentally meets with some ladies and knights-errant, and is immediately seized with a love of adventure. After making his mother repeat to him the history of his family, he instantly sets off to beg the honour of knighthood from the King.

> Biaux fils, fait elle, diex vos doint
> Joie ; plus que ne m'en remaint,
> Vous doint-il où que vous aillez. . . . .
> Quand li varlet fut eloigné,
> Le giet d' une pierre menue
> Se regarda, et vit chaüe
> Sa mère, au chief du pont arrière,
> Et fut pasmée en tel manière
> Comme s'el fut pasmée morte.

In another celebrated Romance, by the same Christian de Troyes, the author, with vast simplicity, delivers his opinion, that France had arrived at that period of glory and science which so greatly distinguished Rome and Greece. The passage is to be found at the commencement of the Romance of Alexander, the descendant of King Arthur. *Biblioth. manusc.* 7498. 3.

> Ce nos ont nos livres appris
> Que Grèce eut de chevalerie
> Le premier loz, et de clergie (*savoir*) ;
> Puis vint chevalerie à Rome

tures are recounted by different Romance writers, with a curious mixture of simplicity, grandeur, gallantry and superstition. The Romance of Lancelot of the Lake was commenced by Christian de Troyes, but continued, after his death, by Godfrey de Ligny. The Romance of Tristan, son of King Meliadus of Leonois, the first which was written in prose, and which is most frequently cited by ancient authors, was written, in 1190, by a Trouvère whose name is forgotten.*

When we examine this numerous family of heroes, and the scenes in which their achievements are laid, we feel confirmed in the opinion that the Normans are the real inventors of this new school of poetry. Of all the people of ancient Europe,

---

Et ja de clergie la some,
Qui ore est en France venue,
Dieu doint qu'elle y soit retenue
Et que li leus li abellisse,
Tant que ja de France ne isse
L'onor qui s'y est arrêtée,
Dont elle est prisée et dotée
Mieux des Gréjois et des Romains.

* In the edition of Paris, 1533, in small folio, the first chapter thus commences: "Je Luce chevalier, seigneur du chasteau du Gast, voysin prochain de Salesbiere en Angleterre, ay voulu rediger et mettre en volume l'histoire autentique des vertueux nobles et glorieux faits du très-vaillant et renommé chevalier Tristan, fils du puyssant roy Meliadus de Leonnoys." The Chevalier Luce, however, is a new editor, and not the original author.

the Normans shewed themselves, during the period which preceded the rise of the Romance literature, to be the most adventurous and intrepid. Their incursions, from Denmark and Norway, on the coasts of France and England, in open vessels, in which they traversed the most dangerous seas, and sailing up the rivers, surprised nations in the midst of peace, who were not even aware of their existence, astonish and confound the imagination, by the audacity which they display. Other tribes of Normans, passing through the wild deserts of Russia, sword in hand, and cutting their way through a perfidious and sanguinary nation, arrived at Constantinople, where they became the guards of the Emperor. They purchased, with their blood, the luxurious fruits of the South; and, even at the present day, "the love of figs" is a phrase in Iceland, signifying the most vehement appetite; an appetite, which impelled their forefathers to the wildest adventures. Others of the Normans established themselves in Russia; and their unconquerable bravery, seconded by the natives, soon rendered them exceedingly powerful. They there founded the dynasty of the Warags or the Warangians, which lasted until the invasion of the Tartars. A powerful colony of Normans, who established themselves in France, and gave their own name to Neustria, adopted the language and the laws of the people, in the midst of whom they lived; without, however, abandoning their taste for foreign incursions. The conquests of these Normans astonish us by their hardihood, and by the adventurous spirit which seems to have actuated every individual. At the commencement of the eleventh century, a few pilgrim adventurers, who were drawn by devotion and curiosity into the kingdom of Naples, successively conquered La Puglia, Calabria, and Sicily. Scarcely fifty years had elapsed from the period when the Normans first discovered the way to these distant lands, when Robert Guiscard beheld, in the same year, the Emperors of the East and the West flying before him. In the middle of the eleventh century, a Duke of Normandy conquered England; and at the commencement of the next century, Boemond, another Norman, founded the principality of Antioch. The adventurers of the North were thus established in the centre of Syria.

A people so active, so enterprising, and so intrepid, found no other delight in their leisure hours,* than listening to tales of adventures, dangers and battles. Their ungovernable imaginations were dissatisfied, unless they were engaged in a game of hazard, at which the stakes were human lives. Nothing delighted them so much as to see some hero wandering alone, combating alone, and gaining the victory by his single arm, as William Bras-de-fer, Osmond, Robert, Roger and Boemond had done, at a period which was then recent. Courage was valued by them, above every other quality. The other chivalric virtues were held in little estimation; and the nation, whose great hero had assumed the surname of Guiscard (the cunning, or the thief), by no means punished treachery with the same severity as cowardice. Thus, in the romance of Lancelot, it is said that "his father had a neighbour, who lived near him in the county of Berry, then called the Desert. This neighbour's name was Claudas, and he was lord of Bourges and the adjacent country. Claudas was a king, chivalric and wise, but wonderfully treacherous."* Love, which is to be found in the poetry of every nation, formed a part of their narratives. But it was not love, with that mixture of constancy, purity, and delicacy which the Spanish romance writers have thrown around it; and which, when awakened amongst the nations of the South, is the most tender and ardent of all passions. Nor was the supernatural world represented with that beauty, which, from a better acquaintance with the fictions of the South, distinguishes the later romances. There were none of those genii, who dispensed, at will, all the wonders of art and nature; who created enchanted palaces at their beck, while every thing that can dazzle or

* Lancelot of the Lake, p. 1. chap. 1. Paris, 1533. 3 vols. fol. *lit. Goth.*

charm the senses, started up at the word of a magician. They had only a kind of fays, powerful, yet dependant beings, who influenced the destinies of men, and yet had themselves, occasionally need of human protection. Their existence had been an article in the creed of all the northern nations, even during the reign of paganism. The priestesses of the sombre divinities of the woods were then their interpreters and their organs. Christianity had not as yet taught the Normans to disbelieve in the existence of these beings. It merely attributed to them another origin. The ancient worship was considered as a magical art and the powers, attributed to the fays, were a modification of those possessed by the devil. "At this time*," says the author of the romance of Lancelot, "all those were called *fays*, who dealt in enchantments and charms; and there were many of them, principally in Great Britain

* "En celui temps, étoient appelées fées toutes celles qui s'entremettoient d'enchantemens et de charmes; et moult en estoit pour lors, principalement en la Grande-Bretaigne; et savoient la force et la vertu des paroles, des pierres, des herbes, parquoi elles estoient tenues en jeunesse, en beauté et en grandes richesses: celle-ci avoit appris tout ce qu'elle savoit de nygromancie de Merlin le prophète aux Anglois qui sçut toute la sapience qui des diables peut descendre. Or fut le dit Merlin ung homme engendré en femme par ung diable, et fut appelé l'enfant sans père." Part I fol. 6.

They knew the power and virtue of words, and of stones, and of herbs, whereby they preserved themselves in youth and beauty, and got great riches. They learned all the necromancy of Merlin, the English prophet, who possessed all the wisdom that the devil can bestow. The said Merlin was a man engendered between a woman and the devil, and he was called the fatherless child."

The heroes of chivalry were never tired of roaming through France, Brittany, England, Scotland, and Ireland. Many kingdoms are named; and the kings of Logres, of Léonois, of Cornwall, and twenty other places, are introduced; but all their territories might be comprised within a very small circle. The provinces of France, whither the scene is often transported, are generally those which, in the eleventh and twelfth centuries, belonged to the English, or which were well known to that people. We meet with no knightly adventures in that portion of France where the Langue d'Oc was spoken, nor in the countries beyond Paris. Sometimes the Romans are obscurely mentioned, as if that nation still existed; but the knights never passed into Italy, nor do any of the chivalry of that country ever make their appearance amongst them.*

* "Durant ce temps estoient le roy de Cornouailles et celui de Leonnois subjects au roi de Gaule. Cornouailles rendoit au roy de Gaule cent jouvenceaux et cent damoyselles, et cent chevaux de

Neither Spain nor the Moors are mentioned, nor is any notice taken of Germany and the inland countries of the North. The most perfect ignorance, indeed, of every other part of the world, is manifested. In addition to their native country, the Romance writers appear to have been only acquainted with the places mentioned in Scripture. Joseph of Arimathea passes, without any difficulty, from Judæa to Ireland; and the kingdom of Babylon, the native country of the mother of Tristan de Léonois, is represented to have bordered upon Brittany. The countries within which the Norman Romance writers confined themselves, did not exist at the period when they wrote, and, at no time, resembled the picture which is there given. The gross chronological errors which they committed, prevent our referring their fables to any one period of history;

---

prix, et le roy de Leonnois autant. Et tenoit le roy de Gaule de la seigneurie de Rome. Et sachez que alors rendoient tribut à Rome toutes les terres du monde, N'en Gaule n'avoit encore nul chrétien, ains estoient tous payens. Le roy que adoneques estoit en Gaule, estoit Maronéus (no doubt, Marovéus), que moult estoit prud'homme de sa loi. Et après sa mort, vint saint Remy en France, que convertit Clovis à la loi chrétienne." (*Tristan de Leonnois*, fol. 5.) This passage is copied from the edition of Paris, 1533; but the oldest editions are modern when compared with the manuscripts, and bear evident traces of more recent times. It is only in the manuscripts of the Royal Library, that we find the unmixed and genuine picture of the twelfth century.

and the political state which they describe, in all probability, never had any existence. In their fictions, they yet appear to have proceeded upon some fixed notions; for the geography of their romances is not altogether so confused and fantastic as that of Ariosto. The wanderings of their heroes are not absolutely impossible, and might, perhaps, be traced upon the map; unlike those of Orlando, of Rinaldo, and of Astolpho. The political state and the independence of the little princes of Armorica, had some foundation in history. A confused account is preserved of a league amongst the people of Armorica, for their common defence against the barbarians, at the period of the fall of the Western Empire, which coincides with the reign of Arthur, and the expiring efforts of the Britons to repel the Saxons.*

The scene in which these romances are always

* The league of Armorica, or the maritime countries situated between the mouth of the Seine and of the Loire, was entered into, in the disastrous reign of Honorius, about 420, and continued until the subjection of those provinces by Clovis, posterior to the year 497. The long contests between the Anglo-Saxons and the Britons, for the possession of England, lasted from 455 to 582. Arthur, Prince of the Silures, who was elected king by the British, appears to have succeeded Vortimer and Vortigern, who long led the British armies to victory. His reign must therefore be placed about the end of the fifth century; and, if he ever lived at all, he must have been the contemporary of Clovis.

laid, appears to leave little doubt as to their Norman origin. It may, perhaps, be asked why the Normans have always chosen foreigners for their heroes? and why, if they were the inventors of the romances of chivalry, they have not attached themselves to the real chivalric achievements of their own leaders? We have, however, seen that such an attempt was made, and that the *Rou,* or *Raoul,* of the Normans, was written at the same period as the romance of *Brutus,* with the intention of exalting the fame of the founder of the Duchy of Normandy, and of his ancestors and companions in arms. We may conclude that this romance did not display much talent. It made little impression, and the attempt was never imitated. But, when the romances of Saint Gréaal, of Merlin, of Tristan de Léonois, and of Lancelot of the Lake, appeared, they furnished models for all subsequent writers. The characters were ready formed to their hands, and all that remained for them to do, was to vary the adventures. It is possible, too, that the Normans, who were enemies of the conquered Saxons, regarded themselves as the avengers of the vanquished Britons, whose glory they thus wished to re-establish.

In the second class of chivalric romances, we find the Amadises; but whether those romances belong to French literature has been reasonably disputed. The scene is placed nearly in the same countries as in the romances of the Round Table; in Scotland, England, Brittany, and France. But the exact spots are less decidedly marked, and there is a want of locality about them; while the names are generally borrowed from prior romances. The times are absolutely fabulous. The reigns of Perion, king of France, of Languines, king of Scotland, and of Lisvard, king of Brittany, correspond with no period of history; nor do the adventures of the Amadises refer to any revolution, or great public event. Amadis of Gaul, the first of these romances, and the model of all the rest, is claimed, by the people to the south of the Pyrenees, as the work of Vasco Lobeira, a Portuguese, who lived between 1290 and 1325. If, indeed, this be the production of a Portuguese, it is remarkable that he has laid the scene in France, precisely in the same country which the romances of the Round Table have selected; that he has never led his hero into Spain, nor introduced any adventures with the Moors, the contests with whom possessed the highest interest for every Spaniard; and, lastly, that he should only differ from his predecessors in his superior delicacy and tenderness, and in a somewhat greater mysticism upon the topic of love. If, on the contrary, as the French contend, Amadis of Gaul was only worked up, by Lobeira, from a French romance of still higher antiquity, it is strange that the latter should have had no connexion with the romances of the Round Table, and that it should display a new set of characters, and a totally different fable.*

No doubt exists with regard to the continuations, and the numerous imitations of the Amadis of Gaul. All these romances, as the Amadis of Greece, and the others of that name, Florismart of Hircania, Galaor, Florestan, and Esplandian, are incontestably of Spanish origin, the character of which they bear. Oriental ornaments supersede the ancient simplicity of style; the imagination is extravagant, and yet weak; love is refined away; valour is changed into rhodomontade; religion assumes a more conspicuous place, and the persecuting spirit of fanaticism begins to display itself. These works were in their highest repute, at the time when Cervantes produced his inimitable Don Quixote; and, when we arrive at that epoch of Spanish literature, we shall again refer to them.

The third class of chivalric romances is entirely French, although their celebrity is chiefly

* I have merely looked at the Spanish Amadis, printed at Seville, in 1547, in folio, and the French Amadis, translated by Nicholas de Herberay from the Spanish, folio, 1540. We must look amongst the Manuscripts, both for the original of this romance in French verse, and for the genuine work of Vasco Lobeira, which we scarcely recognise in the Spanish editions of the sixteenth century.

lue to the renowned Italian poet, who availed himself of their fictions. The court of Charlemagne and his Paladins are the subjects of these romances. The history of that monarch, the most brilliant of all during the middle ages, excited the astonishment and admiration of subsequent times. His long reign, his prodigious activity, his splendid victories, his wars with the Saracens, the Saxons, and the Lombards, his influence in Germany, Italy, and Spain, and the re-establishment of the empire of the West, rendered his name popular throughout Europe, long after the achievements, by which he had signalised himself, were forgotten. He was a brilliant star in that dark firmament; the true hero of chivalry, to whom a thousand fantastic adventures might be ascribed.

It is difficult to fix the precise period of these fables. The most ancient monument of the marvellous history of Charlemagne, is the pseudonymous Chronicle of Turpin, or Tilpin, Archbishop of Rheims. It is universally admitted, that the name of this prelate, who is supposed to be contemporary with Charlemagne, is fictitious; and some writers have dated this imposture as far back as the tenth century.* As the Chronicle

* I have some doubts with regard to this. In the introduction, Turpin says, that his friend Leoprand, to whom his book is addressed, was unable to find all the details he wanted, respecting

is written in Latin, the greater or less purity of the language does not enable us to distinguish the period of its composition. The most ancient manuscripts, preserved in the Royal and Vatican libraries, appear to be of the eleventh or twelfth centuries. The translations, imitations, and continuations, commenced only in the reign of Philip Augustus, whom his courtiers wished to flatter, by comparing him to Charlemagne.

But, it is by internal evidence, that we must endeavour to ascertain the age of this fabulous chronicle, which bears, no doubt, the impress of the times in which it was written. The most striking characteristic of this romance, and indeed of all the others to which it has given birth, is the enthusiastic feeling which it displays with regard to the holy wars, of which we observe no traces in the romances of the Round Table. But, what is scarcely less remarkable, is the frequent mention of the wars and the Moors of Spain, and of every thing Spanish, which is not at all in accordance

---

Charlemagne, in the Chronicle of St. Denis. The book is, therefore, posterior to that work, which is thought to have been commenced in the reign of Louis VII. In the 18th chapter it is said, that Charlemagne gave *Portugal* to the Danes and Flemish ; *terram Portugallorum Danis et Flandris.* But that name is only of equal date with the monarchy, in the twelfth century. The Chronicle of Turpin is divided into thirty-two chapters, and only occupies twenty-five folio pages, in the edition of Echardt. *Germanicarum rerum celebriores vetustioresque Chronographi.* 1 vol. fol. Francf. 1566.

with the spirit of the first crusade, and which has given rise to conjectures that this work was the production of a monk of Barcelona. The Chronicle of Archbishop Turpin contains only the history of Charlemagne's last expedition into Spain, whither he was miraculously invited by St. James, bishop of Galicia; his victories over the Moorish king, Argoland; the single combats of Orlando and Ferragus; the death of Orlando at Roncevalles, and the revenge of Charlemagne. Almost all the heroes, who afterwards made so splendid a figure in Ariosto, are named and described in this romance; from which subsequent writers have borrowed the outline of their fables.

If it be true that manuscripts of the Chronicle of Turpin are in existence, written in the eleventh century, I should confidently refer its composition to the time when Alfonso VI. king of Castile and Leon, conquered Toledo and New Castile, in 1085. He was accompanied on this expedition by numbers of French knights, who passed the Pyrenees for the sake of combating the infidels, under the banners of so great a king, and of beholding the Cid, the hero of the age. The war against the Moors of Spain originated in a very different sort of religious zeal, from that which, twelve years later, lighted up the flame of the first crusade. The object of the former was, to succour Christian brethren and neighbours, who adored the same God and avenged common injuries, of which the author seems to be unwilling that the remembrance should perish. But the design of the crusade was to deliver the Holy Sepulchre, to recover the inheritance of the Messiah, and to succour God rather than man; as a Troubadour, whom we have already cited, expresses himself. This zeal for the Holy Sepulchre, and this enthusiastic devotion directed to the East, are not to be found in the Chronicle of Archbishop Turpin, which is, nevertheless, full of ardent fanaticism, and loaded with miracles.

If this Chronicle, to which Ariosto is so fond of alluding, and which has received from him its poetical celebrity, be anterior to the first romances of the Round Table, yet the romances of the court of Charlemagne, which are imitations of the former, are decidedly of a later date. The Chronicle of Turpin, however fabulous it may be, can scarcely be considered as a romance. We are presented, alternately, with incredible martial achievements, the fruits of monkish credulity; and with miracles, the result of monkish superstition. We are, also, entertained with enchantments. The sword of Orlando, Durandal, or Durindana cannot strike without wounding; the body of Ferragus is rendered invulnerable by enchantments; and the terrible horn of Orlando, with which he blew a blast, at Roncevalles, for succour, is heard as far as Saint-Jean-Pied-de-Port, where Charlemagne lies with his army; but the traitor Ganelon prevents the monarch from repairing to the assistance of his nephew. Orlando, abandoning all hope, attempts to break his sword, to prevent its falling into the hands of the enemy, and being stained with Christian blood. He strikes it against trees and rocks, but nothing can resist the enchanted blade, when wielded by so powerful an arm. The trees are cut down and the rocks fly into splinters, but Durandal still remains unbroken. At last, Orlando drives it up to the hilt in a hard rock, and bending it violently, it breaks in his hand. He again sounds his horn, not in hope of succour, but to announce to the Christians that their hour is come; and he blows so violent a blast, that his veins burst, and he expires, weltering in his blood. This is extremely poetical, and indicates a brilliant imagination; but to make it into a chivalric romance, it would be necessary to introduce women and love; subjects which are entirely excluded.

The author of the Chronicle of Turpin had no intention of laying claim to the fame of a creative genius, or of amusing the idle, by tales obviously fictitious. He presented to the French all the wonderful facts, which he related, as purely historical; and the reader of such fabulous legends was accustomed to give credit to still more marvellous narratives. Many of these fables were, therefore, again brought forward in the ancient

Chronicle of Saint Denis, the compilation of which was commenced by the command of the Abbé Suger, minister to Louis the young (1137—1180,) although the work was written without any idea of imposing fictions upon the world, and as an authentic history of the times. Thus we find that it contains, in an abridged form, the same account as in Turpin, of Orlando, and his duel with Ferragus; of the twelve peers of France; the battle of Roncevalles, and the wars of Charlemagne against the Saracens. The portrait of the monarch is borrowed, almost word for word, from the Chronicle of Turpin.—"He was a man of strong heart and great stature, but not too great; seven feet, of the measure of his own foot, was he in height; his head was round; his eyes large, and so clear, that, when he was angry, they sparkled like carbuncles. He had a large straight nose, rising a little in the middle; his hair was brown, and his face fresh-coloured, pleasant, and cheerful. He was so strong that he could easily straighten three horseshoes at once, and raise an armed knight on the palm of his hand from the earth. *Joyeuse*, his sword, could cut an armed knight in two," &c.*

* "Homs fut de cors fort, et de grant estature, et ne mie de trop grant; sept piez avoit de long à la mesure de ses piez; le chief avoit roont, les yeux grans et gros, et si clers que quant il étoit courrouciés, ils resplendissoient ainsi comme escarboucles; le nez avoit grant et droit, et un petit hault au milieu,

But all these marvellous narratives, which then passed for history,* furnished materials for the romances at the conclusion of the crusades, which had introduced a knowledge of the East, at the end of the thirteenth century, and during the reign of Philip the Bold (1270-1285). Adenez, the king-at-arms of this monarch, wrote the romances of Bertha-au-grand-pied, the mother of Charlemagne, Ogier the Dane, and Cleomadis, in verse; and Huon de Villeneuve, the romance of Renaud de Montauban. The four sons of

---

brune chevelure, la face vermeille, lie et haligre; de si grant force estoit, que il estendoit trois fers de chevaux tous ensemble légierement, et levoit un chevalier armé sur sa paume de terre jusques amont. De joyeuse, s'épée, coupoit un chevalier tout armé," &c.

* When the ancient romance writers touch upon the subject of the court of Charlemagne, they assume a more elevated tone. They are not then repeating fables, but celebrating their national history, and the glory of their ancestors; and they claim the right of being heard with respect. The romance of Gerard de Vienne, one of the Paladins of Charlemagne, thus commences: (*Manuscript in the Royal Library*, 7498.3.)

Une chançon plait nos, que je vos die
De haut estoire. et de grand baronie;
Meillor ne peut être dite ne oie.
Cette n'est pas d'orgueil et de follie,
De trahison ou de losengerie,
Mais du Bar'nage que Jésus bénie,
Del plus très fier qui oncques fut en vie.
A Saint Denys à la maître abbayie
Dedans un livre de grant anciennerie
Trovons écrit, etc.

Aymon, Huon de Bordeaux, Doolin de Mayence, Morgante the Giant, Maugis the Christian Enchanter, and many other heroes of this illustrious court, have found, either at that or a subsequent period, chroniclers, who have celebrated the characters and the events of that glorious age, which has been consecrated by the divine poem of Ariosto.

The invention of this brilliant system of romantic chivalry was, however, perfected, as early as the conclusion of the thirteenth century; and all its characteristics are to be found in the romances of Adenez. The knights no longer wandered like the cavaliers of the Round Table, through the dark forests of a semi-barbarous country covered with mists and white with frosts. The whole universe was exposed to their eyes. The Holy Land, indeed, was the grand object of their pilgrimages; but, by that means, they established an intercourse with the extensive and wealthy kingdoms of the East. Their geography, like all their information, was much confused. Their voyages from Spain to Carthage, and from Denmark to Tunis, were accomplished with a facility and rapidity, even more surprising than the enchantments of Maugis or Morgana. These fantastic voyages furnished the Romance writers with opportunities of adorning their narrative with the most splendid descriptions. All the luxury and perfumes of the most highly-favoured countries were at their command. The pomp and magnificence of Damascus, of Bagdad, and of Constantinople, swelled the triumph of their heroes. But the most precious of all their acquisitions, was the imagination of the people of the South and the East; that brilliant and playful faculty, so well calculated to give animation to the sombre mythology of the North. The *fays* were no longer hideous wretches, the object of popular hatred and dread, but the rivals or allies of those enchanters, who, in the East, disposed of the seal of Solomon, and of the Genii who waited upon it. To the art of prolonging life, they added that of multiplying pleasures. They were, in a manner, the priestesses of nature, and all her pomps. At their voice, magnificent palaces started up in the deserts; enchanted gardens and perfumed groves of oranges and myrtles burst forth amid the sands, or on the rocks of the ocean. Gold, and diamonds, and pearls, sparkled upon their garments, or along the walls of their palaces; and their love, far from being considered sacrilegious, was the sweetest recompense of a warrior's toils. Ogier the Dane, the valiant Paladin of Charlemagne, was thus welcomed by the fay Morgana to her castle of Avalon. Morgana, taking a crown of gold ornamented with jewels, representing the leaves of the laurel, the myrtle, and the rose, tells the knight that she had, with five of her sisters, endowed him from his birth, and that she had then chosen him for he favourite.—" Here reign," says she, " and receiv this crown, a symbol of the authority which yo shall ever exercise here." Ogier permits her t place upon his head the fatal crown, to which be longed the gift of immortal youth; but, at the sam time, every sentiment was effaced from his mind except love for Morgana. The hero forgets th court of Charlemagne, and the glory he had gained in France; the crowns of Denmark, o England, of Acre, of Babylon, and of Jerusalem, which he had successively worn; the battles he had fought, and the many giants he had conquered. He passes two hundred years with Morgana, intoxicated with love, without noting the lapse of time; but, upon his crown accidentally falling into a fountain, his memory is restored. He believes that Charlemagne is still alive, and he eagerly asks for intelligence of the brave Paladins, his companions in arms.* When

* Morgana, who meets Ogier on a loadstone rock, which attracts his vessel, in the first place restores his youth to him. " Then she approached Ogier and gave him a ring, which was of such virtue, that, though he had numbered a hundred years, he was immediately restored to the age of thirty." She thus prepared him for an introduction into an assembly of the " finest nobles that were ever seen." In fact, King Arthur and all the peers of ancient chivalry, for three hundred years past, were assembled in the delicious spot into which the knight of Charlemagne was admitted.

we peruse this pleasing fiction, we easily perceive that it was written after the crusade had mingled the nations of the East and the West, and enriched the French with all the treasures of Arabian imagination.

" Or quand Morgue approcha du château, ses fées vindrent au-devant d'Ogier, chantant le plus mélodieusement qu'on sauoit jamais ouïr ; puis entra dedans la salle pour soi deduyre totalement. Adonc vit plusieurs dames fées aornées, et toutes couronnées de couronnes très-somptueusement faites, moult riches ; et long du jour chantoient, dansoient, et menoient joyeuse vie, sans penser à quelque chose, fors prendre leurs mondains plaisirs. Et ainsi que Ogier, il devisoit avec les dames, tantôt arriva le roi Arthus, auquel Morgue la fée dit : Approchez-vous, monseigneur mon frère, et venez saluer la fleur de toute chevalerie, l'honneur de toute la noblesse de France, celui où bonté, loyauté, et toute vertu est enclose. C'est Ogier de Danemarck, mon loyal ami et mon seul plaisir, auquel régit toute l'espérance de ma liesse. Adonc le roi vint embrasser Ogier très-amiablement. Ogier, très-noble chevalier, vous soyez le très-bien venu, et regratie très-grandement notre Seigneur de ce qu'il m'a envoyé un si très-notable chevalier. Si le fit servir incontinent au siége de Machar, par grant honneur, dont il remercia le roi Arthus très-grandement ; puis Morgue la fée lui mit une couronne dessus son chef, moult riche et prétieuse, si que nul vivant ne la sauroit priser nullement. Et avec ce qu'elle étoit riche, elle avoit en elle une vertu merveilleuse ; car tout homme qui la portoit sur son chef, il oublioit tout deuil, mélancolie et tristesse, ne jamais ne lui souvenoit de pays ni de parens qu'il eut ; car tant qu'elle fut sur son chef, n'eut pensement quelconque ne de la dame Clarice, ne de Guyon son frère, ne de son neveu Gautier, ne de créature qui fût en vie, car tout fut mis lors en oubli." *Fol. G. Lit. Goth.* Ogier-le-Danois. Printed by Alain Lotrian and Denys Janot, without name of place or year, in 12mo.

CHAPTER VIII.

On the various Poetry of the Trouvères; their Allegories; Fabliaux; Lyrical Poems; Mysteries and Moralities.

Although the literature of France is entirely distinct from the Romantic literature, having adopted a different set of rules, and a different spirit and character, yet the literature of the Langue d'Oil and of the Trouvères, which was that of ancient France, had the same origin as that of the South. It owed its birth, in the same manner to the mixture of the Northern nations with the Romans. Chivalry and the feudal system, the manners and opinions of the middle ages, gave it its peculiar character; and not only did it belong to the same class as the literature of Provence, of Italy, and of Spain, but it even exercised a very perceptible influence over those countries. It is amongst the Trouvères that we must look for the origin of the chivalric poems, the tales, the allegories, and the dramatic compositions, of southern Europe. Thus, although none of their works have obtained a high reputation, or deserve to be ranked amongst the masterpieces of the human intellect, they are still worthy of our attention, as monuments of the progress of the mind, and as gleams of that rising taste which has since been fully developed.

Nothing is more difficult than to define the constituent qualities of poetry. As the peculiar object of this divine art is to captivate the whole soul, to allure it from its seat, and to transport it to a higher sphere, where it may enjoy delights which seem reserved for more perfect beings, every one is only sensible, in poetry, to that which is in unison with his own character, and values it in proportion to its power of exciting the feelings which most strongly affect him, and which most largely contribute to his own enjoyments. Hence some regard imagination as the essence of poetry. Others have supposed it to consist in feeling, in reflection, in enthusiasm, or in liveliness. It appears, then, that if we are desirous of being correctly understood, we must apply the name of poetry to every composition in which men, gifted with genius, express their various emotions; that we must give that name to every production which unites harmony and rich expression; and that we must admit that all the powers of the mind may, in their turn, be clothed in that brilliant form, that melodious and figurative language, which captivates all the senses at once, striking upon the ear with a regular cadence, and presenting to the mind's eye all the pictures of its marvellous creation.

When we thus adopt the name of poetry, as descriptive of the form of expression only, we shall be better able to comprehend how the poetry of one nation differs, in its essential characteristics, from that of another; and how strictly it is in accordance with those qualities, which are most powerfully developed amongst the nation by whom it is cultivated. The character of a people is always communicated to their poetry. Amongst the Provençals, it is full of love and gallantry; amongst the Italians, it abounds with playful imagination. The poetry of the English is remarkable for its sensibility; that of the Germans, for its enthusiasm. In the Spanish poetry, we remark a wildness of passion, which has suggested gigantic ideas and images; while, in the Portuguese, there is a spirit of soft melancholy and pastoral reflection. All these nations considered those subjects alone to be adapted to poetry, which were accordant with their own dispositions; and they all agreed in considering the character of the French nation as anti-poetical The latter, again, even from the earliest period, have testified their aversion to the more contemplative qualities of the mind, and have given the preference to wit and argument, cultivating the imagination only inasmuch as it assists the faculty of invention. The witty and argumentative taste of this nation has gradually increased. The French have attached themselves almost exclusively, in their poetry, to the narrative style, to wit, and to argument; and they have, therefore, become such complete strangers to romantic poetry, that they have detached themselves from all the other modern nations, and have placed themselves under the protection of the ancients. Not because the ancients, like them, confined themselves to the elegant arrangement of the action, to conventional proprieties, and to argumentative conclusions, but because they developed all the human faculties at one and the same time; and because the French discovered in the classical authors, which are the admiration of all Europe, those qualities upon which they themselves set the highest value. Hence, modern writers have been divided into two parties so diametrically opposite to each other, that they are each incapable of comprehending the principles upon which the other proceeds.

But, before the French had raised the standard of Aristotle, which occurred about a century and a half ago, poetry was not an art which was practised by rule, but rather an inspiration. The works of the Trouvères already differed from those of the Troubadours, without any opposition having arisen between them. The poets of the South, on the contrary, perceiving nothing revolting to their taste in the difference of style, profited by the circumstance, and enriched their poems with the inventions of the people who were situated to the north of the Loire.

The French certainly possessed, above every other nation of modern times, an inventive spirit Complaints, and sighs, and passionate expressions, were more fatiguing to them than to any other people. They required something more real, and more substantial, to captivate their attention. We have seen that amongst them the rich and brilliant inventions of the romances of chivalry originated. We shall soon see that they were the inventors of the *Fabliaux*, or tales of amusement, and that it was they, also, who inspired more life into their narrations, by placing the circumstances before the eyes of the spectators in their mysteries; a dramatic invention, which owes its rise to them. On the other hand, we find them, at the same period, producing some tedious works of a different kind; those allegorical poems, which were subsequently imitated by all the romantic nations, but which seem to be more immediately the offspring of French taste, and which, even to the present day, find some imitators amongst our poets. This allegorical form of composition gratified, at once, the national taste for narrative pieces, and the still more national attachment to compositions which unite wit and argument to a moral aim. The French are the only people who, in poetry, look to the object of the composition; and they, perhaps, understand better than any other nation how to accomplish their purpose. They, therefore, always write with a definite aim in view; whilst other nations conceive it to be the essence of poetry not to seek any certain object, but to abandon themselves to unpremeditated and spontaneous transports, courting poetry from inspiration alone.

The most celebrated, and perhaps the most ancient, of these allegorical poems, is the Romance of the Rose; a name known to every one, although few persons are acquainted with the nature and object of the work itself. It is necessary to premise, that the Romance of the Rose, is not a romance in the sense which we attach, at the present day, to that word. At the period at which it was composed, the French was still called the Romance language, and all the more voluminous productions in that tongue were consequently called *Romans*, or Romances. The Romance of the Rose contains twenty thousand verses; and it is the work of two different authors. Four thousand one hundred and fifty verses were written by Guillaume de Lorris; while his continuator, Jean de Meun, produced the remainder of the poem, fifty years later.

Guillaume de Lorris proposed to treat on the same subject, which Ovid had adopted in his Art of Love. But the dissimilarity between the two works very plainly marks the distinction which existed between the spirit of the two ages. Guillaume de Lorris makes no appeal to lovers; h speaks not either from his own feelings, or hi own experience: he relates a dream; and thi eternal vision of his, which would certainly hav occupied not a few nights, in no point resemble a real dream. A crowd of allegorical personage appear before him, and all the incidents of a tedious passion are converted into real beings, anc endowed with names. There is first *Dam Oiseuse*, or Lady Idleness, who inspires the love with the desire of finding the *Rose*, or the rewarc of Love. Then there are *Male-bouche* and *Dangier* who mislead him; and *Felonie, Bassesse, Haine*, anc *Avarice*, who impede his pursuit. All humar virtues and vices are thus personified and introduced upon the scene. One allegory is linkec to another, and the imagination wanders amongs these fictitious beings, upon whom it is impossibl to bestow any corporeal attributes. This fatiguing invention is necessarily destructive of al interest. We are far more willing to bestow ou attention upon a poem which relates to humar feelings and actions, however insignificant they may be, than upon one which is full of abstrac sentiments and ideas, represented under the name of men and women. At the period, however when the Romance of the Rose first appeared, th less it interested the reader as a narrative, th more it was admired as a work of intellect, as a fine moral conception, and as philosophy clothed in the garb of poetry. Brilliant passages struck the eye at every line; the object of the author was never out of sight; and since poetry was regarded by the French as the vehicle of agreeable instruction, they must necessarily have been of opinion, that the Romance of the Rose was admirably calculated for attaining this end, as it contained a rich mine of pleasing information. Upon this question of instruction and moral discipline, we should decide very differently at the present day. It is no longer thought, that, in recommending virtue, it is necessary to paint vice with grossness, as is frequently done by Guillaume de Lorris. We should no longer tolerate the cynical language, and the insulting manner, in which he, and especially his successor, Jean de Meun, speak of the female sex; and we should be shocked at their indecency, so opposed to every idea of love and chivalric gallantry which we now entertain. Our ancestors were, doubtless, much less delicate than we. No book was ever more popular than the Romance of the Rose. Not only was it admired as a masterpiece of wit, invention, and practical philosophy, but the reader attempted to discover in it matters which had never entered into the contemplation of the author. One allegory was not sufficient, and a second was sought for. It was pretended that Lorris had veiled, in this poetical form, the highest mysteries of theology. Learned commentaries were written upon it, which are appended to the Paris edition, (folio, 1531), and in which a key is given to this divine allegory, which is said to pourtray the grace of God and the joys of Paradise, in those licentious passages which describe terrestrial love. It must be confessed, that this admiration of a work which contained many immoral passages, excited, at length, the animadversions of some of the fathers of the Church. Jean Gerson, Chancellor of the University of Paris, and one of the most respected of the Fathers of the Council of Constance, published a Latin treatise against the Romance of the Rose. From this period, many preachers fulminated their censures against the corrupting volume; whilst others did not scruple to cite passages from it in the pulpit, and to mingle the verses of Guillaume de Lorris with texts of holy writ.

Whilst the national character of the French was thus manifested in the allegorical form which Guillaume de Lorris gave to this didactic poem, it was likewise recognized in the style which he selected. To narrate with neatness, clearness, and a degree of simplicity, to which, at the same time, elegance, precision of expression, and a mixture of abstract sentiment are united, appeared to the French, at that time, to be the essence of the poetical art. Even yet, they regard as poetical, those compositions in which other na-ions can distinguish nothing but rhymed prose. The Romance of the Rose, and its numberless imiations, are of this class. The language is never igurative; it presents nothing to the eye; it neither proceeds from, nor affects, the heart; and f the measure of the verse were taken away, it vould be impossible to recognize it as poetry. n the note, some of the best passages of the poem re extracted.*

* The origin of royalty is represented in the following nes:—

Les homs la terre se partirent,
Et au partir, bornes y mirent;
Mais quand les bornes y mettoient,
Maintes fois s'entrecombattoient,
Et se tollurent ce qu'ils purent;
Les plus forts les plus grands parts eurent....
Lors, convint que l'on ordonnât
Aucun qui les bornes gardât,
Et qui les malfaiteurs tous prit,
Et si bon droit aux plaintifs fit
Que nul ne l'osàt contredire;
Lors s'assemblèrent pour l'élire....
Un grand vilain entr'eux élurent,
Le plus ossu de quant qu'ils furent,
Le plus corsu, et le *greigneur (plus grand)*
Et le firent prince et seigneur....
Cil jura que droit leur tiendroit,
Se chacun en droit soit lui livre
Des biens dont il se puisse vivre....
De là vint le commencement
Aux rois et princes terriens
Selon les livres anciens.

Guillaume de Lorris commenced the Romance of the Rose, in the earlier part of the thirteenth century, and died in 1260. His successor, Jean

---

The following is a celebrated representation of Time, which has been often quoted:

Le Temps qui s'en va nuit et jour
Sans repos prendre et sans séjour;
Et qui de nous se part et emble
Si secrètement qu'il nous semble
Que maintenant soit en un point,
Et il ne s'y arrête point;
Ains ne *fine* d'outre passer *(cesse)*,
Sitôt que ne sauriez penser
Quel temps il est présentement:
Car avant que le pensement
Fut fini, si bien y pensez
Trois temps seroient déjà passés.

The next lines contain the portrait of Love, which, in a poem written in his honour, ought certainly to be the most admirable passage in the book:

Le dieu d'amour, cil qui départ
Amourettes à sa devise,
C'est cil qui les amans attise,
Cil qui abbat l'orgueil des braves,
Cil fait les grands seigneurs esclaves,
Et fait servir royne et princesse,
Et repentir none et abbesse.

A portrait of Dame Beauty:

Celle dame avoit nom Beauté,
Qui point n'étoit noire ne brune,
Mais aussi clère que la lune
Est envers les autres estoiles

de Meun, surnamed Clopinel, was not born until 1280. The continuation of the Romance of the Rose is posterior to the great poem of Dante, which is, like it, a vision. Guillaume de Lorris is, however, the true inventor of that style of writing, and the innumerable poetical visions,

---

Qui semblent petites chandelles.
Tendre chair eut comme rosée ;
Simple fut comme une épousée,
Et blanche comme fleur de lys.
Le *vis (visage)* eut bel, donx et *alys (poli)* ;
Et estoit grêle et alignée,
Fardée n'estoit ne pignée,
Car elle n'avait pas mestier
De soi farder et nettoyer ;
Cheveux avoit blonds et si longs
Qu'ils lui battoient jusqu'aux talons ;
Beaux avoit le nez et la bouche.
Moult grand douleur au cuer me touche
Quand de sa beauté me remembre
Pour la façon de chacun membre. . . .
Jeune fut et de grand faconde,
Saige plaisante, gaie et *cointe (agréable)*,
Gresle, gente, frisque et *accointe (adroite)*.

Even the title of the work was in rhyme :

Cy est le rommant de la Rose
Où tout art d'amour est enclose.
Histoires et autorités,
Et maints beaux propos usités.
Qui a été nouvellement
Corrigé suffisantement,
Et coté bien à l'avantaige
Com on voit en chacune paige.

which occupy so large a space in modern literature, are all imitations of the Romance of the Rose.

The first imitations of this poem appeared in French, and, like their model, they bear the title of romances. One of these romances, which was very famous in its day, and copies of which are frequently met with in libraries, is that of the *Trois Pelerinages*, composed by Guillaume de Guilleville, a Cistercian monk, between 1330 and 1358. This is, also, a dream of a most appalling length; for each pilgrimage occupies a poem of ten or twelve thousand verses, forming a quarto volume. The first is the pilgrimage of man, or human life; the second, the pilgrimage of the soul after it has left the body, or the life to come; the third, the pilgrimage of Jesus Christ, or the life of our Lord. Guilleville tells us in his poem, that the Romance of the Rose was his model; but it is easy to perceive that he has likewise imitated Dante, whose immortal poem had appeared in the interval. Thus, in his orthodox visions, Guilleville takes Ovid for his guide, as Dante was conducted by Virgil through the regions of the dead. But Virgil was in reality the master of the Florentine, and had inspired him with the perception and the enthusiasm of poetry; whilst Guilleville owes nothing to Ovid, and has no connexion with the guide whom he pretends to follow.

About the same time, appeared the *Bible Guyot,** the work of Hugues de Bercy, surnamed Guyot, a bitter satire against all classes of society. It contains the Book of *Mandevie,* or the amendment of the life; the Book of *Clergie,* or of the sciences; and many others of the same kind, in which tiresome allegories partially conceal morals no less fatiguing. We should feel astonished at the patience of our forefathers, who could thus devour these long and stupid works, did we not remember that the people of that day were almost entirely without books, and that there was nothing around them which could extend or awaken their ideas. A single work, a single volume, was the

---

* The following is a fragment of this poem. The title of *Bible* is merely synonymous with *Book.*

Contre les Femmes.

Nulli ne pot oncqu' accomplir
Voloir de femme; c'est folie
De cherchier lor être et lor vie,
Quand li sages n'y voient goute....
Femme ne fut oncques vaincue
Ne apertement bien cognue:
Quand li œil pleure li cuer rit,
Peu pense à ce qu'elle nous dit,
Moult mue souvent son courage,
Et tost a déçu le plus sage
Quand me *membre* (*souvient*) de Salomon,
De Costantin et de Samson
Que femmes inganièrent si,
Moult me *tuit* (*convient*) d'être esbahi.

treasure of a whole mansion. In unfavourable weather, it was read to a circle around the fire; and when it was finished, the perusal was again commenced. The wit of the company was exercised in discovering its applications, and in speculating upon its contents. No comparison with other works enabled them to form a judgment upon its merits. It was reverenced like holy writ, and they accounted themselves happy in being able to comprehend it; as though it were a great condescension in the author, to accommodate himself, sometimes, to their capacities.

Our ancestors likewise possessed another species of poetry, which, though it might not display greater inventive talents, nor a more considerable portion of that inspiration and fire, upon which other nations have bestowed the epithet of poetical, was, at least, exceedingly amusing. Such are the *fabliaux*, the brilliant reputation of which has been revived in the present age. They have been represented as treasures of invention, originality, simplicity, and gaiety, of which other nations can furnish no instances, but by borrowing from the French. A vast number of these ancient tales, written in verse, in the twelfth and thirteenth centuries, are preserved in the Royal Library at Paris. M. de Caylus has given an account of them in his entertaining papers, published in the Transactions of the Academy of Inscriptions. M. Grand d'Aussy has, likewise, made a selection, which he has presented to the public in a more modern dress; and, lastly, M. M. Barbazan and Méon have published four large volumes of these Tales, in the original language, and often with their original grossness. This important portion of the literature of the middle ages merits our attention, as affording an insight into the manners and spirit of the times, and as pointing out the origin of many of those inventions, to which men of other ages and other nations have subsequently laid claim. But researches of this kind are not suited to every one. The dictates of delicacy, decency, and modesty, were little respected in the good old times; and the Trouvères, to excite the gaiety of the knights and ladies who received them at their courts, would often amuse them with very licentious wit. The grossness of their language was esteemed pleasantry, and the most dissolute manners were the most inviting subjects of their verse.

The French, who always accounted elegance and easiness of style to be the essence of poetry, availed themselves, with eagerness, of every tale of gallantry, and every adventure and anecdote, which could awaken curiosity or excite mirth. These, they put into verse, and then called themselves poets, whilst every other nation reserved such subjects for prose. A collection of Indian tales, entitled *Dolopathos*, or the King and the Seven Wise Men, having been translated into

Latin, about the tenth or eleventh century, was the first storehouse of the Trouvères. The Arabian tales, which were transmitted by the Moors to the Castilians, and by the latter to the French, were in their turn versified. Even the romantic adventures of the Provençal Knights and Troubadours, furnished the Trouvères with subjects for their tales. But, above all, the anecdotes which they collected in the towns and castles of France; the adventures of lovers; the tricks which were played upon the jealousy and credulity of husbands; the gallantries of priests, and the disorders of convents, supplied the reciters of tales with inexhaustible materials for their ludicrous narratives. These were treasures common to them all. We seldom know the name of the Trouvère by whom these anecdotes have been versified. Others related them anew, adapting them to their own taste, and adding to, or retrenching from them, according to the impression which they wished to make upon their auditors. Thus it is, that we find, in the fabliaux, every variation of the language. At the period we are discussing, there were neither theatrical entertainments, nor games at cards, to fill up the leisure hours of society. It was found necessary to devise some means of passing the long evenings in courts and castles, and even in private houses; and the Trouvères, or relaters of tales, were therefore welcomed, with an eagerness proportioned to the store of anecdotes which they brought with them to enliven conversation. Whatever was the subject of their verse, they were equally acceptable. Legends, miracles, and licentious anecdotes, were related by the same men to the same companies; and, in the collections of the ancient fabliaux, we find stories of the most opposite kind immediately succeeding each other. The most numerous are those tales, properly so called, which were the models of those of Boccaccio, of the Queen of Navarre, and of La Fontaine. Some of these old fabliaux have had great fame. They have been successively reproduced by all who have any pretensions to the narrative art, and they have passed from age to age, and from tongue to tongue, down to our own days. Several of them have even been introduced upon the theatre, and have furnished fresh food for French gaiety. The fabliau of the *Faucon* gave rise to the opera of *Le Magnifique*. That of the *Myre* produced *Le Medecin malgré lui*, and to *La Housse partie* we are indebted for the comedies of *Conaxa* and *Les Deux Gendres*. In the fabliaux, we find the originals of Parnell's poem of the *Hermit*, of the *Zadig* of Voltaire, and of the tale of *Renard*, which Goëthe has converted into a long poem, under the title of *Reinecke Fuchs*. *Le Castoyement d'un Père à son Fils*, is a collection of twenty-seven fabliaux, connected with one another, and forming a manual of instruction, presented by a father to his son, on his entrance into the world. The *Ordène de Chevalerie* is a simple and interesting recital of the mode, in which the Sultan Saladin caused himself to be dubbed a knight, by the Crusaders whom he had vanquished. In that poem, we find many authentic and contemporary details respecting the order of knighthood, the various ceremonies which accompanied the presentation of the different pieces of armour to the new-made knight, and the signification of these various chivalric customs, which are not to be met with elsewhere. Some of the fabliaux very nearly approach the romances of chivalry; describing, like them, the heroic manners of the nobles, and not the vices of the common people. These alone are really poetical, and display a creative imagination, graceful pictures, elevated sentiments, lively representations of character, and that mixture of the supernatural, which so completely seduces the imagination. It is in a fabliau of this class, *Le Lay de l'Oiselet**, that we meet with the following comparison between the worship of God and of Love.

> And, in truth, you well may see,
> God and Love do both agree: †

* *Fabliaux*, vol. iii. p. 119.

† Et pour vérité vous record
Dieu et Amour sont d'un accord,

God loves truth and reverence,
Nor with those will Love dispense;
God hates pride and treachery,
And Love likes fidelity;
God loves honour and courtesy,
So does Love as well as he;
God to prayers will give an ear,
Nor does Love refuse to hear.

To the same class belongs, also, the Lay of Aristotle, by Henri d'Audeley*, from which we have derived the entertaining opera of *Aristote Amoureux*. In the middle ages, antiquity was represented in the garb of chivalry. The people of that day could scarcely comprehend, how there could have existed manners and a mode of life different from their own. Ancient Greece, moreover, was only known to the people of the West, through the medium of the Arabians. The Lay of Aristotle was, in all probability, itself of eastern origin; for that philosopher, and his disciple, Alexander, were in the number of those Greeks, whose praises the Arabians had the greatest pleasure in celebrating.

Dieu aime sens et honorance,
Amour ne l'a pas en viltance;
Dieu hait orgueil et fausseté,
Et Amour aime loyauté;
Dieu aime honneur et courtoisie,
Et bonne Amour ne hait-il mie;
Dieu écoute belle prière,
Amour ne la met pas arrière, etc.

* *Fabliaux*, vol. i. p. 96.

Alexander, according to the poet, is arrested by Love, in the midst of his conquests. He dreams of nothing, but how he may amuse his mistress with festivals, and testify his passion. All his barons, his knights, and his soldiers, lament over his inactivity.

But of this he took no care ;
For he found his Love so fair,
Past his hopes, that his desire
Never after mounted higher
Than with her to live in bliss.
Love a powerful master is,
Since of man so great and brave
He can make a humble slave,
Who no other care shall take
Than for his sweet lady's sake.*

No one dares to inform Alexander of the discontent of his army. His master, Aristotle, alone, whose authority over his pupil was the result of his vast knowledge and profound wisdom, reproaches the conqueror of the world with for-

---

* Dont il ne se repentoit mie,
Car il avoit trouvé sa mie
Si belle qu'on put souhaiter.
N'avoit cure d'ailleurs plaider,
Fors qu'avec lui manoir et être.
Bien est Amour puissant et maître,
Quand du monde le plus puissant
Fait si humble et obéissant
Qu'il ne prend plus nul soin de lui,
Ains s'oublie tout pour autrui.

etting himself for love, with suffering his army o lie inactive in the midst of his conquests, and vith disgusting the whole order of knighthood. Alexander, touched with these reproaches, promises to forsake his mistress, and remains some lays without seeing her:

> But her pleasant memory
> Did not, with her presence, flee;
> Love recalls each lovely grace,
> Her sweet manner, her fair face
> In whose features you could trace,
> Nought of malice or of ill;
> Her bright forehead, like some chill
> And crystal fountain; her fine form,
> Fair hair, and mouth, with beauty warm:
> How, in mischief's name, he cries,
> Can I live, without this prize? *

At last, he can no longer resist the desire of gain beholding her; and he returns to her, excusing his absence by relating how sharply he ad been reprimanded by his master. The lady

---

* Mais il n'a pas le souvenir
Laissé ensemble avec la voie;
Qu'Amour lui ramembre et ravoie
Son clair visage, sa façon,
Où il n'a nulle retraçon
De vilenie ni de mal;
Front poli, plus clair que cristal,
Beau corps, belle bouche, blond chef.
Ah, fait-il, comme à grand meschef
Veulent toutes gens que je vive?

swears to revenge herself, and to make Aristotle himself bow to the power of her charms. She seeks him in the garden where he is studying, and employs all the arts of coquetry to seduce him. The philosopher in vain calls to mind his age, his grey head, and his discoloured and meagre features. He perceives that he has devoted himself uselessly to study, and that all his learning will not preserve him from love. He humbly throws himself upon the compassion of the lady, and declares himself her slave. She does not upbraid him, but imposes a penance, to punish him for the rebellious counsels which he had given to his pupil.

Said the lady, you must bring
Yourself to do another thing;
If, indeed, you feel love's fire,
You must do what I desire:
Know, then, that it is my pride
This day, on your back to ride,
Through the grass and garden gay;
If you answer not with nay,
I will straightway saddle you,
That will be the best to do.*

---

* Dit la Dame; vous convient faire
Pour moi un moult divers affaire,
Si tant êtes d'amour surpris;
Car un moult grand talent m'a pris
De vous un petit chevaucher
Dessus cette herbe, en ce verger:
Et si veux, dit la Demoiselle,
Qu'il ait sur vos dos une selle,
Si serai plus honnêtement.

The philosopher can refuse nothing to the lady, whom he so passionately loves. He falls on all fours, and suffers her to place a saddle on his back. The lady mounts, and guides him, with a string of roses, to the foot of the tower, where Alexander is waiting for her, and where he witnesses the triumph of love over "the most skilful clerk in all the world." *

But the most interesting, and, perhaps, the most celebrated of all the fabliaux, is that of Aucassin and Nicolette †, which Legrand has given under the title of *Les Amours du bon vieux temps,* and which has furnished the subject for a very agreeable opera, full of the splendours of chivalry. The original is written alternately in prose and verse, with a few lines of music occasionally interspersed. The language, which resembles that of Ville-Hardouin, seems to belong to the earlier part of the thirteenth century, and is the dialect of Champagne. The Provençals have, however, laid claim to this tale, the scene of which is laid in their territories. Aucassin, the son of the Count de Beaucaire, falls passionately in love with Nicolette, a young girl whose parents are unknown, and whom his father is unwilling he should marry. In the mean

* [The Lay of Aristotle is to be found in Way's Fabliaux, vol. ii. p. 159; but the passage given by M. de Sismondi is not sufficiently literal, in the translation, to authorize its insertion. *Tr.*]

† *Fabliaux*, vol. i. p. 380.

time, the Count of Valencia, the enemy of Beaucaire, besieges the city, which is on the point of being taken; and the Count de Beaucaire in vain solicits his son to place himself at the head of the troops. Aucassin refuses to fight, unless his father will promise him Nicolette, as the reward of his valour. Having extorted this promise from the Count, he makes a sally, and returns victorious. The Lord of Beaucaire, relieved from his terror, forgets his promise, and being indignant at the idea of his son's unworthy alliance, he causes Nicolette to be carried off.

* Soon as her doom this hapless orphan spied,
To a small casement with quick step she hied,
And o'er the garden cast her wishful sight,
All gay with flowers it seem'd, a garden of delight;
On every spray the merry birds did sing,
And hail'd the season's prime with fluttering wing:
"Ah, woe is me!" she cried, in doleful cheer,
"Lo! here I bide, for ever prison'd here!
"Sweet love! sweet Aucassin! for thee confined!
"For that dear love which fills our mutual mind!
"Yet shall their deeds ne'er shake my constant will,
"For I am true of heart, and bent to love thee still!" †

---

* [This translation is extracted from Mr. Way's Fabliaux, where the reader will find the story of Aucassin and Nicolette very beautifully paraphrased. See vol. i. p. 5. *Tr.*]

† Nicolette est en prison mise,
Dans une chambre à voûte grise,
Bâtie par grand artifice,
Et empeinte à la mosaïce.

It is unnecessary to make any further extracts from this fabliau, which the opera of Aucassin

---

Contre la fenêtre marbrine
S'en vint s'appuyer la mesquine ;
Chevelure blonde et poupine
Avoit, et la rose au matin
N'étoit si fraîche que son teint.
Jamais plus belle on ne vit.
Elle regarde par la grille,
Et voit la rose épanouie,
Et les oiseaux qui se dégoisent.
Lors se plaint ainsi l'orpheline :
Las, malheureuse que je suis !
Et pourquoi suis-je en prison mise ?
Aucassin, damoiseau, mon sire,
Je suis votre fidele amie,
Et de vous ne suis point haie :
Pour vous je suis en prison mise,
En cette chambre à voûte grise.
J'y traînerai ma triste vie
Sans que jamais mon cœur varie,
Car toujours serai-je sa mie.

The preceding version has been selected, as approaching nearest to the modern language. In the manuscripts printed by M. Méon, the poem is in verses of seven syllables, and commences thus:

Nicole est en prison mise
En une canbre vautie
Ki faite est par grant devises,
Panturée à miramie.
A la fenêtre marbrine
La s'apoya la mescine ;
Elle avoit blonde la crigne
Et bien faite la sorcille, etc.

and Nicolette has rendered sufficiently known. Nicolette, escaping from her prison, takes refuge with the King of Torreloro (Logodoro, or Le Torri, in Sardinia), and afterwards in Carthage. Her birth is, in the mean while, ascertained to be illustrious, and she returns to Provence in disguise, where she is discovered by her lover, and all ends happily. The latter part of the tale is confused, and badly put together; but the first twenty pages of the poem are written with a simplicity, a purity, and a grace, which have, perhaps, never been equalled by any poet of the good old times.

The Trouvères likewise possessed a few lyrical poets. Although their language was less harmonious than that of the people of the South, and although their imagination was less lively, and their passions less ardent, yet they did not absolutely neglect a species of composition which formed the glory of their rivals. They attempted to introduce into the Langue d'Oil all the various forms of versification, which the Troubadours had invented for the Langue d'Oc. Lyrical poetry was more especially cultivated by the powerful nobility, and we have scarcely any other songs remaining, than such as are the composition of sovereign princes. Thibaud III., Count of Champagne, who flourished from 1201 to 1253, and who ascended the throne of Navarre in 1234, is the most celebrated of the French poets of the middle ages, not only on account of his regal dignity, but of his attachment, real or supposed, to Blanche of Castile, the mother of Saint Louis, and of the influence which his romantic amours had upon the affairs of his kingdom. The poems of the King of Navarre are exceedingly difficult to comprehend. Antique words were long considered in France as more poetical than modern ones; and thus, while the language of prose was polished and perfected, that of poetry retained all its early obscurity. The lyric poets, moreover, seem to have attached greater importance to the sound, to the alternation of the rhymes, and to the rigorous observation of the laws established by the Troubadours for regulating the construction of the stanza in their songs, their tensons, and their sirventes, than to the sense and the sentiments which they were expressing. The two volumes, therefore, of the King of Navarre's poems, which have been published by La Ravallière, are a curious monument of the language and manners of the times, but present few attractions to the reader.

Amongst the princes who led their troops to the later crusades, and whose verses have been preserved, may be mentioned Thierry de Soissons, of the ancient house of Nesle, who was made prisoner in Egypt, at the battle of Massoura; the Vidame de Chartres, of the ancient house of Vendôme; the Count of Brittany, Jean the son of Pierre de Dreux, called Mauclerc; the

Lord Bernard de la Ferté; Gaces Brulés, a knight and gentleman of Champagne, and a friend of the King of Navarre; and Raoul II. de Coucy, killed in 1249, at the side of Saint Louis, at the battle of Massoura. His grandfather, Raoul I. de Coucy, the hero of the tragedy of Gabrielle de Vergy, was slain in Palestine, in 1191. The companions of St. Louis, the valorous knights who accompanied him to the crusade, were delighted with listening to the tales of the Trouvères, who, during the festivals, related to them amusing, and often licentious anecdotes, and diverted them with marvellous adventures. When, however, they assumed the lyre themselves, their own sentiments and their own passions were their theme. They sang of love or war, and they left to inferior bards the task of mere narration. In order to give some idea of this kind of composition, I shall extract, not in its original form, but in the shape which M. de Montcrif has given it, one of the tender and almost languishing songs of Raoul de Coucy, his *Lay de departie*, when he followed Saint Louis to the crusade.

How cruel is it to depart,
Lady! who causest all my grief!
My body to its lord's relief
Must go, but thou retain'st my heart.
To Syria now I wend my way,
Where Paynim swords no terror move;
Yet sad shall be each lingering day,
Far from the side of her I love.

We learn from many a grave divine
That God hath written in his laws,
That, to avenge his holy cause,
All earthly things we must resign.
Lord! I surrender all to thee!
No goods have I, nor castle fair;
But, were my lady kind to me,
I should not know regret nor care.

At least, in this strange foreign land,
My thoughts may dwell by night and day,
(Fearless of what detractors say)
On her whose smile is ever bland.*

---

* Que cruelle est ma départie,
Dame qui causez ma langueur!
Mon corps va servir son seigneur,
Mon cœur reste en votre balie;
Je vais soupirant en Syrie,
Et des Payens n'ai nulle peur.
Mais dure me sera la vie
Loin de l'objet de mon ardeur.

L'on nous dit et l'on nous sermonne
Que Dieu, notre bon Créateur,
Veut que pour venger son honneur
Tout dans ce monde on abandonne.
A sa volonté je m'adonne;
Je n'ai plus ni château ni bien,
Mais que ma belle me soit bonne,
Et je n'aurai regret à rien.

Du moins dans cette étrange terre
Pourrai-je penser jour et nuit
A ma dame au charmant souris,
Sans craindre la gent mauparlière;

And now I make my will—and here
I give, and fully do devise,
My heart to her I hold so dear,
My soul to God in Paradise.

Amongst the songs of the Châtelain de Coucy, preserved in the Royal Library, I know not whether I am correct in imagining that I have discovered the original of the piece given by M. de Montcrif. The song, which is subjoined in the note,* is on the same subject, and has even many

---

Et pour ma volonté dernière,
Je lègue, et clairement le dis,
Mon cœur à celle qui m'est chère,
Mon âme au Dieu de paradis.

* Oimi amors si dure départie
Me convendra faire de la moillor
Qui oncques fust amée ne servie.
Dex me ramoint à lui por sa douçor
Si voirement que j'en part à dolor.
Dex ! qu'ai-je dit, je ne m'en part je mie ;
Se li cors va servir notre seignor,
Tout li miens cuers remaint en sa baillie.

Por li m'en vois sopirant en surie,
Que nul ne doit faillir son Creator;
Qui li faudra à cest besoing d ahie,
Sachié de voir, faudra li à greignor,
Et saichiez bien li grant et li minor
Que là doit-on faire chétive vie.
Là se conquiert paradis et honor,
Et pers et los et l'amor de sa mie.

of the same rhymes; and yet it is not exactly the same thing. Another poem, likewise, on his departure, displays much sensibility at the commencement, but has no resemblance to the first

---

Lonc tems avons esté prou paix oiseuze,
Or partira qui acertes iert preu;
Vescu avons à honte doloreuze,
Dont tous li monz est iriez et honteus;
Quant à nos tens est perdu li sains leus
Où Dex por nos soffrit mort angoisseuse,
Or ne nos doit retenir nule honeus
D'aller vengier cette perte honteuse.

Qui vuet avoir honre et vie enviouse
Se voist morir liez et bauz et joiauz,
Car cele mort est douce et savoreuse
Où conquis est paradis et honors;
Ne ja de mort n'en i morra i tous,
Ains vivront tuit en vie gloriouse,
Et saichiez bien, qui ne fust amorouz,
Moût fust la voie et bele et delitouze.

Tuit li clergie, et li home d'aaige,
Que de bienfaiz et d'aumosnes vivront,
Partiront tuit à cest pelerinaige;
Et les Dames qui chastes se tendront,
Et léauté portent à ces qui iront.
Et se les font per mal conseil folage,
Ha! les quelx gens mauvaises les feront?
Car tuit li bons iront en cet viage.

Dex est assis en son haut héritage:
Or parra bien co cil le secorront,
Cui il geta de la prison ombrage,
Quant il fut mis en la croix que tuit ont.

piece.* The manuscript songs of these early French poets are not to be found in regular order, in the volumes in which we look for them. They are dispersed amongst a thousand other poems, and after having turned over many volumes, we cannot be confident that we have seen them all.

This race of heroes† was succeeded by other

Certes tuit cil sont honnis que n'i vont
S'ils n'ont pov'té, ou vieillesse ou malage.
Et cil qui jove et sain, et riche sont
Ne porront pas demorer sans hontage.

* Another song of the Châtelain de Coucy thus begins :

S'oncques nuls homs por dure departie
Ot cuer dolant, je l'aurai por raison,
Oncques tortre qui pert son compaignon
Ne remest jor de moi plus esbahie.
Chacuns plore sa terre et son pays,
Quand il se part de ses coraux amis ;
Mais nuls partir, saichiez, que que nuls die,
N'est dolorous, que d'ami et d'amie.

† The interest attached to the names of distinguished men, and to our historical recollections, gives a value to all the little poems, which have been written by the heroes of the crusades. We endeavour to discover in them the spirit and intimate thoughts of those *preux chevaliers*. This must be my excuse for inserting, in their modern form, a few stanzas of the third song of the Vidame de Chartres, in which he gives us the portrait of his mistress :

Ecoutez, nobles chevaliers,
Je vous tracerai volontiers

poets, who polished the language of the Trouvères, and who, like their predecessors, confirmed the national taste for tales, allegories, and verses, in which wit and information were mingled. No extracts from these authors are given, because it is the object of this work to treat of French litera-

---

L'image de ma belle.
Son nom jamais ne le saurez,
Mais si parfois la rencontrez,
Aisément la reconnoîtrez
A ce portrait fidèle.

Ses cheveux blonds comme fil d'or
Ne sont ni trop longs ni trop cort,
Tous repliés en onde;
Sous son front blanc comme le lys,
Où l'on ne voit taches ni plis,
S'élèvent deux sourcils jolis,
Arcs triomphans du monde.

Ses yeux bleus, attrayans, rians
Sont quelquefois fiers et poignans,
Clignotans par mesure;
Par l'amour même ils sont fendus,
De doux filets y sont tendus,
Et tombent cœurs gros et menus
Par si belle ouverture.

The following is the last stanza:

S'en savois plus, ne le dirois,
Car mon trop parler grêveroit
D'amor la confiance;
Si ne peut chevalier d'honnour
Manquer à Dame et à Seignour
Sans de Dieu mériter rigour
Et rude pénitence.

ture only in connexion with the Romantic poetry, and as it exerted an influence over the nations of the South. Instead of employing ourselves upon the poems of the historian Froissart, of Charles Duke of Orléans, of Alain Chartier, of Villon, and of Coquillart, who, however largely they contributed to the improvement of the French, had no share in forming the other languages of the South, we shall investigate the origin of the Mysteries, or the Romantic Drama, which first arose in France, and served as a model for the dramatic representations both of Spain and England.

The French justly claim the merit of being the first discoverers of a form of composition, which has given such a lively character to the works of the imagination. They define poetry and the fine arts, by calling them *imitative arts*, whilst other nations consider them as the effusion of the sentiments of the heart. The object of the French authors, in their tales, their romances, and their fabliaux, is to present a faithful picture of the characters of others, and not to develope their own. They were the first, at a period when the ancient drama was entirely forgotten, to represent, in a dramatic form, the great events which accompanied the establishment of the Christian religion; the mysteries, the belief in which was inculcated, as a part of that system; or the incidents of domestic life, to excite the spectators to laughter, after the more serious representations.

The same talent which enabled them to versify a long history in the heroic style, or to relate a humorous anecdote with the spirit of a jester, prompted them to adopt, in their dramas, similar subjects and a similar kind of versification. They left to those who had to recite these dialogues, the care of delivering them with an air of truth, and of accompanying them with the deception of scenic decoration.

The first who awakened the attention of the people to compositions, in which many characters were introduced, were the pilgrims who had returned from the Holy Land. They thus displayed to the eyes of their countrymen all which they had themselves beheld, and with which every one was desirous of being acquainted. It is believed, that it was in the twelfth, or at all events in the thirteenth century, that these dramatic representations were first exhibited in the open streets. It was not, however, until the conclusion of the fourteenth century, that a company of pilgrims, who, by the representation of a brilliant spectacle, had assisted at the solemnization of the nuptials between Charles VI. and Isabella of Bavaria, formed an establishment in Paris, and undertook to amuse the public by regular dramatic entertainments. They were denominated the Fraternity of the Passion; from the Passion of our Saviour being one of their most celebrated representations.

This mystery, the most ancient dramatic work of modern Europe, comprehends the whole history of our Lord, from his baptism to his death. The piece was too long to be represented without interruption. It was, therefore, continued from day to day; and the whole mystery was divided into a certain number of *journées*, each of which included the labours or the representation of one day. This name of *journée*, which was abandoned in France, when the mysteries became obsolete, has retained its place in the Spanish language, although its origin is forgotten. Eighty-seven characters, successively, appear in the Mystery of the Passion, amongst whom we find the three persons of the Trinity, six angels or archangels, the twelve apostles, six devils, Herod and his whole court, and a host of personages, the invention of the poet's brain. Extravagant machinery seems to have been employed, to give to the representation all the pomp which we find in the operas of the present day. Many of the scenes appear to have been recited to music, and we likewise meet with choruses. The intermingled verses indicate a very perfect acquaintance with the harmony of the language. Some of the characters are well drawn, and the scenes occasionally display a considerable degree of grandeur, energy, and tragic power. Although the language sometimes becomes very prosaic and heavy, and some most absurd scenes are introduced, we yet cannot fail to recognize the very high talents which must have been employed in the conception of this terrible drama, which not only surpassed its models, but, by placing before the eyes of a Christian assembly all those incidents for which they felt the highest veneration, must have affected them much more powerfully than even the finest tragedies can do, at the present day.

A few lines and quotations cannot give a clear idea of a work so long and various as this; a work which, when printed in double columns, fills a large folio volume, and exceeds, in length, the united labours of our tragic authors. Still, as it is our object to enable the reader to judge for himself, and as we shall have occasion to present him with extracts from compositions no less barbarous in the earlier stage of the Spanish drama, and which are merely imitations of the great French Mystery, it will be as well to introduce, at least, some verses from this astonishing production, and to give an idea of the various styles, both tragic and comic, of the author. The clearness of the language, which is much more intelligible than that of the lyrical poets of the same period, immediately strikes us. Those poets attributed, not only more simplicity, but also more pomp to the antique phraseology. But this stately style of expression was excluded from poetry which was intended to become popular. The grandeur of the ideas and of the language of the Mystery of Passion, might be thought, in some instances, to belong to a more cultivated age. Thus, in the council of the Jews, in which many of the Pharisees deliver their opinions at considerable length, Mordecai expresses himsel in the following terms :

When the Messiah shall command,
We trust that, with a mighty hand,
In tranquil union, he shall rule the land ;
His head shall with a diadem be crown'd,
Glory and wealth shall in his house abound ;
In justice shall he sway it, and in peace ;
And should the strong oppress or rob the poor,
Or tyrant turn the vassal from his door,
When Christ returns, these evils all shall cease.*

Saint John enters into a long discourse, and we can only account for the patience with which our forefathers listened to these tedious harangues, by supposing that their fatigue was considered by them to be an acceptable offering to the Deity ; and that they were persuaded that every thing which did not excite them to laughter or tears,

---

* Quant Messias, quant le Crist règnera,
Nous espérons qu'il nous gouvernera
En forte main, en union tranquille ;
Couronne d'or sur son chef portera,
Gloire et richesse en sa maison aura,
Justice et paix régira sa famille.
Et si le fort le povre oppresse ou pille,
Si le tyran son franc vassal exille,
Quant Crist viendra tout sera mis en ordre.

was put down to the account of their edification. The following scene in dialogue, in which Saint John undergoes an interrogation, displays considerable ability :—

ABYAS.

Though fallen be man's sinful line,
Holy Prophet! it is writ,
Christ shall come to ransom it,
And by doctrine, and by sign
Bring them to his grace divine.
Wherefore, seeing now the force
Of thy high deeds, thy grave discourse,
And virtues shewn of great esteem,
That thou art he, we surely deem.

SAINT JOHN.

I am not Messiah !—No!
At the feet of Christ I bow.*

---

* ABYAS.

Sainct Prophète! il nous est escript
Que le Crist, pour nous racheter,
Se doit à nous manifester,
Et réduyre par sa doctrine
Le peuple en sa grace divine.
Par quoi, veu les enseignemens
Les haulx faits et les prêchemens
Dont tu endoctrines tes proesmes ;
Nous doultons que ce soit toy-mesmes
Qui montres tes belles vertus.

SAINT JEHAN.

Non suis ; je ne suis pas Christus,
Mais desouls lui je m'humilie.

ELYACHIM.

Why, then, wildly wanderest thou,
Naked, in this wilderness?
Say! what faith dost thou profess?
And to whom thy service paid?

BANNANYAS.

Thou assemblest, it is said,
In these lonely woods, a crowd
To hear thy voice proclaiming loud,
Like that of our most holy men.
Art thou a king in Israel, then?
Know'st thou the laws and prophecies?
Who art thou? say!

NATHAN.

Thou dost advise
Messiah is come down below.
Hast seen him? say, how dost thou know?
Or art thou he?

ELYACHIM.

D'où te vient doncques la folie
De toi tenir en ces déserts,
Tout nu; dis nous de quoi tu sers,
Et quelle doctrine tu presches?

BANNANYAS.

On nous a dit que tu t'empesches
D'assembler peuples par ces bois
Pour venir escouter ta voix,
Comme d'un homme solemnel.
Es-tu donc maître en Israël?
Scai-tu les lois et prophéties,
Qu'est-ce de toi?

NATHAN.

Tu nous publies
Que Messyas est jà venu;
Comme le scai-tu? l'as-tu vu?
Est-ce toi?

SAINT JOHN.

I answer, No!

NACHOR.

Who art thou? Art Elias then?
Perhaps Elias?

SAINT JOHN.

No!—

BANNANYAS.

Again!
Who art thou? what thy name? Express
For never surely shall we guess.
Thou art the Prophet!

SAINT JOHN.

I am not—

ELYACHIM.

Who and what art thou? Tell us what!

SAINT JEHAN.

Ce ne suis-je mye.

NACHOR.

Et quel homme es-tu donc? Helye?
Te dis-tu Helyas?

SAINT JEHAN.

Non.

BANNANYAS.

Non?
Qui es tu donc? quel est ton nom?
Imaginer je ne le puis.
Tu es le Prophête!

SAINT JEHAN.

Non suis.

ELYACHIM.

Qui es-tu donc? or te dénonce,

That true answer we may bear
To our lords, who sent us here
To learn thy name and mission.

SAINT JOHN.

Ego
Vox clamantis in deserto.
A voice, a solitary cry
In the desert paths am I!
Smooth the paths, and make them meet,
For the great Redeemer's feet,
Him, who brought by our misdoing,
Comes for this foul world's renewing.

The result of this scene is the conversion o the persons to whom Saint John addresses himself. They eagerly demand to be baptized, anc the ceremony is followed by the baptism of Jesu: himself. But the versification is not so remarkable as the stage directions, which transpor us to the very period of these Gothic representations.

Afin que nous donnons réponse
Aux grans Princes de notre foi,
Qui nous ont transmis devers toi
Pour savoir qui tu es.

SAINT JEHAN.

Ego
Vox clamantis in deserto.
Je suis voix au désert criant,
Que chacun soit rectifiant
La voie du Sauveur du Monde,
Qui vient pour notre coulpe immonde
Réparer sans doubte quelconque.

"Here Jesus enters the waters of Jordan, all naked, and Saint John takes some of the water in his hand and throws it on the head of Jesus—

SAINT JOHN.

Sir, you now baptized are,
As it suits my simple skill,
Not the lofty rank you fill;
Unmeet for such great service I;
Yet my God, so debonair,
All that 's wanting will supply.*

"Here Jesus comes out of the river Jordan, and throws himself on his knees, all naked, before Paradise. Then God the Father speaks, and the Holy Ghost descends, in the form of a white dove, upon the head of Jesus, and then returns into Paradise:—and note, that the words of God the Father be very audibly pronounced, and well sounded, in three voices; that is to say, a treble, a counter-treble, and a counter-bass, all in tune: and in this way must the following lines be repeated—

Hic est filius meus dilectus,
In quo mihi bene complacui.
C'estui-ci est mon fils amé Jésus,
Que bien me plaist, ma plaisance est en lui."

---

* SAINT JEHAN.

Sire, vous êtes baptizé.
Qui à votre haute noblesse
N'appartient ne à ma simplesse,
Si digne service de faire;
Toutefois mon Dieu débonnaire
Veuille suppléer le surplus.

As this mystery was not only the model of subsequent tragedies, but of comedies likewise, we must extract a few verses from the dialogues of the devils, who fill all the comic parts of the drama. The eagerness of these personages to maltreat one another, or, as the original expresses it, *à se torchonner* (to give one another a wipe), always produced much laughter in the assembly.

BERITH.

Who he is I cannot tell—
This Jesus; but I know full well
That in all the worlds that be,
There is not such a one as he.
Who it is that gave him birth
I know not, nor from whence on earth
He came, or what great devil taught him,
But in no evil have I caught him;
Nor know I any vice he hath.

SATAN.

Haro! but you make me wroth;
When such dismal news I hear.*

---

* BERITH.

Je ne sçay qui est ce Jésus,
Mais je croy qu'en l'universel
N'en y-a point encore ung tel;
Qui que l'ait en terre conçu,
Je ne sçay d'où il est issu,
Ne quel grant dyable l'a presché;
Mais il n'est viçe ne péché
De quoi je le sçusse charger.

SATHAN.

Haro, tu me fais enrager
Quand il faut que tels mots escoute.

BERITH.

Wherefore so?

SATAN.

Because I fear
He will make my kingdom less.
Leave him in the wilderness,
And let us return to Hell
To Lucifer our tale to tell,
And to ask his sound advice.

BERITH.

The imps are ready in a trice;
Better escort cannot be.

LUCIFER.

Is it Satan that I see,
And Berith, coming in a passion?

ASTAROTH.

Master! let me lay the lash on.
Here's the thing to do the deed.

BERITH.

Et pourquoi?

SATHAN.

Pour ce que je doubte
Qu'en la fin j'en soie désert.
Laissons-le ici en ce désert,
Et nous en courons en enfer
Nous conseiller à Lucifer,
Sur les cas que je lui veulx dire.

BERITH.

Les dyables vous veulent conduire,
Sans avoir meilleur sauf conduit.

LUCIFER.

J'aperçoy Sathan et Berith,
Qui reviennent moult empêchés.

ASTAROTH.

Si vous voulez qu'ils soient torchés,
Vecy les instrumens tous prêts.

LUCIFER.

Please to moderate your speed,
To lash behind and lash before ye,
Ere you hear them tell their story,
Whether shame they bring, or glory.

As soon as the devils have given an account to their sovereign, of their observations and their vain efforts to tempt Jesus, Astaroth throws himself upon them with his imps, and lashes them back to earth from the infernal regions.

The example which was set by the author of the Mystery of the Passion, was soon followed by a crowd of imitators, whose names, for the most part, have been lost. The Mystery of the Conception, and the Nativity of our Lord, and of the Resurrection, are amongst the most ancient of these. The legends of the saints were, in their turn, dramatised and prepared for the theatre; and, in short, the whole of the Old Testament was brought upon the stage. In the same mystery, the characters were often introduced at various stages of life, as infants, youths, and old men, represented by different actors; and in the margin of some of the mysteries we find, *Here enter the second, or the third, Israel or Jacob.* When the mystery was founded on histo-

LUCIFER.

Ne te hâte pas de si près,
A frapper derrière et devant;
Ouir faut leur rapport avant,
Sçavoir s'il nous porte dommage.

rical facts not generally known, the poets exercised their own invention more freely, and did not hesitate to mingle comic scenes in very serious pieces. Thus, when they exhibited the saints triumphing over temptation, and their contempt for the allurements of the flesh, they often introduced language and scenes quite at variance with the serious nature of these sacred dramas.

The theatre, on which the mysteries were represented, was always composed of an elevated scaffold, divided into three parts; heaven, hell, and the earth between them. It was in this central portion that Jerusalem was sometimes represented, or occasionally the native country of some saint or patriarch, whither angels descended or devils ascended, as their interference in mundane affairs was called for. In the higher and the lower parts of the theatre, the proceedings of the Deity and Lucifer might be discerned. The pomp of these representations continued increasing for the space of two centuries; and, as great value was set on the length of the piece, some mysteries could not be represented in less than forty days.

The *Clercs de la Bazoche,* or Clerks of the Revels, who were an incorporated society at Paris, and whose duty it was to regulate the public festivities, at length resolved to amuse the people with some dramatic representations themselves. But, as the fraternity of the Passion had obtained, in 1402, a royal licence to represent mysteries, the clerks were compelled to abstain from that kind of exhibition, and they, therefore, invented a new one, which differed in name, rather than in substance, from the former. These were the *Moralities*, which were also borrowed from the historical parts, or the parables of the Bible, as that of the Prodigal Son. Sometimes they were purely allegorical compositions, in which God and the devil were introduced, accompanied by the virtues or vices. In a morality entitled *Le bien advisé et le mal advisé*, almost forty allegorical characters appear, and, amongst others, the different tenses of the verb *to reign*—as *Regno*, *Regnavi*, and *Regnabo*. In the course of this work, we shall have occasion to notice, in speaking of the Spanish drama, even during the times of Lope de Vega and Calderon, the *Autos sacramentales*, which were allegorical pieces, evidently of the same nature as the ancient Moralities.

It is to the Clerks de la Bazoche, likewise, that we owe the invention of comedy. Whilst the fraternity of the Passion conceived themselves bound only to present edifying pieces to the public, the Clerks de la Bazoche, who did not consider themselves as ecclesiastics, mingled with their moralities, farces, of which the sole object was to excite the laughter of the spectators. All the gaiety and vivacity of the French character was displayed, in the ludicrous representations of such real adventures as had perhaps been the conversation of the town. The versification was managed with great care, and one of these farces, the *Avocat Pathelin*, which was represented for the first time in 1480, and has been attributed to an ecclesiastic of the name of Pierre Blanchet de Poitiers, may still be considered as a model of French gaiety and comic powers. None of these farces were more successful than this, and none have so well maintained their celebrity. It was translated into Latin, in 1512, by Alexander Connibert, and was imitated by the famous Reuchlin. Brueys remodelled it, and it was again brought forward in 1706, and is represented to the present day.

In the reign of Charles VI., likewise, and at the commencement of the fifteenth century, a third comic company was established, the *Enfans sans souci*, who, under the command of the chief, *le Prince des sots*, undertook to make the French laugh at their own follies, and introduced personal, and even political satire upon the stage.

Thus, every species of dramatic representation was revived by the French. This was the result of that talent for imitation, which seems peculiar to the French people, assisted by a pliancy of thought, which enables them to conceive new characters, and a correctness of intellect, which always carries them directly to the object at which they aim, or to the effect which they wisl to produce. All these discoveries, which led ii other countries to the establishment of the Ro mantic drama, were known in France more thai a century before the rise of the Spanish or Italiai theatre, or even before the classical authors were first studied and imitated. At the end of the sixteenth century, these new pursuits acquired a more immediate influence over the literature o France. They wrought a change in its spiri and its rules; but without altering the nationa character and taste, which had been manifest ed in the earliest productions of the Trouvères It is here that the history of the literature o France has its commencement; and, at the same period, we shall abandon it. But, in examining the literature of the South, which, from the *Romance* languages, has been called the *Romantic*, it was necessary to bestow some attention upon one o the most celebrated of the Romance dialects and one, too, which boasts of poets who display so superior a fertility of invention. If it should be thought deficient in sensibility, in enthusiasm, in ardour, or in depth and truth of thought, it has yet surpassed all other languages in its in ventive genius. We are now about to proceec to the History of Italian Poetry, from its rise, tc the present times. Yet, even there, we shall re cognise the spirit of the Trouvères in the majes tic allegories of Dante, who, although he has infinitely surpassed it, has yet taken the Romance of the Rose for his model. We shall, likewise, trace the same spirit in the tales of Boccaccio, which are frequently nothing more than the ancient fabliaux. In the poems of Ariosto, also, and in all those chivalric epics, for which the romances of Adenez and his contemporaries prepared the way, the Trouvères will meet us. In the Spanish school, as late as the seventeenth century, we shall discover imitations of the ancient mysteries of the Trouvères; and Lope de Vega, and Calderon, will remind us of the fraternity of the Passion. Even amongst the Portuguese, Vasco Lobeira, the author of Amadis, seems to have been educated in this early French school. It is not, therefore, without sufficient reason, that, in a View of the Literature of the South, we have thought ourselves compelled to bestow some attention on the language, the spirit, and the poetry of our ancestors.

CHAPTER IX.

On the Italian Language—Dante.

THE language of Provence had attained its highest degree of cultivation; Spain and Portugal had already produced more than one poet; and the *Langue d'Oil*, in the north of France, was receiving considerable attention, while the Italian was not yet enumerated amongst the languages of Europe, and the richness and harmony of its idiom, gradually and obscurely formed amongst the populace, were not as yet appreciated. But a great poet, in the thirteenth century, arose to immortalize this hitherto neglected tongue, and, aided by his single genius, it soon advanced with a rapidity which left all competition at a distance.

The Lombardian Duchy of Benevento, comprising the greater part of the modern kingdom of Naples, had preserved, under independent princes, and surrounded by the Greeks and the Saracens, a degree of civilization, which, in the earlier part of the middle ages, was unexampled throughout the rest of Italy. Many of the fine arts, and some branches of science, were cultivated there with success. The schools of Salerno communicated to the West the medical skill of the Arabs, and the commerce of Amalfi, introduced into those fertile provinces, not only wealth, but knowledge. From the eighth to the tenth century, various historical works, written, it is true, in Latin, but distinguished for their fidelity, their spirit, and their fire, proceeded from the pen of several men of talent, natives of that district, some of whom clothed their compositions in hexameter verses, which, compared with others of the same period, display superior facility and fancy. The influx of foreigners consequent upon the invasion of the Norman adventurers, who founded a sovereignty in Apulia, was not sufficiently great to effect a change in the language; and, under their government, the Italian or Sicilian tongue first assumed a settled form. The court of Palermo, early in the twelfth century, abounded in riches, and consequently indulged in luxurious habits; and there the first accents of the Sicilian muse were heard. There, too, at the same period, the Arabs acquired a degree of influence and credit which they have never possessed in any other christian court. The palace of William the First, like those of the monarchs of the East, was guarded by Mahometan eunuchs. From them he selected his favourites, his friends, and sometimes even his ministers. To attach themselves to the arts and to the various avocations which contribute to the pleasures of life, was the peculiar province of the Saracens, by whom half of the island was still occupied. When Frederick the Second, at the end of the twelfth century, succeeded to the throne of the Norman monarchs, he transported numerous colonies of Saracens into Apulia and the Principality, but he did not banish them from either his service or his court. Of them his army was composed: and the governors of his provinces, whom he denominated Justiciaries, were chosen almost exclusively from their number. Thus was it the destiny of the Arabians, in the East as well as in the West of Europe, to communicate to the Latin nations their arts, their science, and their poetry.

From the history of Sicily, we may deduce the effects produced by Arabian influence on the Italian, or as it was then considered, the Sicilian poetry, with no less certainty than that with which we trace its connexion, in the county of Barcelona, and in the kingdom of Castile, with the first efforts of the Provençal and Spanish poets. William the First, an effeminate and voluptuous prince, forgot, in his palace of Palermo, amidst his Moorish eunuchs, in the song and the feast, those commotions which agitated his realms. The regency of the kingdom devolved, at his decease, upon his widow, who intrusted the government to Gayto Petro, the chief of the eunuchs, connected with the Saracens of Africa. All the commerce of Palermo was monopolized by the infidels. They were the professors of every art, and the inventors of every variety of luxury. The nation accommodated itself to their customs; and in their public festivals, it was usual for Christian and Moorish women to sing in concert, to the music of their slaves. We may safely conclude that on these occasions each party adopted their mother tongue; and that the Italian females who responded, in melancholy cadence, to the tambours of their Moorish attendants, would, in all probability, adapt Sicilian words to African airs and measures.*

A complete separation had now taken place between the ordinary language of the country and the Latin tongue. Of the latter, the women were ignorant. The general adoption of the language to which their delicacy gave new graces, and in which alone they were accessible to the gallantry of their admirers, was a necessary result. It was now submitted to rules, and enli-

---

* On the death of William the First of Sicily, says Hugo Falcandus, a celebrated contemporary historian, "Per totum autem hoc triduum mulieres, nobilesque matronæ, *maxime Saracenæ*, quibus ex morte regis dolor non fictus obvenerat, saccis opertæ, passis crinibus, et die noctuque turmatim incedentes, ancillarum præeunte multitudine, totam civitatem ululatu complebant, ad pulsata tympana cantu flebili respondentes." *Muratori*, Script. Rer. Italic. t. vii. p. 303.

vened by that sensibility of expression, of whicl a dead and pedantic language ceases to be sus ceptible. For a century and a half, in fact, i would seem that the Sicilians confined themselve: to the composition of love-songs alone. Thes‹ primitive specimens of Italian poetry have bee! studiously preserved, and they have been ana· lyzed by M. Ginguené, with equal talent an‹ learning. To his work, such of our readers a: may wish to obtain a more particular knowledg‹ of these relics, will have satisfaction in referring nor can they apply to a better source of informa tion, for more complete and profound details, o! the subject of Italian poetry, than can possibl; find a place in a condensed history of the genera literature of the South.

The merit of amatory poetry consists, almos entirely, in its expression. Its warmth and ten derness of sentiment is injured by any exertio! of mere ingenuity and fancy, in the pursui of which the poet, or the lover, seems to los‹ sight of his proper object. Little more is re quired from him than to represent with sensibilit; and with truth, the feelings which are commo! to all who love. The harmony of language is th‹ best means of expressing that of the heart. Bu this principle seems almost entirely to have es caped the notice of the first Sicilian and Italia! writers. The example of the Arabs and of th‹ Provençals induced them to prefer ostentation t‹

simplicity, and to exercise a false and affected taste in the choice of their poetical ornaments. In the best specimens of this school, we should find little to reward the labour of translating them; and we feel still less inclined to draw the inferior pieces from their deserved obscurity. It is, therefore, principally with a view to the history of the language, and of the versification, that we turn over the pages of Ciullo d'Alcamo, the Sicilian; those of Frederick the Second, and of his Chancellor, Pietro delle Vigne, of Oddo delle Colonne, of Mazzeo di Ricco, and of other poets of the same class.

The form of their versification was modelled upon that of the Provençals, or, perhaps, derived its origin from the same source as the latter. The verse was determined, not by the quantity, but by the accent of the syllables, and was always rhymed. Of all the feet employed by the ancients in the combination of syllables of different quantity, the iambic alone still continued in use; five of them being comprised in the heroic verse, and three or four, in verses of a shorter measure. In the former, ten syllables were thus contained, exclusive of the mute; of which the fourth, the eighth, and the tenth, or the sixth and the tenth, were accented. The rhymes were governed by the rules of the Provençals, and were, as in the poems of that country, intermingled in such a manner as to anticipate recurring terminations at certain passages of the poem, and by thus connecting the composition, to give it a stronger hold upon the memory. The piece was generally divided into stanzas or couplets, and the ear of the reader was taught to appreciate, not only the musical charm of each individual line, but the general harmony of the whole.

The language employed by the Sicilians in their poetical attempts, was not the popular dialect, as it then existed amongst the natives of the island, and as we still find it preserved in some Sicilian songs, scarcely intelligible to the Italians themselves. From the Imperial court, and that of the kings of Sicily, it had already received a more elegant form; and those laws of grammar, which were originally founded upon custom, had now obtained the ascendancy over it, and prescribed their own rules. The *lingua cortigiana*, the language of the court, was already distinguished as the purest of the Italian dialects. In Tuscany, it came into general use; and, previous to the end of the thirteenth century, it received great stability from several writers of that country, in verse as well as in prose, who carried it very nearly to that degree of perfection which it has ever since maintained. For elegance and purity of style, Ricordano Malaspina, who wrote the History of Florence in 1280, may be pronounced, at the present day, to be in no degree inferior to the best writers now extant.

No poet, however, had yet arisen, gifted with absolute power over the empire of the soul; no philosopher had yet pierced into the depths of feeling and of thought; when Dante, the greatest name of Italy, and the father of her poetry, appeared, and demonstrated the mightiness of his genius, by availing himself of the rude and imperfect materials within his reach, to construct an edifice resembling, in magnificence, that universe whose image it reflects. Instead of amatory effusions, addressed to an imaginary beauty; instead of madrigals, full of sprightly insipidity, sonnets laboured into harmony, and strained or discordant allegories, the only models, in any modern language, which presented themselves to the notice of Dante; that great genius conceived, in his vast imagination, the mysteries of the invisible creation, and unveiled them to the eyes of the astonished world.

In the century immediately preceding, the energy of some bold and enthusiastic minds had been directed to religious objects. A new spiritual force, surpassing in activity and fanaticism, all monastic institutions before established, was organized by Saint Francis and Saint Dominick, whose furious harangues and bloody persecutions revived that zeal, which, for several centuries past, had appeared to slumber. In the cells of the monks, nevertheless, the first symptoms of reviving literature were seen. Their studies had now assumed a scholastic character. To the imagination of the zealot, the different conditions of a future state were continually present; and the spiritual objects, which he saw with the eyes of faith, were invested with all the reality of material forms, by the force with which they were presented to his view in detailed descriptions, and in dissertations displaying a scientific acquaintance with the exact limits of every torment, and the graduated rewards of glorification.

A very singular instance of the manner in which these ideas were impressed upon the people, is afforded by the native city of Dante, in which the celebration of a festival was graced by a public representation of the infernal tortures; and it is not unlikely that the first circulation of the work of that poet gave occasion to this frightful exhibition. The bed of the Arno was converted into the gulf of perdition, where all the horrors, coined by the prolific fancy of the monks, were concentrated. Nothing was wanting to make the illusion complete; and the spectators shuddered at the shrieks and groans of real persons, apparently exposed to the alternate extremes of fire and frost, to waves of boiling pitch and to serpents.*

It appears, then, that when Dante adopted, as the subject of his immortal poem, the secrets of

---

* This scene occurred at Florence on the 1st May, 1804.

the invisible world, and the three kingdoms of the dead, he could not possibly have selected a more popular theme. It had the advantage of combining the most profound feelings of religion, with those vivid recollections of patriotic glory and party contentions, which were necessarily suggested by the re-appearance of the illustrious dead on this novel theatre. Such, in a word, was the magnificence of its scheme, that it may justly be considered as the most sublime conception of the human intellect.

At the close of the century, in the year 1300, and in the week of Easter, Dante supposes himself to be wandering in the deserts near Jerusalem, and to be favoured with the means of access to the realm of shadows. He is there met by Virgil, the object of his incessant study and admiration, who takes upon himself the office of guide, and who, by his own admirable description of the heathen hell, seems to have acquired a kind of right to reveal the mysteries of these forbidden regions. The two bards arrive at a gate, on which are inscribed these terrific words:—

> "Through me you pass into the city of woe:
> Through me you pass into eternal pain:
> Through me, among the people lost for aye.
> Justice the founder of my fabric mov'd:
> To rear me was the task of power divine,

Supremest wisdom, and primeval love*.
Before me things create were none, save things
Eternal, and eternal I endure.
All hope abandon, ye who enter here." †

By the decree of the Most High, the companions are, however, enabled to pass the gates of hell, and to penetrate into the dismal sojourn.

Here sighs, with lamentations and loud moans,
Resounded through the air, pierc'd by no star,
That e'en I wept at entering. Various tongues,
Horrible languages, outcries of woe,
Accents of anger, voices deep and hoarse,
With hands together smote that swell'd the sounds,
Made up a tumult, that for ever whirls
Round through that air, with solid darkness stain'd,
Like to the sand that in the whirlwind flies. ‡

Notwithstanding their afflictions, these sufferers were not such as had been positively wicked, but

---

* The three persons of the blessed Trinity. The English versions of the extracts from Dante, are taken from Cary's Translation.

† *Inferno*, canto iii. v. i.

Per me si va nella Città dolente :
  Per me si va nell' eterno dolore :
  Per me si va tra la perduta gente.
Giustizia mosse 'l mio alto fattore :
  Fece mi la divina potestate,
  La somma sapienza e 'l primo amore.
Dinanzi a me non fur cose create
  Se non eterne, ed io eterno duro :
  Lasciate ogni speranza, voi ch' entrate.

‡ *Inferno*, canto iii. v. 22.

such as, if they had lived without infamy, had yet no claims to virtue.

> "This miserable fate
> Suffer the wretched souls of those, who liv'd
> Without or praise or blame, with that ill band
> Of angels mix'd, who nor rebellious prov'd,
> Nor yet were true to God, but for themselves
> Were only. From his bounds Heaven drove them forth,
> Not to impair his lustre; nor the depth
> Of Hell receives them, lest th' accursed tribe
> Should glory thence with exultation vain."
>
> * * * * *
>
> "Fame of them the world hath none,
> Nor suffers; mercy and justice scorn them both.
> Speak not of them, but look, and pass them by." *

Leaving this ignoble multitude, the poets arrive at the gloomy banks of Acheron, where are assembled, from every part of the earth, such as have died in the displeasure of God. Divine justice pursues their steps, and terror, more powerful than desire, hurries them on. The reprobate souls are transported across the melancholy waters, in the boat of Charon; for Dante, in common with many fathers of the church, under the supposition that paganism, in the person of its infernal Gods, represented the evil angels, made no scruple to adopt its fables. He thus blended with the terrors of the catholic faith, all the brilliant colouring of the Greek mythology, and all the force of poetical asso-

---

* *Inferno*, canto iii. v. 34, &c.

ciation. In his picture of the Last Judgment, Michael Angelo drew from Dante his ideas of hell. We there see Charon carrying over the condemned souls; and forgetting that he is introduced, not as an infernal God, but as the evil spirit of the stream, it has been objected to the painter of the Sestine Chapel, that he has confounded the two religions, when, in fact, he has not transgressed the strict faith of the church.

The poets, proceeding into the depths of the regions of darkness, arrive at the abode of the wise and just of antiquity, who having been necessarily precluded, in their lives, from receiving the benefits of baptism, are condemned, by the catholic creed, to eternal pains. Their tears and groans are extorted, not by actual tortures, but by their eternal sense of the want of that bliss which they are destined never to attain. Their habitation is not unlike the shadowy Elysium of the poets, and affords a kind of fainter picture of earthly existence, where the place of hope is occupied by regret. We may here observe, that M. de Chateaubriand, after having expressed an inclination to exempt virtuous heathens from eternal punishment, has since experienced some scruples of conscience; and in the third edition of his Martyrs, has penitently retracted a sentiment so pure, so benevolent, and

› consistent with every attribute of a God of ıfinite goodness.

After surveying the heroes of antiquity, Dante, ı his descent into the abyss, next encounters ıose whom love seduced into crime, and who ied before they had repented of their sin; for ıe distinction between Hell and Purgatory does ot consist in the magnitude of the offence, but ı the circumstances of the last moments of the ffender. The first reprobate shades with which ›ante meets, are treated with the greatest share f indulgence, and the punishments become more ıtense, in proportion as he penetrates deeper ıto the bosom of hell.

Into a place I came
Where light was silent all. Bellowing, there groan'd
A noise, as of a sea in tempest torn
By warring winds. The stormy blast of hell
With restless fury drives the spirits on,
Whirl'd round and dash'd amain, with sore annoy.*

In the midst of this unhappy throng, Dante ɜcognises Francesca di Rimini, daughter of Gui-o da Polenta, one of his patrons, who became ıe wife of Lancillotto Malatesti, and being de-ɜcted in an adulterous intrigue with Paolo, her rother-in-law, was put to death by her husband. 'he reputation of this striking episode has made : familiar to every language; but the beauty and

* *Inferno*, canto v. v. 28.

finished harmony of the original remain without a rival:

> "Bard! willingly
> I would address those two together coming,
> Which seem so light before the wind." He thus:
> "Note thou, when nearer they to us approach.
> Then by that love which carries them along,
> Entreat; and they will come." Soon as the wind
> Sway'd them toward us, I thus fram'd my speech:
> "O wearied spirits! come, and hold discourse
> With us, if by none else restrain'd." As doves
> By fond desire invited, on wide wings
> And firm, to their sweet nest returning home,
> Cleave the air, wafted by their will along;
> Thus issu'd, from that troop where Dido ranks,
> They, through the ill air speeding: with such force
> My cry prevail'd, by strong affection urg'd.
> "O gracious creature and benign! who go'st
> Visiting, through this element obscure,
> Us, who the world with bloody stain imbru'd;
> If, for a friend, the King of all, we own'd,
> Our pray'r to him should for thy peace arise,
> Since thou hast pity on our evil plight.
> Of whatsoe'er to hear or to discourse
> It pleases thee, that will we hear, of that
> Freely with thee discourse, while e'er the wind,
> As now, is mute. The land, that gave me birth,
> Is situate on the coast, where Po descends
> To rest in ocean with his sequent streams.
> "Love, that in gentle heart is quickly learnt,
> Entangled him by that fair form, from me
> Ta'en in such cruel sort, as grieves me still:
> Love, that denial takes from none belov'd,
> Caught me with pleasing him so passing well,
> That, as thou see'st, he yet deserts me not.

Love brought us to one death: Caina waits
The soul, who spilt our life."

fter a pause, Dante exclaims:

"Alas! by what sweet thoughts, what fond desire
Must they at length to that ill pass have reach'd!"
Then turning, I to them my speech address'd,
And thus began: "Francesca! your sad fate
Even to tears my grief and pity moves.
But tell me; in the time of your sweet sighs,
By what, and how Love granted, that ye knew
Your yet uncertain wishes?" She replied:
"No greater grief than to remember days
Of joy, when mis'ry is at hand. That kens
Thy learn'd instructor. Yet so eagerly
If thou art bent to know the primal root,
From whence our love gat being, I will do
As one, who weeps and tells his tale. One day,
For our delight we read of Lancelot,
How him love thrall'd. Alone we were, and no
Suspicion near us. Oft times by that reading
Our eyes were drawn together, and the hue
Fled from our alter'd cheek. But at one point
Alone we fell. When of that smile we read,
The wished smile, so rapturously kiss'd
By one so deep in love, then he, who ne'er
From me shall separate, at once my lips
All trembling kiss'd. The book and writer both
Were love's purveyors. In its leaves that day
We read no more." While thus one spirit spake,
The other wail'd so sorely, that heart-struck
I, through compassion fainting, seem'd not far
From death, and like a corse fell to the ground.*

* *Inferno*, canto v. v. 73. It has not been thought necessary, every instance, to give these extracts in the Italian also, when

In the third circle of Hell, whose capacious gulf is divided into seven concentric circles, Dante finds those who are punished for their gluttony. Extended upon the fetid mire, these wretches are eternally exposed to showers of ice. The poet is recognised by one of them, and receives from him tidings of several of his countrymen. The opposite vices of avarice and prodigality suffer a common punishment, in the fourth circle; the inhabitants of which attack

---

the original is so easy of access. A portion, however, of this exquisite passage, the reader will, it is hoped, excuse us for here inserting:

Si tosto come l' vento a noi gli piega,
  Muovo la voce: O anime affannate!
  Venite a noi parlar, s' altri nol niega.
Quali colombe dal disio chiamate,
  Coll' ali alzate e ferme, al dolce nido
  Vengon per aere, da voler portate;
Cotali uscir della schiera ov' è Dido,
  A noi venendo per l' aere maligno;
  Sí forte fu l' affettuoso grido.
O animal grazioso e benigno,
  Che visitando vai per l' aere perso
  Noi, che tignemmo 'l mondo di sanguigno,
Se fosse amico il Re dell' universo,
  Noi pregheremmo lui per la tua pace,
  Da ch' hai pietà del nostro mal perverso.
Di quel ch' udire e che parlar ti piace,
  Noi udiremo, e parleremo a vui.
  Mentre che l' aura, come fà, si tace.

each other with mutual reproaches. A disgusting slough swallows up those who have abandoned themselves to their choleric passions; and the heresiarchs have a place reserved for them, within the precincts of the city of Pluto. A number of tombs are scattered over a wide plain, partially open, and glowing like a heated furnace. From these, over which the coverings remain suspended, the most dreadful shrieks proceed. As he passes by one of the tombs, Dante is thus saluted by its tenant:

> "O Tuscan! thou, who through the city of fire
> Alive art passing, so discreet of speech;
> Here, please thee, stay awhile. Thy utterance
> Declares the place of thy nativity
> To be that noble land, with which, perchance,
> I too severely dealt."*

The person who thus addresses him from the midst of the flames, proves to be Farinata de' Uberti, the chief of the Ghibeline faction at Florence, who triumphed over the Guelphs at the battle of Arbia, and saved his country, which the Ghibelines were about to sacrifice, to secure their own safety. Farinata was one of those great characters, of which antiquity, or the middle ages, alone, afford us any example. Controlling, with the hand of a master, the course of events, as well as the minds of men, destiny itself seems

---

* *Inferno*, canto x. v. 23.

to submit to his will, and the very torments of hell are insufficient to disturb the haughty tranquillity of his spirit. He is admirably portrayed in the conversation which Dante has assigned to him. Every passion is concentrated in his attachment to his country and his party; and the exile of the Ghibelines inflicts upon him far greater torments than the burning couch upon which he is reposing.

On descending into the seventh circle, Dante perceives a vast pool of blood, into which tyrants and homicides are plunged. Centaurs, armed with darts, traverse its margin, and compel the wretches, who raise their heads above the surface, to hide them again in the bloody stream. Proceeding farther, he finds those who have committed suicide, suffering transformation into the shape of trees, and retaining nothing of their human character but the power of speech, and the sense of pain. As a punishment for having once turned their hands against themselves, they are deprived of all capacity of action. On a plain of scorching sand, and exposed to showers of fire, the poet finds a company of shades, whose disgraceful vices had incurred this penalty; but who, in many respects, were entitled to his affection and respect. Amongst these, he distinguishes Brunetto Latino, his instructor in eloquence and poetry; Guido Guerra, Jacopo Rusticucci, and Tegghiaio Aldobrandi, the most virtuous and disinterested republicans of Florence, in the preceding century. Dante observes :

> If from the fire
> I had been shelter'd, down amidst them straight
> I then had cast me ; nor my guide, I deem,
> Would have restrain'd my going : but that fear
> Of the dire burning vanquish'd the desire,
> Which made me eager of their wish'd embrace.
> I then began : ———
> " I am a countryman of yours, who still
> Affectionate have utter'd, and have heard,
> Your deeds and names renown'd." *

He proceeds to give them some intelligence of he affairs of Florence, in whose prosperity these ictims of eternal torture still continue to take he deepest interest.

It is not our design to follow the steps of the oet from circle to circle, from gulf to " lower gulf." To render the description of these terible scenes at all supportable, we must call to ur aid the magical powers of style and of verse ; hat vehement and picturesque genius, which laces distinctly before our eyes the new world, ummoned into being at the will of the poet. bove all, we cannot dispense with that interest a the personages introduced upon the scene, of hich Dante availed himself, when, in anticipation f the Divine judgments, he described individuals ell known to his fellow-citizens by their vices,

* *Inferno*, canto xvi. v. 47.

and by the recent consequences of their crimes, as inhabiting the various mansions of hell, recognizing the Florentine bard, and losing, for a moment, the sense of their own agonies, in the remembrance of their country and their friends.

As this great work does not possess any regular action, and derives no support from the enthusiasm of human passion, it is impossible to take any lively interest in the hero of the story; if, indeed, Dante is not to be considered rather as the mere spectator of the pictures conjured up by his imagination, than as the hero of his own tale. It cannot, however, be said that the poem is altogether divested of dramatic interest. Unassisted and alone, we see Dante advance into the midst of demons and condemned souls. The Divine will has, it is true, opened to him the gates of Hell; and Virgil, who bears the mandate of omnipotence, attends his steps. But the demons are not the less active in opposing, with their utmost malignity, the superior decrees of fate. At one time, they violently close the gates of Hell upon him; at another, they rush towards him, with the design of tearing him in pieces. They deceive him with false information, and endeavour to lead him astray in the infernal labyrinth. We are sufficiently absorbed in his narrative, to feel interested in the dangers to which he is perpetually exposed; and the truth of his descriptions, added to the deep horror inspired

›y the objects which he depicts, seldom fails to nake a strong and painful impression on the nind. Thus, in the twenty-fifth canto, we hudder at the tortures, which he supposes to be nflicted upon robbers. These miserable offend-rs inhabit a valley, filled with horrible serpents. Before the very face of Dante, one of these mon-ters springs upon Agnolo Brunelleschi, enve-ɔpes him in its folds, and pours its poisonous ɔam over his features. The two bodies soon ap-ear to blend into one; the distinction of colours isappears; the limbs undergo a gradual change; nd when they are disengaged, Brunelleschi is ransformed into a snake, and Cianfa, who had ttacked him, recovers the human shape. Imme-iately after, Buoso de' Abbati is wounded by nother serpent, which relinquishes its hold, and tretches itself out at his feet. Buoso fixes his yes upon it, but cannot utter a word. He taggers and gasps, as if overpowered by lethargy r fever. The eyes of the man and of the reptile re steadfastly fixed on each other. From the ound of the former and the mouth of the latter, ɔick volumes of smoke proceed, and as soon s these unite, the nature of the two beings is hanged. Arms are seen to issue from the body f the serpent, while the limbs of the man con-ract and disappear under the scaly figure of his dversary. While one erects himself, the other rovels upon the earth; and the two accursed souls, who have interchanged their punishments, separate with mutual execrations.

The general conception of this unknown world, which Dante has revealed to our eyes, is, considered in itself, full of grandeur and sublimity. The existence of the three kingdoms of the dead, in which the sufferings, at least, were all of a physical nature, and to which the language of scripture and of the fathers was always literally applied, was a point of faith which, at the time when the poet flourished, admitted of no dispute. The creed of the church had not, however, fixed, with exact precision, the different abodes of departed spirits, and it was difficult to form an idea of the separation as well as of the degree of rewards and punishments. The future state described by the poets of antiquity is confused, and almost incomprehensible. That of Dante, on the contrary, strikes the imagination by the order, regularity, and grandeur with which it is depicted. It is impossible, when once impressed with his conceptions, to figure his scenes to our fancy in any other form. A horrible abyss occupies the interior of our earth. The declivity is not uniform, but broken, as it were, into steps, and terminates in the centre of the globe. This is the kingly station of Lucifer, the despotic ruler of these realms of pain, who waves his six gigantic wings over a frozen ocean, in which he is half submerged, and is at once the servant and the victim of Almighty vengeance. Like him, the other spirits of darkness who espoused his cause, are incessantly employed in exercising their diabolical malignity on the reprobate souls, whose agonies they inflict and partake. From the centre of the earth, a long cavern reconducts the poet to the light of day. It opens at the base of a mountain, situated on the opposite hemisphere. In figure, this mountain is the exact reverse of the infernal regions. It forms an immense cone, divided into distinct departments, in which are distributed those souls who are undergoing the judgments of purgatory. Its avenues are guarded by angels; and whenever they permit a purified soul to ascend into heaven, the whole mountain rings with the joyous thanksgivings of its remaining inhabitants. On its summit is situated the terrestrial Paradise, which forms the communicating link between heaven and earth. The celestial regions constitute the third portion of this universe, ascending in spiral rings, from sphere to sphere, to the throne of Almighty power. The same unity of design is thus visible in the conception of the different worlds; upon which the genius of Dante has conferred a diversified symmetry, combining, at once, perfect consistency with perpetual novelty, and approaching to that which characterizes the works of the creation.

The Divine Comedy is divided into a hundred

cantos, each containing from one hundred and thirty to one hundred and forty verses. The first canto is intended as a kind of introduction to the whole work. Thirty-three cantos are then devoted to each of the three topics of Hell, Purgatory, and Paradise. Proceeding with our rapid sketch, we shall not at present particularize the terrific punishments which the poet contemplates in the ocean of ice, swept by the wings of Lucifer. Dante issues from the abyss by placing himself upon the body of the fiend, and at the same time revolving round the centre of the earth, towards which all matter gravitates. His position is then changed, and he ascends by the path which appeared to him to be a declivity. Emerging to the light of day in the opposite hemisphere, he discovers a vast ocean, in the midst of which is placed the steep mountain to which we have already alluded. After purifying himself from the infernal stains, Dante proceeds to attempt the spiral ascent, under the guidance of Virgil, who never forsakes his side. As he passes along, he sees the souls of the elect chastened by long and severe sufferings. But in the midst of their agonies, they are filled with holy raptures, having exchanged faith for certainty, and having always before their eyes those heavenly rewards, which they are destined at last to attain. The angels who guard the various districts of the mountain, or who visit it, in their robes of light, as messengers of the Supreme will, continually remind the sufferers that their temporary chastisement will be succeeded by the joys and the splendours of paradise.

In this portion of the work, however, the interest is not equally supported. All apprehension of danger to the person of the hero is at an end. He walks in safety with the guardian angels of the place. There is little novelty in the punishments; and, such as they are, they do not strike the imagination, after those which we have already witnessed. Our sympathy, too, for the persons introduced to our notice, begins to languish. Their present state of existence is rendered indifferent to them by the vivacity of their hopes; their recollections of the past are absorbed in the future; and, experiencing no vehement emotions themselves, they have little power to excite them in us. Nor did this defect escape the observation of the poet. He endeavours to repair it, by entering into philosophical and theological discussions, and by detailing all the learning of the schools on the most subtle questions of metaphysics. But his style of argument, which was respected as profound at the period when he wrote, produces a very different effect upon minds which do not allow the authority of the doctors to supersede that of reason. These disquisitions, moreover, are always at variance with true poetry, and weary the reader, by interrupting the progress of the action.

Some interest is, however, occasionally excited by those whom Dante here encounters. Thus, on his first entrance into Purgatory, we are affected by the tender friendship of the musician, Casella, who endeavours to throw himself into the poet's arms. A striking incident occurs, also, in the third canto, where he is accosted by Manfred, the natural son of Frederick, and the greatest prince who has filled the throne of the Two Sicilies. He enjoins Dante to seek his daughter Constance, wife of Peter the Third of Aragon, and mother of Frederick, the avenger of the Sicilians, for the purpose of satisfying her as to his doom, and dissipating the painful doubts which the Pope and the priesthood had excited. Not contented with persecuting him during his life, with defaming his character, and precipitating him from his throne, they took upon themselves to pronounce the sentence of his eternal damnation. His body was torn from the grave, and exposed on the banks of a river, as that of a rebellious and excommunicated son of the Church. Yet the Divinity, whose mercy is not as the mercy of man, had accepted him, pardoned him, and given him promise of an eternity of bliss; neither the maledictions of the priests, nor the imposing forms of excommunication, possessing power to deprive sinners of the benefits of infinite love. It was thus that this singular poem might be said to convey tidings from parents to their children, and to afford grounds for hope, by giving, as it were, an authentic description of the state of the soul after dissolution.

In his sixth canto, Dante introduces us to the spirit of Sordello, the Troubadour of Mantua, of whom we have spoken in the fourth chapter. We behold him solitary, haughty, and contemptuous. He is recognized by Virgil, and the conference which ensues between them gives occasion to a fine invective against Italy, one of the most eloquent passages in the Purgatory. To enter, however, fully into the feelings of the poet, we must bear in mind the political storms by which Italy was, at that time, devastated; the long anarchy of the Empire, which, in the middle of the thirteenth century, had broken all the bonds by which its component states had before been united; the ambition of the Popes, who were only eager to aggrandize themselves at the expense of the ancient temporal sovereigns of the state; and the turbulent passions of the citizens, who continually sacrificed the liberty of their country to the indulgence of their private revenge. To all these sources of indignation, we must add the personal situation of Dante, then exiled from Florence by the triumphant faction of his enemies, and compelled to fly for succour to the Emperors, who were then beginning to re-establish their authority in Germany, but were unable to direct their attention, in any considerable degree, to the affairs of Italy. The poet thus fervently apostrophizes his country:

> Ah, slavish Italy! thou inn of grief!
> Vessel, without a pilot, in loud storm!
> Lady no longer of fair provinces,
> But brothel-house impure! this gentle spirit,
> Ev'n from the pleasant sound of his dear land,
> Was prompt to greet a fellow-citizen
> With such glad cheer: while now thy living ones
> In thee abide not without war; and one
> Malicious gnaws another; ay! of those
> Whom the same wall and the same moat contains.
> Seek, wretched one! around thy sea-coasts wide;
> Then homeward to thy bosom turn; and mark,
> If any part of thee sweet peace enjoy.
> What boots it, that thy reins Justinian's hand
> Refitted, if thy saddle be unpress'd?
> Nought doth he now but aggravate thy shame.——
> O German Albert! who abandon'st her
> That is grown savage and unmanageable,
> When thou should'st clasp her flanks with forked heels,
> Just judgment from the stars fall on thy blood;
> And be it strange and manifest to all;
> Such as may strike thy successor with dread;
> For that thy sire and thou have suffer'd thus,
> Through greediness of yonder realms detain'd,
> The garden of the empire to run waste.*

* *Purgat.* canto vi. v. 76.

After having rebuked the Emperor for permiting the discord of the Ghibeline chiefs, the oppression of his noble partizans, and the desolation of Rome, he appeals to Providence against the universal confusion, which seems to contradict the scheme of its benevolence. He concludes with an address, conceived in a spirit of the bitterest irony, to his native country, in which he reproaches her with her ambition, with that inconstant temper which induces her to make perpetual alterations in her laws, her coinage, and her civil offices, and with the ostentatious and affected display of those virtues which she has long ceased to practise.

In the twentieth canto, and in the fifth circle of Purgatory, where the sin of avarice is expiated, Dante meets with Hugh Capet, father of the king of that name; and in the conversation which takes place between them, the hatred which the poet entertains for the kings of France, who had extended their protection to his oppressors, and occasioned the downfall of his faction, is sufficiently manifest.

"I was root
Of that ill plant, whose shade such poison sheds
O'er all the Christian land, that seldom thence
Good fruit is gather'd. Vengeance soon should come,
Had Ghent and Douay, Lille and Bruges power;
And vengeance I of heav'n's great Judge implore.
Hugh Capet was I hight: from me descend

The Philips and the Louis, of whom France
Newly is govern'd; born of one, who ply'd
The slaughterer's trade at Paris. When the race
Of ancient kings had vanish'd (all save one
Wrapt up in sable weeds) within my gripe
I found the reins of empire, and such powers
Of new acquirement, with full store of friends,
That soon the widow'd circlet of the crown
Was girt upon the temples of my son,
He, from whose bones th' anointed race begins.
Till the great dower of Provence had remov'd
The stains, that yet obscur'd our lowly blood,
Its sway indeed was narrow; but howe'er
It wrought no evil: there, with force and lies,
Began its rapine: after, for amends,
Poitou it seiz'd, Navarre and Gascony.
To Italy came Charles; and for amends,
Young Conradine, an innocent victim, slew;
And sent th' angelic teacher back to heaven,
Still for amends. I see the time at hand,
That forth from France invites another Charles
To make himself and kindred better known.
Unarm'd he issues, saving with that lance,
Which the arch-traitor tilted with; and that
He carries with so home a thrust, as rives
The bowels of poor Florence. No increase
Of territory hence, but sin and shame
Shall be his guerdon; and so much the more
As he more lightly deems of such foul wrong.
I see the other, (who a prisoner late
Had stept on shore,) exposing to the mart
His daughter, whom he bargains for, as do
The Corsairs for their slaves. O avarice!
What canst thou more, who hast subdued our blood
So wholly to thyself, they feel no care

Of their own flesh? To hide with direrer guilt
Past ill and future, lo! the flower-de-luce
Enters Alagna; in his Vicar, Christ
Himself a captive, and his mockery
Acted again. Lo! to his holy lip
The vinegar and gall once more applied;
And he 'twixt living robbers doom'd to bleed." *

The Purgatory of Dante is, in some respects, a ainter picture of the infernal regions. The same rimes are there corrected by punishments of a imilar nature, but limited in their duration, insmuch as the sinner gave proofs of penitence revious to his death. Dante has, however, intro-uced much less variety into the offences and the enal inflictions. After remaining a considerable ime with those souls which linger at the outside f Purgatory, as a punishment for having deferred, n their lifetime, the period of their conversion, he roceeds in regular order through the seven moral sins. The proud are overwhelmed with enornous weights; the envious are clothed in garnents of horsehair, and their eyelids are closed vith an iron thread; clouds of smoke suffocate he choleric; the indolent are compelled to run vithout ceasing; the avaricious are prostrated vith their faces on the earth; the cravings of unger and thirst afflict the epicure; and those

* *Purgat.* canto xx. v. 43.

who have given themselves up to incontinence, expiate their crime in fire. It will appear, from this slight sketch, that the scene of the Purgatory is more contracted, and its action more tardy; and as Dante determined to make the Purgatory equal in length to the two other divisions of his work, the execution is perhaps necessarily languid. We find the cantos overloaded with visions and reveries, fatiguing to the reader, who looks forward with impatience to the termination of this mysterious excursion.

After having traversed the seven circles of Purgatory, Dante, in his twenty-eighth canto, reaches the terrestrial Paradise, situated on the summit of the mountain. His description of this place is full of beauty, and all that can be objected to it is, that he has too frequently digressed into scholastic dissertations. In this earthly Paradise, Beatrice, the object of his earliest affection, descends from heaven to meet him. She appears as the minister of grace, and the organ of divine wisdom; and the passion which he entertains for her, exists only in the noblest sentiments and in the most elevated feelings. It is only as a manifestation of the goodness of God, that she presents herself to his thoughts, after her translation to the skies. In this view, she occupies the first place in his poem. From her, Virgil received his orders to escort the bard on his journey; by her influence, the gates of Hell were opened before him ; her care removed every obstacle which opposed his progress ; and her mandates are implicitly obeyed, throughout the three kingdoms of the dead. Such is the glory with which her lover surrounds her, that we are sometimes inclined to suspect that she is merely an allegorical character, and that the individual object of his affections is lost in a personification of theology. Whilst she is advancing towards him, and whilst, even before he has recognized her, he already trembles in her presence, from the power of his first love, Virgil, who had hitherto accompanied him, disappears. Beatrice reproves the early errors of the poet, and attempts to purify his heart; but her discourse is, perhaps, not altogether equal to the situation. As Dante approaches nearer to Heaven, he aims at something beyond the ordinary language of the world; and, in this attempt, he frequently becomes so obscure, that it is difficult to detect the beauties which still remain. To give us an idea of the language of Heaven, he borrows that of the church; and he intersperses such a number of Latin verses and hymns in his poetry, that the difference between the prosody, sound, and turn of expression of the two languages, arrests, at every moment, the attention of the reader.

In ascending into Heaven, Dante no longer avails himself of human machinery or human power; and he is, therefore, transported thither by fixing his eyes steadfastly on the sun, and by the mere vehemence of his spiritual aspirations. It is here difficult to understand him; and whilst we are endeavouring to discover the meaning of his enigmatical words, we cease to sympathise with his feelings and to accompany him on his way. In his account of the infernal world, there is nothing supernatural, which is not in strict accordance with our own nature. He only exaggerates those forces and those evils of which we have real experience. When he issues from Purgatory and enters into Heaven, he presents us, on the contrary, with supernatural appearances like those of our wildest dreams. He supposes the existence of faculties, with which we have no acquaintance. He neither awakens our associations, nor revives our habits. We never thoroughly understand him; and the perpetual state of astonishment in which we are placed, tends only to fatigue us.

The first abode of the blessed, is the heaven of the Moon, which revolves with the most tardy motion, and at the greatest distance from the glory of the Most High. Here inhabit the souls of such as, after having pronounced the vows of celibacy and religious seclusion, have been compelled to renounce them. But, although Dante distributes the beatified souls into distinct classes, their bliss, which is entirely of a contemplative nature, seems not to be susceptible of such a livision. He represents one of these spirits as hus expressing herself:—

> "Brother! our will
> Is, in composure, settled by the power
> Of charity, who makes us will alone
> What we possess, and nought beyond desire:
> If we should wish to be exalted more,
> Then must our wishes jar with the high will
> Of him, who sets us here."*

This may be very true; but the state of indif-erence, in which these souls exist, throws an air of coldness on the remainder of the poem; the nterest of which is still farther impaired by fre-quent theological disquisitions. All the doubts of Dante, on the union of the body and the soul, on the nature of vows, on free will, and on other intricate points, are readily solved by Bea-rice; but it is not so easy to satisfy the minds of his readers on these obscure topics. The most philosophical prose is not always successful on hese subjects; and we cannot, therefore, be surprised, if the poetical form of Dante's argu-nents, and the authority of Beatrice, to whose livine mission we are not always disposed to give mplicit faith, throw still greater obscurity over questions, which are beyond all human compre-ension.

We find very few descriptions in the Paradise

---

* *Parad.* canto iii. v. 70.

of Dante. The great artist, whose sketches of the infernal realms possess such appalling sublimity, has not attempted to delineate the scenery of the skies. We leave the heaven of the Moon, with a very imperfect knowledge of its nature; and our visit to that of Mercury is no less unsatisfactory. In each successive kingdom, however, the poet excites our curiosity, by assigning a prominent station to some character of distinguished celebrity. In the sixth canto, and in the second heaven, he is accosted by the Emperor Justinian, who is represented in a light as favourable as that in which the civilians have always delighted to view the great father of their science, and very different from that in which he is exhibited, with all his frailties and his vices, in the Secret History of Procopius.

In the third heaven, which is that of the planet Venus, Dante meets with Cunissa, the sister of Azzolino da Romano, who forewarns him of the revolutions of the Marca Trivigiana. Saint Thomas Aquinas and Saint Bonaventura are found in the fourth heaven, which is placed in the Sun; and they narrate the glorified actions of Saint Dominick and Saint Francis. The souls of those who have combated for the true faith, are rewarded in the heaven of Mars. Amongst these, he observes his ancestor, Cacciaguida de' Elisei, who perished in the crusades; and from whom he receives an account of the early greatness of his own family. Cacciaguida proceeds to describe the ancient severity of manners maintained in Florence, in the time of Conrad the Third, and gives a catalogue, with a few characteristic remarks, of the noble houses which then flourished; of those which had, in later times, fallen into decay, and of those which had more recently risen to distinction. He then predicts to Dante his approaching exile:

> "Thou shalt leave each thing
> Belov'd most dearly: this is the first shaft
> Shot from the bow of exile. Thou shalt prove
> How salt the savour is of others' bread;
> How hard the passage, to descend and climb
> By others' stairs. But that shall gall thee most,
> Will be the worthless and vile company,
> With whom thou must be thrown into these straits." *

Cacciaguida then encourages Dante to disclose to the world all that he has witnessed in the realm of shadows, and to elevate his mind above the unworthy apprehension of giving offence to those, who might deem themselves disgraced by his narrations.

The sixth heaven is that of Jupiter, in which those, who have administered justice with impartiality, receive their reward. The seventh is in Saturn, and contains such as devoted themselves to a life of contemplation or seclusion. In the

---

* *Parad.* canto xvii. v. 55.

eighth heaven, Dante beholds the triumph of Christ, which is attended by a host of beatified souls and by the Virgin Mary herself. He is then examined by Saint Peter in point of faith, by Saint James in hope, and by Saint John in charity, from all of whom he obtains honourable testimonials of their approbation. Adam, also, here informs him what language was spoken in the terrestrial Paradise.

The poet then ascends into the ninth sphere, where he is favoured with a manifestation of the Divine Essence, which is, however, veiled by three hierarchies of surrounding angels. The Virgin Mary, and the Saints of the Old and New Testament, are also visible to him in the tenth heaven. All his doubts are finally resolved by the saints or by the Deity himself; and this great work concludes with a contemplation of the union of the two natures in the Divine Being.

The measure in which this poem is written, and of which Dante was, in all probability, the original inventor, has received the name of *terza rima*. It has since been especially appropriated to philosophical poetry, to satires, and to epistolary and allegorical compositions. But it is applicable, with no less success, to epic poetry. The position of the recurring rhymes keeps the attention alive, and admits of a regular flow of the narrative; an advantage, to which the *ottava rima*, or stanza of the later Italian writers, and even the *quatrains* of French poetry, cannot lay claim. The *terza rima* consists of three verses, disposed in such a manner, that the middle line of each couplet rhymes with the first and third verses of the succeeding. From the way in which the lines are thus perpetually interwoven, the memory derives very material assistance. Whatever couplet we may select from the poem, will afford us, by two of its rhymes, a clue to the preceding passage, and by one of them, to the following couplet. The verses, thus interlinked, are all endecasyllables, which are exclusively used in the epic poetry of Italy; and they are divided, or supposed so to be, into five iambics, of which the last is followed by a short syllable.

As a specimen of the *terza rima*, I have attempted to translate into French verse the celebrated Episode of Ugolino, from the thirty-third canto of the *Inferno*. In this, I have found very great difficulty. The French language, compared with the Italian, is very poor in rhymes, which are not easily found for three verses, placed at a regular and invariable distance. The rule which compels the French writer not to employ two feminine rhymes in succession, and which is not observed in Italian composition, presents an additional obstacle. It may, perhaps, also be said, that the French language has a natural tendency, in its versification, to the use of the couplet, and that a continued union of rhyme is as repugnant to its genius as the running of one line into another. If not absolutely insurmountable, the constraint imposed by these various difficulties, is, at least, such, as almost to destroy the magnificent spirit of the celebrated passage in question. In the last circle of the infernal world, Dante beholds those who have betrayed their native land, entombed in everlasting ice. Two heads, not far distant from each other, raise themselves above the frozen surface. One of these is that of Count Ugolino della Gherardesca, who, by a series of treasons, had made himself absolute master of Pisa. The other head is that of Ruggieri de' Ubaldini, archbishop of that state, who, by means not less criminal, had effected the ruin of the count, and having seized him, with his four children, or grandchildren, had left them to perish, by famine, in prison. Dante does not at first recognize them, and shudders when he sees Ugolino gnawing the skull of his murderer, which lies before him. He inquires into the motive of this savage enmity, and with the count's reply the thirty-third canto commences.*

---

* *Inferno*, Canto xxxiii. v. i. [As the object of M. Sismondi is to shew the peculiarities of the *terza rima*, and to try how far its adoption is practicable in French versification, it has been thought expedient to present the reader with his version below; the perusal of which will probably convince him, that the objections stated by that gentleman are not overcharged. Without detracting from the spirit and ingenuity with which he

His mouth upraising from his hideous feast,
And brushing, with his victim's locks, the spray
Of gore from his foul lips, that sinner ceas'd:
Then thus: "Will'st thou that I renew the sway
Of hopeless grief, which weighs upon my heart
In thought, ere yet my tongue that thought betray?
But, should my words prove seeds from which may start
Ripe fruits of scorn for him, whose traitor head
I gnaw, then words and tears, at once, shall part.

---

has executed his laborious task, it is not too much to say, that he admirer of the unequalled original will turn with pleasure, heightened by the contrast, to the excellent translation of this episode by Mr. Cary.

Disclaiming any intention of entering into competition with either of these versions, the Editor has ventured to attempt an original translation, in which he has preserved, in the English, the form of the Italian terza rima, and has adhered as literally as possible, and line for line, to the original. This species of verse is certainly difficult in our own language, to which, however, it is much more congenial than to the French. It has been employed with considerable success by Lord Byron, in his Prophecy of Dante, where the reader will be enabled fully to estimate all that it is capable of effecting in our language. *Tr.*]

Ce pécheur, soulevant une bouche altérée,
Essuya le sang noir dont il était trempé,
A la tête de mort qu'il avait dévorée.
Si je dois raconter le sort qui m'a frappé,
Une horrible douleur occupe ma pensée,
Dit-il, mais ton espoir ne sera point trompé.
Qu'importe ma douleur, si ma langue glacée,
Du traître que tu vois comble le déshonneur,
Ma langue se ranime, à sa honte empressée.

I know thee not; nor by what fortune led
Thou wanderest here; but thou, if true the claim
Of native speech, wert in fair Florence bred.
Know, then, Count Ugolino is my name,
And this the Pisan prelate at my side,
Ruggier.—Hear, now, my cause of grief—his shame.
That by his arts he won me to confide
In his smooth words, that I was bound in chains,
Small need is, now, to tell, nor that I died.
But what is yet untold, unheard, remains,
And thou shalt hear it—by what fearful fate
I perish'd. Judge, if he deserves his pains.
When, in those dungeon-walls emmew'd, whose gate
Shall close on future victims, called the Tower
Of Famine, from my pangs, the narrow grate
Had shewn me several moons, in evil hour
I slept and dream'd, and our impending grief
Was all unveil'd by that dread vision's power.

Je ne te connais point, je ne sais quel bonheur
Te conduit tout vivant jusqu'au fond de l'abîme;
N'es-tu pas Florentin? vois, et frémis d'horreur!
Mon nom est Ugolin, Roger est ma victime;
Dieu livre à mes fureurs le prélat des Pisans;
Sans doute tu connais et mon sort et son crime:
Je mourus par son ordre avec tous mes enfans;
Déjà la renommée aura pu t'en instruire;
Mais elle n'a point dit quels furent mes tourmens.
Écoute, et tu verras si Roger sut me nuire.
Dans la tour de la Faim, où je fus enfermé,
Où maint infortuné doit encor se détruire,
Le flambeau de la nuit plusieurs fois rallumé,
M'avait de plusieurs mois fait mesurer l'espace,
Quand d'un songe cruel mon cœur fut alarmé.

This wretch, methought, I saw, as lord and chief,
  Hunting the wolf and cubs, upon that hill
  Which makes the Pisan's view towards Lucca brief.
With high-bred hounds, and lean, and keen to kill,
  Gualandi, with Sismondi, in the race
  Of death, were foremost, with Lanfranchi, still.
Weary and spent appear'd, after short chace,
  The sire and sons, and soon, it seem'd, were rent
  With sharpest fangs, their sides. Before the trace
Of dawn, I woke, and heard my sons lament,
  (For they were with me), mourning in their sleep,
  And craving bread. Right cruel is thy bent,
If, hearing this, no horror o'er thee creep;
  If, guessing what I now began to dread,
  Thou weep'st not, wherefore art thou wont to weep?
Now were they all awake. The hour, when bread
  Was wont to be bestow'd, had now drawn near,
  And dismal doubts, in each, his dream had bred.

  Vieux tyran des forêts, on me force à la chasse;
  Cet homme, avec Gualande et Sismonde, et Lanfranc,
Changés en chiens cruels, se pressaient sur ma trace,
  Je fuyais vers les monts l'ennemi de mon sang;
Mes jeunes louvetaux ne pouvaient plus me suivre,
Et ces chiens dévorans leur déchiraient le flanc.
  De ce songe un réveil plus affreux me délivre;
Mes fils dans leur sommeil me demandaient du pain,
Un noir pressentiment paraissait les poursuivre.
  Et toi, si, prévoyant mon funeste destin,
Tu t'abstiens, étranger, de répandre des larmes,
Aurais-tu dans ton cœur quelque chose d'humain?
  Mes fils ne dormaient plus; mais de sombres alarmes
Avaient glacé leurs sens; le geôlier attendu
N'apportait point ce pain que nous trempions de larmes.

Then lock'd, below, the portals did we hear
 Of that most horrible Tower. I fix'd my eye,
 Without one word, upon my children dear:
Harden'd like rock within, I heav'd no sigh.
 They wept; and then I heard my Anselm say,
 'Thou look'st so, Sire! what ails thee?' No reply
I utter'd yet, nor wept I, all that day,
 Nor the succeeding night, till on the gloom
 Another sun had issued. When his ray
Had scantily illum'd our prison-room,
 And in four haggard visages I saw
 My own shrunk aspect, and our common doom,
Both hands, for very anguish, did I gnaw.
 They, thinking that I tore them through desire
 Of food, rose sudden from their dungeon-straw,
And spoke; "Less grief it were, of us, O Sire!
 If thou would'st eat—These limbs, thou, by our birth,
 Didst clothe—Despoil them now, if need require."

Tout à coup des verroux le bruit est entendu,
Notre fatale tour est pour jamais fermée:
Je regarde mes fils, et demeure éperdu.
 Sur mes lèvres la voix meurt à demi formée;
Je ne pouvais pleurer: ils pleuraient, mes enfans!
Quelle haine par eux n'eût été désarmée?
 Anselme, me serrant dans ses bras caressans,
S'écriait: que crains-tu, qu'as-tu donc, ô mon père!
Je ne te connais plus sous tes traits pâlissans.
 Cependant aucuns pleurs ne mouillaient ma paupière,
Je ne répondais point; je me tus tout un jour.
Quand un nouveau soleil éclaira l'hémisphère,
 Quand son pâle rayon pénétra dans la tour,
Je lus tous mes tourmens sur ces quatre visages,
Et je rongeai mes poings, sans espoir de secour.

Not to increase their pangs of grief and dearth,
I calm'd me. Two days more, all mute we stood:
Wherefore didst thou not open, pitiless Earth!
Now, when our fourth sad morning was renew'd,
Gaddo fell at my feet, outstretch'd and cold,
Crying, 'Wilt thou not, father! give me food?'
There did he die; and as thine eyes behold
Me now, so saw I three, fall, one by one,
On the fifth day and sixth: whence, in that hold,
I, now grown blind, over each lifeless son,
Stretch'd forth mine arms. Three days, I call'd their names;
Then Fast achiev'd what Grief not yet had done."

Mes fils, trompés sans doute à ces gestes sauvages,
D'une féroce faim me crurent consumé.
Mon père, dirent-ils, suspendez ces outrages!
Par vous, de votre sang notre corps fut formé,
Il est à vous, prenez, prolongez votre vie;
Puisse-t-il vous nourrir, ô père bien aimé!
Je me tus, notre force était anéantie!
Ce jour ni le suivant nous ne pûmes parler:
Que ne t'abîmais-tu, terre notre ennemie!
Déjà nous avions vu quatre soleils briller,
Lorsque Gaddo tomba renversé sur la terre.
Mon père, cria-t-il, ne peux-tu me sauver!
Il y mourut. Ainsi que tu vois ma misère,
Je les vis tous mourir, l'un sur l'autre entassés,
Et je demeurai seul, maudissant la lumière.
Trois jours, entre mes bras leurs corps furens pressés;
Aveuglé de douleur, les appelant encore,
Trois jours je réchauffai ces cadavres glacés,
Puis la faim triompha du deuil qui me dévore.

CHAPTER X.

On the influence of Dante over his age.—Petrarch.

THE power of the human mind was never more forcibly demonstrated, in its most exquisite masterpieces, than in the poem of Dante. Without a prototype in any existing language, equally novel in its various parts, and in the combination of the whole, it stands alone, as the first monument of modern genius, the first great work which appeared in the reviving literature of Europe. In its composition, it is strictly conformable to the essential and invariable principles of the poetical art. It possesses unity of design and of execution; and bears the visible impress of a mighty genius, capable of embracing, at once, the parts and the whole of its scheme; of employing, with facility, the most stupendous materials, and of observing all the required niceties of proportion, without experiencing any difficulty from the constraint. In all other respects, the poem of Dante is not within the jurisdiction of established rules. It cannot with propriety be referred to any particular class of composition, and its author is only to be udged by those laws which he thought fit to .mpose upon himself. His modesty induced him to give his work the title of a *Comedy*, in order to place it in a rank inferior to the Epic, to which he conceived that Virgil had exclusive claims. Dante had not the slightest acquaintance with the dramatic art, of which he had, in all probability, never met with a single specimen; and from this ignorance proceeded that use of the word, which now appears to us to be so extraordinary*. In his native country, the title which he gave to his work was always preserved, and t is still known as *The Divine Comedy*. A name so totally different from every other, seems to be happily bestowed upon a production which stands without a rival.

The glory which Dante acquired, which commenced during his lifetime, and which raised him, in a little time, above the greatest names of Italy, contributed but little to his happiness. He was born in Florence in 1265, of the noble and distinguished family of the Alighieri, which was attached, in politics, to the party of the Guelphs. Whilst yet very young, he formed a strong attachment to Beatrice, the daughter of

* [Mr. Cary observes, in his preface, "Dante himself, I believe, termed it simply *The Comedy*, in the first place, because the style was of the middle kind; and in the next, because the story (if story it may be called) ends happily."—*Tr.*]

Folco de' Portinari, whom he lost at the age of twenty-five years. Throughout his future life, he preserved a faithful recollection of the passion, which, during fifteen years, had essentially contributed to the happy developement of his feelings, and which was thus associated with all his noblest sentiments and his most elevated thoughts. It was, probably, about ten years after the death of Beatrice, when Dante commenced his great work, which occupied him during the remainder of his life, and in which he assigned the most conspicuous station to the woman whom he had so tenderly loved. In this object of his adoration, he found a common point of union for images both human and divine; and the Beatrice of his Paradise appears to us sometimes in the character of the most beloved of her sex, and sometimes as an abstract emblem of celestial wisdom. Far from considering the passion of love in the same light as the ancients, the father of modern poetry recognizes it as a pure, elevated, and sacred sentiment, calculated to ennoble and to sanctify the soul; and he has never been surpassed, by any who have succeeded him, in his entire and affecting devotion to the object of his attachment. Dante was, however, induced by considerations of family convenience, to enter into a new engagement. In 1291, a year after the death of Beatrice, he married Gemma de' Donati, whose obstinate and violent disposition

:mbittered his domestic life. It is remarkable .hat, in the whole course of his work, into which ıe introduces the whole universe, he makes no ›ersonal allusion to his wife; and he was ac-:uated, no doubt, by motives of delicacy towards ıer and her family, when he passed over, in si-nilar silence, Corso Donati, the leader of the 'action of his enemies, and his own most formid-ıble adversary. In the battle of Campaldino, in 1289, Dante bore arms for his country against the Aretini, and, also, against the Pisans, in the campaign of 1290; the year subsequent to that in which the catastrophe of Count Ugolino occurred. He subsequently assumed the magisterial functions, at the period so fatal to the happiness of his country, when the civil wars, between the Bianchi and the Neri, broke out. He was accused of a criminal partiality to the interest of the former faction, during the time when he was a member of the Supreme Council; and when Charles de Valois, the father of Philip the Sixth, proceeded to Florence, to appease the dissensions of the two parties, Dante was sentenced, in the year 1302, to the payment of an oppressive fine and to exile. By the subsequent sentence of a revolutionary tribunal, he was condemned, during his absence, to be burned alive, with all his partizans. From that period, Dante was compelled to seek an asylum at such of the Italian courts as were attached to the Ghibeline interest, and were not unwilling to extend their protection to their ancient enemies. To that party, which he had opposed in the outset of his career, his perpetual exile and his misfortunes compelled him, ultimately, to become a convert. He resided, for a considerable time, with the Marquis Malaspina, in the Lunigiana, with the Count Busone da Gubbio, and with the two brothers, Della Scala, lords of Verona. But, in every quarter, the haughty obstinacy of his character, which became more inflexible in proportion to the difficulties with which he was surrounded, and the bitterness of his wit, which frequently broke out in caustic sarcasms, raised up against him new enemies. His attempts to re-enter Florence with his party, by force of arms, were successively foiled; his petitions to the people were rejected; and his last hope, in the Emperor Henry the Seventh, vanished on the death of that monarch. His decease took place at Ravenna, on the 14th of September, 1321, whilst he was enjoying the hospitable protection of Guido Novello da Polenta, the lord of that city, who had always treated him rather as a friend than as a dependant, and who, a short time before, had bestowed upon him an honourable mark of his confidence, by charging him with an embassy to the Republic of Venice.

On the death of her great poet, all Italy appeared to go into mourning. On every side copies of his work were multiplied, and enriched with numerous commentaries. In the year 1350, Giovanni Visconti, Archbishop and Prince of Milan, engaged a number of learned men in the laborious task of illustrating and explaining the obscure passages of the *Divina Commedia*. Six distinguished scholars, two theologians, two men of science, and two Florentine antiquaries, united their talents in this undertaking. Two professorships were instituted for the purpose of expounding the works of Dante. One of these, founded at Florence, in the year 1373, was filled by the celebrated Boccacio. The duties of the other, at Bologna, were no less worthily discharged by Benvenuto d'Imola, a scholar of eminence. It is questionable whether any other man ever exercised so undisputed an authority, and so direct an influence, over the age immediately succeeding his own.

An additional proof of the superiority of this great genius, may be drawn from the commentaies upon his works. We are there surprised to ee his most enthusiastic admirers incapable of ppreciating his real grandeur. Dante himself, n his Latin treatise, entitled *De Vulgari Elouentiâ* appears to be quite unconscious of the xtent of his services to the literature of his ountry. Like his commentators, he principally alues himself upon the purity and correctess of his style. Yet he is neither pure nor correct; but, what is far superior to either, he had the powers of creative invention. For the sake of the rhyme, we find him employing a great number of barbarous words, which do not occur a second time in his verses. But, when he is himself affected, and wishes to communicate his emotions, the Italian language of the thirteenth century, in his powerful hands, displays a richness of expression, a purity, and an elegance, which he was the first to elicit, and by which it has ever since been distinguished. The personages whom he introduces, are moving and breathing beings; his pictures are nature itself; his language speaks at once to the imagination and to the judgment; and it would be difficult to point out a passage in his poem, which would not form a subject for the pencil. The admiration of his commentators has, also, been abundantly bestowed upon the profound learning of Dante; who, it must be allowed, appears to have been master of all the knowledge and accomplishments of the age in which he lived. Of these various attainments, his poem is the faithful depository, from which we may infer, with great precision, the progress which science had, at that time, made, and the advances which were yet necessary, to afford full satisfaction to the mind.

It would here become our duty to take a summary view of the poets, who flourished contemporaneously with Dante, and who either adopted him as their model, or pursued the path already opened by the Provençal writers. In this object, however, we have been anticipated by M. Ginguené, in his excellent *History of Italian Literature.* In speaking of the great prototypes of literature, with which I am myself acquainted, and which I have studied with enthusiasm, I express the opinions which are the result of my own ideas and sentiments. In every individual, opinions, thus formed, will possess a certain degree of novelty and peculiarity ; and so far, the field lies as open to one critic as to another. But in treating of those authors who hold only a secondary rank, of whom I have only a very partial knowledge, and that knowledge, in some instances, acquired from M. Ginguené himself, I cannot, for a moment, hesitate in referring the reader, for complete information on this head, to the labours of that distinguished writer, who has devoted his whole life to the study of Italian literature, and whose correct and elegant taste, added to his learning, as extensive as it is accurate, have deservedly given to his work universal circulation and applause.

From this source, then, the reader will derive more ample information respecting Jacopone di Todi ; of whom we shall only here observe, that he was a monk, who was induced, by motives of humility, to assume the outward appearances of insanity. He was fond of being insulted by children, and followed in the streets. During many years, he was persecuted by his superiors, and languished in confinement; where, however, amidst all his miseries, he composed religious hymns, which are not deficient in transports of enthusiasm, but which are frequently rendered quite unintelligible by the subtleties of mystical sentiment. To the same period, belongs Francesco di Barberino, the disciple, like Dante, of Brunetto Latini, and author of a treatise, in verse, on moral philosophy, which, in conformity with the affected spirit of the times, he entitled *I Documenti d'Amore*. Cecco d'Ascoli was also the contemporary of Dante, and his personal enemy. His poem, in five books, called *L'Acerba*, or rather, according to M. Ginguené, *L'Acerva*, the heap, is a collection of all the sciences of his age including astronomy, philosophy, and religion. It is much less remarkable for its intrinsic merit, than for the lamentable catastrophe of its author, who was burned alive, in Florence, as a sorcerer, in 1327, at the age of seventy years, after having long held the professorship of judicial astrology in the University of Bologna. Cino da Pistoia, of the house of the Sinibaldi, was the friend of Dante, and was equally distinguished by the brilliancy of his talents in two different departments: as a lawyer, by his commentary on the nine first books of the Code, and, as a poet, by his verses addressed to the beautiful Selvaggia de' Vergiolesi, of whom he was deprived by death, about the year 1307. As a lawyer, he was the preceptor of the celebrated Bartolo, who, if he has surpassed his master, yet owed much to his lessons. As a poet, he was the model which Petrarch loved to imitate; and, in this view, he, perhaps, did his imitator as much injury by his refinement and affectation, as he benefited him by the example of his pure and harmonious style. Fazio de' Uberti, grandson of the great Farinata, and who, in consequence of the hatred which the Florentines entertained for his ancestor, lived and died in exile, raised himself to equal celebrity, at this period, by his sonnets and other verses. At a much later time of life, he composed a poem, of the descriptive kind, entitled *Dettamondo*, in which he proposed to imitate Dante, and to display the real world, as that poet had portrayed the world of spirits. But it need hardly be said, that the distance between the original and the imitation is great indeed.

In some respects, all these poets, and many others, whose names are yet more obscure, have common points of resemblance. We find, in all, the same subtlety of idea, the same incoherent images, and the same perplexed sentiments. The spirit of the times was perverted by an affected refinement; and it is a subject of just surprise, that, in the very outset of a nation, simplicity and natural feeling should have been superseded by conceit and bombast. It is, however, to be considered, that this nation did not form her own taste, but adopted that of a foreign country, before she was qualified, by her own improved knowledge, to make a proper choice. The verses of the Troubadours of Provence were circulated from one end of Italy to the other. They were diligently perused and committed to memory by every poet who aspired to public notice, some of whom exercised themselves in compositions in the same language; and although the Italians, if we except the Sicilians, had never any direct intercourse with the Arabians, yet they derived much information from them by this circuitous route. The almost unintelligible subtleties with which they treated of love, passed for refinement of sentiment; while the perpetual rivalry which was maintained between the heart and the head, between reason and passion, was looked upon as an ingenious application of philosophy to a literary subject. The causeless griefs, the languors, the dying complaints of a lover, became a constituent portion of the consecrated language in which he addressed his mistress, and from which he could not, without impropriety, depart. Conventional feelings in poetry, thus usurped the place of those native and simple sentiments which are the offspring of the heart. But, instead of dwelling upon these defects in the less celebrated poets, we shall attempt to exhibit the general spirit of the fourteenth century, as displayed in the works of the greatest man whom Italy, in that age, produced, whose reputation has been most widely spread, and whose influence has been most extensively felt, not only in Italy, but in France, in Spain, and in Portugal. The reader will easily imagine that it is Petrarch, the lover of Laura, to whom we here allude.

Petrarch was the son of a Florentine, who, like Dante, had been exiled from his native city. He was born at Arezzo, on the night of the nineteenth of July, 1304, and he died at Arqua, near Padua, on the eighteenth of July, 1374. During the century, of which his life occupied the greater portion, he was the centre of Italian literature. Passionately attached to letters, and more especially to history and to poetry, and an enthusiastic admirer of antiquity, he imparted to his contemporaries, by his discourses, his writings, and his example, that taste for the recovery and study of Latin manuscripts, which so eminently distinguished the fourteenth century; which preserved the masterpieces of the classical authors, at the very moment when they were about to be lost for ever; and gave a new impulse, by the imitation of those admirable models, to the progress of the human intellect. Petrarch, tortured by the passion which has contributed so greatly to his celebrity, endeavoured, by travelling, during a considerable portion of his life, to escape from himself and to change the current of his thoughts. He traversed France, Germany, and every part of Italy; he visited Spain; and, with incessant activity, directed his attention to the examination of the remains of antiquity. He became intimate with all the scholars, poets, and philosophers, from one end of Europe to the other, whom he inspired with his own spirit. While he imparted to them the object of his own labours, he directed their studies; and his correspondence became a sort of magical bond, which, for the first time, united the whole literary republic of Europe. At the age in which he lived, that continent was divided into petty states, and sovereigns had not yet attempted to establish any of those colossal empires, so dreaded by other nations. On the contrary, each country was divided into smaller sovereignties. The authority of many a prince did not extend above thirty leagues from the little town over which he ruled; while at the distance of a hundred, his name was unknown. In proportion, however, as political importance was confined, literary glory was extended; and Petrarch, the friend of Azzo di Corregio, Prince of Parma, of Luchino, and of Galeazzo Visconti, Princes of Milan, and of Francesco di Carrara, Prince of Padua, was better known and more respected, throughout Europe, than any of those petty sovereigns. This universal reputation, to which his high acquirements entitled him, and of which he frequently made use, in forwarding the interests of literature, he occasionally turned to account, for political purposes. No man of letters, no poet, was, doubtless, ever charged with so many embassies to great potentates; to the Emperor, the Pope, the King of France, the senate of Venice, and all the Princes of Italy. It is very remarkable that Petrarch did not fulfil these duties merely as a subject of the state which had committed its interests to his hands, but that he acted for the benefit of all Europe. He was entrusted with such missions, on account of his reputation; and when he treated with the different princes, it was, as it were, in the character of an arbitrator, whose suffrage every one was eager to obtain, that he might stand high in the opinion of posterity.

The prodigious labours of Petrarch to promote the study of ancient literature, are, after all, his noblest title to glory. Such was the view in which they were regarded by the age in which he lived, and such also was his own opinion. His celebrity, notwithstanding, at the present day, depends much more on his Italian lyrical poems, than on his voluminous Latin compositions. These lyrical pieces, which were imitated from the Provençals, from Cino da Pistoia, and from the other poets who flourished at the commencement of that century, have served, in their turn, as models to all the distinguished poets of the South. I would gladly make my readers acquainted with some of these poems, if, in my translations, any of those beauties which so essentially depend upon the harmony and colouring of their most musical and picturesque language, could possibly be preserved.

The lyrical style of poetry is the first which is cultivated in every language, on the revival of its literature; for it is that which is most essentially poetical, and in which the poet can abandon himself most freely to his vivid impressions. In an epic poem, the author never ceases to think of his readers. His object is to give a faithful narrative, and to present to their eyes events, in which he can have no personal interest. In the drama, he absolutely loses his identity, and transforms himself into the various persons whom he creates. In the pastoral, it is true, he has an opportunity for the expression of sentiment, but it is not his own; and he is forced to accommodate himself to conventional notions, and to an ideal mode of life. The lyrical poet, on the contrary, is ever himself; he expresses, in his own person, his own peculiar emotions; he sings because he is affected, because he is inspired. Poetry, which is addressed to others, and the object of which is persuasion, should borrow its ornaments from eloquence; but, when it is an effusion of the heart, an overflow of sentiment, its true embellishment is harmony. The ordinary measure of verse is insufficient for the heart which would pour out its feelings, and delight in contemplating them. The verses must be accompanied by music, or by the regular return of the stanza, the natural harmony of language. Verses, which follow one another without being musically disposed, do not seem sufficiently poetical to express the feelings of the writer; and he discovers, by the ear alone, new rules, the observation of which may render the harmonious pleasure more complete.

The ode, in the form in which it existed amongst the ancients, and as it is to be found in the works of many of the poets of Germany, Italy, Spain, and Portugal, is the most perfect model of the lyrical style. The French have retained the same form. Their stanza is sufficiently musical; and the indeterminate length of the poem, and the regularity of each stanza, admit of that mixture of freedom and constraint which the expression of sentiment requires. The short French verse, which is not generally suspected to consist of regular feet, is always composed of long and short syllables, distributed in an harmonious order, and, at least in the hands of ingenious poets, has a good effect upon the ear. Inspiration, however, is wanting to it. Instead of their feelings, our poets have given us their reflections, and philosophy has gained possession of a style of poetry to which it did not seem to have the smallest title.

The Italians have not remained entirely faithful to the genuine style of lyrical composition, but their wanderings have been fewer than ours. It is singular that Petrarch, who was nurtured by th study of the ancients, and who was so much at tached to the Roman poets, should never hav attempted to introduce the ode into the Italiai language. Neglecting the models which Horac has left, and with the value of which he was s well acquainted, Petrarch has clothed all his lyri cal inspirations in two measures, both of whicl are far more strict and fettered; the sonnet, borrowed from the Sicilians, and the canzone of th Provençals. These two forms of versification which have been consecrated by him, and which down to the present day, are much used in Italy confined even his genius in their bonds, and gave a less natural air even to his inspiration. The sonnet, more especially, seems to have had a fatal influence on the poetry of Italy. The inspiration of a lyric poet, however it may be confined as to form, should surely have no limitation as to its length. But this bed of Procrustes, as an Italian has ingeniously called it, confines the poet's thoughts within the stated space of fourteen verses. If the thought should be too short for this extent, it is necessary to draw it out, till it fills the common measure; if, on the contrary, it be too long, it must be barbarously curtailed, in order to introduce it. Above all, it is necessary to set off so short a poem, with brilliant ornaments; and, as warm and passionate sentiments demand a considerable space in which to display ıemselves, ingenious conceits have usurped, in a omposition so essentially lyrical as this, the lace of feeling. Wit, and frequently false wit, ; all that we meet with.

The sonnet is composed of two *quatrains* and wo *tercets*, and has generally four, and never ıore than five rhymes. Its admirers discover he most harmonious grace in the regularity of he measure; in the two *quatrains*, which, with heir corresponding rhymes, open the subject and ›repare the mind of the reader; and in the two *ercets*, which, moving more rapidly, fulfil the ex- ›ectation which has been excited, complete the mage, and satisfy the poetical feeling. The onnet is essentially musical, and essentially ɔunded on the harmony of sound, from which ts name is derived. It acts upon the mind rather hrough the words than by the thoughts. The ichness and fulness of the rhymes constitute a ›ortion of its grace. The return of the same ounds makes a more powerful impression, in pro- ›ortion to their repetition and completeness; and ve are astonished when we thus find ourselves ffected, almost without the power of being able o ascertain the cause of our emotion.

To find a sufficient number of words which vill rhyme together, is a much more laborious ask in French than in Italian. In the latter lan- ·uage, almost all the syllables are simple, and ɔrmed from a few letters, so that the words present a great number of similar terminations. Bu the invariable regularity of the sonnet, in its lengt and in its measures, produces an indescribable monotony in these compositions. The first division o the sonnet is generally filled with some brillian images, while the latter contains an epigram, ar unexpected turn, or a striking antithesis, to excite the mind to momentary admiration. It i to these poems that the Italians owe their *concetti* which proceed from an affectation of wit, employed upon words rather than things. Of these, Petrarch, amongst other authors, affords us many examples.

On the other hand, the brevity of the sonnet has, no doubt, been the cause of much labour an care being bestowed on that kind of composition In a long poem, the portions which connect th more important parts, are often necessarily devoi of interest. The poet, in all probability, calculatin upon the inattention of his readers, is negligen in this part of his task; an indulgence which is frequently fatal to the language and to the poetica spirit of the piece. When Petrarch, however gave to the world a short poem of fourteen lines in this isolated form, which was to be appreciated by its own merits, he bestowed the utmost care upon it, nor suffered it to appear, unless he deemed it worthy of his fame. Thus, the Italian language made a most rapid progres between the times of Dante and Petrarch. More xact rules were introduced; a crowd of barbarous vords were rejected; the nobler were separated rom the more vulgar expressions; and the latter vere excluded for ever from the language of verse. Poetry became more elegant, more melodious, and nore pleasing to the ear of taste; but it lost, at east according to my apprehension, much of the expression of truth and nature.

Petrarch, who founded all his hopes of glory on his Latin compositions, did not place much value upon his Italian verses. The first sonnet which we meet with in his *Canzoniere* is not nerely modest, but expresses a singular sentiment of shame for that which, in fact, constitutes his celebrity.

SONNET I.

* All ye who list, in wildly warbled strain,
Those sighs with which my youthful heart was fed,
Erewhile fond passion's maze I wont to tread,
Erewhile I lived estrang'd to manlier pain;
For all those vain desires, and griefs as vain,
Those tears, those plaints, by am'rous fancy bred,
If ye by love's strong power have e'er been led,
Pity, nay, haply pardon, I may gain.

---

* Voi ch' ascoltate in rime sparse il suono
Di quei sospiri, ond' io nodriva il core
In sul mio primo giovenile errore,
Quand' era in parte altr' huom da quel ch' i sono;
Del vario stile in ch' io piango e ragiono,
Fra le vane speranze, e 'l van dolore,
Ove sia chi per prova intenda amore,
Spero trovar pietà, non che perdono.

Oft on my cheek the conscious crimson glows,
  And sad reflection tells—ungrateful thought!—
How jeering crowds have mock'd my love-lorn woes:
But folly's fruits are penitence and shame;
  With this just maxim, I've too dearly bought,
That man's applause is but a transient dream.*

It is evident that this sonnet was written at a period, when the poet, already on the threshold of age, had given himself up to remorse and religious terrors. He, doubtless, reproached himself with fostering a passion, which had exerted so powerful an influence over his life, which he had nourished, with unsubdued constancy, for one and twenty years, and which still remained sacred to his heart, so long after the loss of its object. This remorse was groundless. Never did passion burn more purely than in the love of Petrarch for Laura. Of all the Erotic poets, he alone never expresses a single hope, offensive to the purity of a heart which had been pledged to

---

Ma ben veggi' hor, sì come al popol tutto
  Favola fui gran tempo; onde sovente
  Di me medesmo meco mi vergogno:
E del mio vaneggiar vergogna è' l frutto
  E 'l pentirsi, e' l conoscer chiaramente
  Che quanto piace al mondo e breve sogno.

* [The translation of this sonnet is taken from a small volume, published in 1777, under the title of "Sonnets, and Odes, translated from the Italian of Petrarch." For the remaining versions, from this poet, the editor only is responsible.—*Tr.*]

another. When Petrarch first beheld her, on the sixth of April, 1327, Laura was in the church of Avignon. She was the daughter of Audibert de Noves, and wife of Hugues de Sade, both of Avignon. When she died of the plague, on the sixth of April, 1348, she had been the mother of eleven children. Petrarch has celebrated, in upwards of three hundred sonnets, all the little circumstances of this attachment; those precious favours which, after an acquaintance of fifteen or twenty years, consisted at most of a kind word, a glance not altogether severe, a momentary expression of regret or tenderness at his departure, or a deeper paleness at the idea of losing her beloved and constant friend. Yet even these marks of an attachment so pure and unobtrusive, and which he had so often struggled to subdue, were repressed by the coldness of Laura, who, to preserve her lover, cautiously abstained from giving the least encouragement to his love. She avoided his presence, except at church, in the brilliant levees of the papal court, or in the country, where, surrounded by her friends, she is described by Petrarch as exhibiting the semblance of a queen, pre-eminent amongst them all in the grace of her figure, and the brilliancy of her beauty. It does not appear that, in the whole course of these twenty years, the poet ever addressed her, unless in the presence of witnesses. An interview with her alone would surely have been celebrated in a thousand verses; and, as he has left us four sonnets on the good fortune he enjoyed, in having an opportunity of picking up her glove, we may fairly presume, that he would not have passed over in silence so happy a circumstance as a private interview. There is no poet, in any language, so perfectly pure as Petrarch, so completely above all reproach of levity and immorality; and this merit, which is due equally to the poet and to his Laura, is still more remarkable, when we consider that the models which he followed were by no means entitled to the same praise. The verses of the Troubadours and of the Trouvères were very licentious. The court of Avignon, at which Laura lived, the Babylon of the West, as the poet himself often terms it, was filled with the most shameful corruption; and even the Popes, more especially Clement V. and Clement VI. had afforded examples of great depravity. Indeed, Petrarch himself, in his intercourse with other ladies, was by no means so reserved. For Laura, he had conceived a sort of religious and enthusiastic passion; such as mystics imagine they feel towards the Deity, and such as Plato supposed to be the bond of union between elevated minds. The poets, who have succeeded Petrarch, have amused themselves with giving representations of a similar passion, of which, in fact, they had little or no experience.

In order to appreciate the full beauty of Pe

trarch's sonnets, it would be necessary to write the history of his attachment, as M. Ginguené has so ably done; and thus to assign to every sonnet, the place to which its particular sentiment destines it. But it would be even more necessary, that I should myself be sensible of the excellence of these poems, and that I should feel that charm which has enchanted every nation and every age. To this, I must acknowledge, that I am a stranger. I could have wished, in order to comprehend and to become interested in the passion of Petrarch, that there should have been a somewhat better understanding between the lovers; that they should have had a more intimate knowledge of each other; and that, by this means, we might ourselves have been better acquainted with both. I could have wished to have seen some impression made upon the sensibility of this loving and long-loved lady; to have seen her heart, as well as her mind, enlarging itself and yielding to the constancy and the purity of true friendship, since virtue denied a more tender return. It is tiresome to find the same veil, always shading not only the figure, but the intellect and the heart of the woman who is celebrated in these monotonous verses. If the poet had allowed us a fairer view of her, he would have been less likely to fall into exaggerations, into which my imagination, at least, is unable to follow him. How desirable would it be, that he should have recalled her to our minds by thought, by feeling, and by passion, rathe than by a perpetual play upon the words *Laur* (the laurel), and *l'aura* (the air). The first o these conceits, more especially, is incessantly re peated, nor merely in the poems alone. Through out Petrarch's whole life, we are in doubt whethe it is of Laura, or of the laurel, that he is enamoured so great is the emotion which he expresses, when ever he beholds the latter; so passionately doe he mention it; and so frequently has he celebrate it in his verses. Nor is that personified heart, t which Petrarch perpetually addresses himself, les fatiguing. It speaks, it answers, it argues, it i ever upon his lips, in his eyes, and yet ever at a distance. He is always absent, and we canno avoid wishing that, during his banishment, h would for once cease to speak of it. Judging fron these *concetti*, and from the continual personifica tion of beings which have no personal attributes it has always appeared to me that Petrarch is by no means so great a poet as Dante, because he i less of a painter. There is scarcely one of his son nets, in which the leading idea is not completely at variance with the principles of painting, an which does not, therefore, escape from the ima gination. Poetry may be called a happy unio of two of the fine arts. It has borrowed its har monies from music, and its images from painting But, to confound the two objects which poetry ha thus in view, is to be equally in error; whether w attempt, by an image, to represent a coincidence in sound, as when the laurel is put for Laura; or whether we wish to call up an image by sounds, as when, neglecting the rules of harmony, we produce a discordance suited to the object we design to paint, and make the serpents, of which we are speaking, hiss in our verses. Waving, however, as far as depends upon myself, my prejudice against Petrarch, of which I feel somewhat distrustful, because it is in opposition to the general taste, I shall translate a few of his sonnets; not for the purpose of criticising them, but in order to lead those, who are but imperfectly acquainted with the Italian language, to a more complete knowledge of them, so that they may read them without fatigue, and may comprehend the sense, while they enjoy the harmony of the sound; and, in short, that they may form their own judgment upon the masterpieces of one of the most celebrated men of modern times.

SONNET XIV.

* With hoary head and locks of reverend grey,
The old man leaves his youth's sweet dwelling-place,
And grief is mark'd on each familiar face,
Which watches him, as forth he takes his way:

---

* Movesi 'l vecchiarel canuto e bianco
Dal dolce loco ov' ha sua età fornita,
E dalla famigliuola sbigottita
Che vede il caro padre venir manco;

And he departs, though from his latest day
  Not distant far, and with an old man's pace,
  With right good will, he enters on the race,
Though travel-tired and broken with decay:
And now, accomplishing his last desires,
  In Rome, he sees the image of that One,
Whom to behold in Heaven his soul aspires:
  Even so have I, sweet lady! ever gone
Searching, in others' features, for some trace
Approaching thy long-lost peculiar grace.

SONNET XVII.

Creatures there be, of sight so keen and high,
  That even on the sun they bend their gaze;
  Others, who, dazzled by too fierce a blaze,
Issue not forth till evening veils the sky;

Indi traendo poi l' antico fianco
  Per l' estreme giornate di sua vita,
  Quanto più può, col buon voler s' aita,
  Rotto dagli anni, e dal cammino stanco:
E viene a Roma seguendo 'l desio,
  Per mirar la sembianza di colui
  Ch' ancor lassu nel ciel vedere spera:
Così lasso talor vo cercand' io
  Donna, quant' è possibile, in altrui
  La desiata vostra forma vera.

* Son animali al mondo di sì altera
  Vista, che 'ncontr' al sol pur si difende;
  Altri, però che 'l gran lume gli offende,
  Non escon fuor se non verso la sera;

Others, who, with insane desire, would try
The bliss which dwells within the fire's bright rays,
But, in their sport, find that its fervour slays;
Alas! of this last heedless band am I:
Since strength I boast not, to support the light
Of that fair form, nor, in obscure sojourn,
Am skill'd to fence me, nor enshrouding night;
Wherefore, with eyes which ever weep and mourn,
My fate compels me still to court her sight,
Conscious I follow flames which shine to burn.

The succeeding sonnet was written at a time, vhen the beauties of Laura began to fade. We ıre astonished at the constancy which Petrarch lisplays, towards one who could no longer :harm the eye of the beholder.

SONNET LXIX.

Waved to the winds were those long locks of gold,
Which in a thousand burnish'd ringlets flow'd,
And the sweet light, beyond all measure, glow'd,
Of those fair eyes, which I no more behold;

Ed altri col desio folle, che spera
Gioir forse nel foco, perchè splende,
Provan l' altra virtù, quella che 'ncende;
Lasso, il mio loco è 'n questa ultima schiera;
Ch' i non son forte ad aspettar la luce
Di questa donna, e non sò fare schermi
Di luoghi tenebrosi, ò d'ore tarde.
Però con gli occhi lagrimosi e 'nfermi
Mio destino a vederla mi conduce:
E sò ben ch' io vò dietro a quel che m' arde.

Nor (so it seem'd) that face, aught harsh or cold
  To me (if true or false, I know not) shew'd:
  Me, in whose breast the amorous lure abode,
If flames consumed, what marvel to unfold?
That step of hers was of no mortal guise,
  But of angelic nature, and her tongue
  Had other utterance than of human sounds;
A living sun, a spirit of the skies,
  I saw her—Now, perhaps, not so—But wounds
  Heal not, for that the bow is since unstrung.*

In the second part of Petrarch's poems, we find those which were written after the death of Laura, who, as we have already mentioned, died in 1548, at the age of forty-one, having been, for twenty-one years, the object of Petrarch's attachment. The poet was, at the time of that event, at Verona; and some of the poems, which were occasioned by this loss, are distinguished by more

* Erano i capei d'oro a l'aura sparsi,
  Che 'n mille dolci nodi gli avolgea:
  E 'l vago lume oltra misura ardea
  Di quei begli occhi, ch' or ne son si scarsi;
E 'l viso di pietosi color farsi,
  Non sò se vero ò falso, mi parea:
  I' che l'esca amorosa al petto avea,
  Qual maraviglia, se di subit', arsi?
Non era l' andar suo cosa mortale,
  Ma d'angelica forma, e le parole
  Sonavan altro che pur voce humana.
Uno spirto celeste, un vivo sole
  Fù quel ch' i vidi: e se non fosse or tale,
  Piaga per allentar d'arco non sana.

natural feelings, and excite in the reader a more lively sympathy. Still, there is, perhaps, too much ingenuity and invention displayed, to be compatible with great grief.

SONNET CCLI.

Those eyes, my bright and glowing theme erewhile,
  That arm, those hands, that lovely foot, that face,
Whose view was wont my fancy to beguile,
  And raise me high o'er all of human race;
Those golden locks that flow'd in liquid grace,
  And the sweet lightning of that angel smile,
Which made a Paradise of every place,
  What are they? dust, insensible and vile!
And yet I live! oh grief! oh rage! oh shame!
  Reft of the guiding star I loved so long,
A shipwreck'd bark, which storms of woes assail.
  Be this the limit of my amorous song:
Quench'd in my bosom is the sacred flame,
  And my harp murmurs its expiring wail.*

---

* Gli occhi, di ch'io parlai si caldamente,
  E le braccia et le mani, e i piedi, e 'l viso,
  Che m' havean sì da me stesso diviso,
  E fatto singular da l'altra gente;
Le crespe chiome d'or puro lucente,
  E 'l lampeggiar de l'angelico riso,
  Che solean far in terra un paradiso,
  Poca polvere son che nulla sente.
Ed io pur vivo: onde mi doglio e sdegno,
  Rimaso senza 'l lume, ch' amai tanto,
  In gran fortune, e 'n disarmato legno.
Or sia qui fine al mio amoroso canto:
  Secca e la vena de l'usato ingegno,
  E la cetera mia rivolta in pianto.

On his return to Vaucluse, where he was never again to behold his Laura, Petrarch wrote the following sonnet.

SONNET CCLXXIX.

I feel the well-known breeze, and the sweet hill
  Again appears, where rose that beauteous light
  Which (while Heaven will'd it) met my eyes, then bright
With gladness, but now dimm'd with many an ill.
Vain hopes! weak thoughts! Now, turbid is the rill;
  The flowers have droop'd; and she hath ta'en her flight
  From the cold nest, which once, in proud delight,
Living and dying, I had hoped to fill:
I hoped, in these retreats, and in the blaze
  Of her fair eyes, which have consumed my heart,
To taste the sweet reward of troubled days.
  Thou, whom I serve, how hard and proud thou art!
Erewhile, thy flame consumed me; now, I mourn
Over the ashes which have ceased to burn.*

---

* Sento l'aura mia antica, e i dolci colli
  Veggio apparir, onde 'l bel lume nacque
  Che tenne gli occhi miei, mentr' al ciel piacque,
  Bramosi e lieti; or li tien tristi e molli.
O caduche speranze, o pensier folli!
  Vedove l'herbe e torbide son l'acque;
  E voto, e freddo 'l nido in ch' ella giacque,
  Nel qual io vivo e morto giacer volli;
Sperando al fin da le soavi piante
  E da' begli occhi suoi, che'l cor m'han arso,
  Riposo alcun da le fatiche tante.
Ho servito a signor crudele e scarso:
  Ch' arsi quanto 'l mio foco hebbe davante;
  Or vò piangendo il suo cenere sparso.

Were I to give more numerous extracts, they would not render the style and the spirit of Petrarch's sonnets better known to those who do not read Italian; and, as examples merely, what are given are sufficient. The other form of his lyrical compositions, the *canzone*, is not unknown to us, although we have no express word for it, in the French; that of *chanson*, derived from it, signifying a poem of a totally different kind. We have seen that, amongst the Troubadours and the Trouvères, the chansons were odes divided into regular stanzas, longer than those of the odes of antiquity. The verses, which had the variety both of measure and rhyme, were disposed according to the rule of harmony which the poet established in the first stanza, and which was scrupulously observed in all the subsequent ones. The Italian *canzone* differed from the Provençal, in not being limited to five stanzas and an envoy, and in the more rare use of those very short lines, which sometimes give such vivacity to the Provençal poetry. There are some of Petrarch's *canzoni*, in which we find stanzas of twenty lines. This extraordinary length, which perhaps renders the harmony less perceptible to the ear, has given a peculiar character to the *canzoni*, and distinguishes the romantic from the classical ode. Modern poets, instead of pursuing the rapid and passionate inspiration of their feelings, dwell upon the same thought; not precisely for the purpose of filling up the stanza, for, to this mechanical process, the true poet will never submit but of preserving the regular and correspondin advance of the stanza and the sentiment. The bestowed more attention upon that reflectiv spirit, which is occupied with its own contemplations; upon that analytical power, whicl subjects every thing to its scrutiny; and upoi that forcible imagination, which places its object before us; but their enthusiasm vanished The translation of a canzone of Petrarch coul never be confounded with the translation of a ode of Horace. We are obliged to class then both under the head of lyrical poems; but w immediately perceive that such a division include very different kinds of compositions.

I feel myself called upon to give, at least, small specimen of those poems which have contributed so greatly to the renown of Petrarch and I shall select a few stanzas from the fift canzone, in which he exhorts the Bishop o Lombez to take up the cross, for the deliver of the Holy Land. This is, in my opinion, on of his most brilliant and enthusiastic poems, an one which approaches nearest to the ancien ode.

> And all who dwell between the salt main-seas
> And Rhone, and Rhine, and all between thy wave,
> Garonne! and the high hills, that Christian train
> Shall join. And if there be who love the brave,

Within that circle which the Pyrenees
Hold in horizon, Aragon and Spain
Shall be left desert. England, with the isles
Sea-girt, between the constellated Bear
And the great-pillar'd streight;
Yea, every land, where yet
The sainted lore of Helicon has charms,
Diverse in language, in attire, in arms,
This deed, for charity's sweet sake, shall dare.
What love so faithful, or what tender age
Of child, or charms of maiden, may compare
With the stern duties of this holy rage!

A region of the world there is afar,
Whelm'd under drifted snows, and bound with frost,
Where, wide remote from the sun's bright career,
In clouds and mist, the day is briefly lost:*

---

* Chiunque alberga tra Garona e 'l monte,
E tra 'l Rodano e 'l Reno e l'onde salse,
L' ensegne Christianissime accompagna:
Et a cui mai di vero pregïo calse,
Dal Pireneo a ultimo orizonte,
Con Aragon lascerà vota Ispagna;
Inghilterra, con l'Isole che bagna
L'Oceano, intra'l carro e le colonne,
Infin là, dove sona
Dottrina del santissimo Helicona,
Varie di lingue, e d'arme, e de le gonne,
A l'alta impresa caritate sprona,
Deh! qual amor si licito, ò si degno,
Quai figli mai, quai donne
Furon materia a si giusto disdegno?

There dwell a race, by nature prone to war,
And, even in death itself, disdaining fear.
Let these, more pious than they yet appear,
Join, with their hardy bands, the German host!
Thenceforth, I deem, not long
The Turk and Arab throng,
With the Chaldee, along the Red Sea coast,
Their own vain force, or their false gods shall boast!
A people naked, timorous, slow,
To grasp the steel, nor skill'd, nor strong,
But wasting on the wind their aimless blow!

We shall not enter into so minute an examinatio of those allegorical poems, to which Petrarch ha given the name of Triumphs. Not because the display any paucity of imagination, or any wan of that pictorial art, by which the poet place the object of his verse before the eyes of hi

---

Una parte del mondo è che si giace
Mai sempre in ghiaccio ed in gelate nevi,
Tutta lontana dal cammin del sole.
Là, sotto giorni nubilosi e brevi,
Nemica naturalmente di pace,
Nasce una gente a cui 'l morir non dole.
Questa, se più devota che non sole
Col Tedesco furor la spada cigne,
Turchi Arabi e Chaldei
Con tutti quei che speran ne gli Dei
Di quà dal mar che fà l'onde sanguigne,
Quanto sian da prezzar, conoscer dei:
Popolo ignudo, paventoso e lento,
Che ferro mai non strigne,
Ma tutti i colpi suoi commette al vento.

reader; but because those compositions are evidently formed on the model of Dante. There is the same metre; the same division into cantos, or chapters, not exceeding a hundred and fifty lines; and there are similar kinds of visions, in which the poet is partly the spectator and partly the actor. He is present, successively, at the Triumph of Love, of Chastity, of Death, of Renown, of Time, and of the Divinity. But the great vision of Dante, occupying a long poem, approaches almost to a second nature. We are struck with the action; we are interested for the characters; and we forget the allegory. Petrarch, on the contrary, never loses sight of his object, or the moral precept which he designs to inculcate. Two things alone are perpetually before our eyes; the advice intended for the reader, and the vanity of the poet; and we feel as little inclined to gratify the latter as to profit by the former.

The Latin compositions, upon which Petrarch rested his fame, and which are twelve or fifteen times as voluminous as his Italian writings, are now only read by the learned. The long poem entitled *Africa*, which he composed on the victories of the elder Scipio, and which was considered, in his own age, as a masterpiece worthy of rivalling the Æneid, is very fatiguing to the ear. The style is inflated, and the subject so devoid of interest, and so exceedingly dull, as absolutely to prevent the perusal of the work.

His numerous epistles in verse, instead of giving interest to the historical events to which they allude, acquire it from that circumstance. The imitation of the ancients, and the fidelity of the copy, which in Petrarch's eyes constituted their chief merit, deprive these productions of every appearance of truth. The invectives against the barbarians who had subjugated Italy, are so cold so bombastic, and so utterly destitute of al colouring suited to the time and place, that we might believe them to be written by some rhetorician, who had never seen Italy; and we might confound them with those which a poetic fury dictated to Petrarch himself, against the Gauls who besieged the capital. His philosophical works amongst which may be mentioned a treatise on Solitary Life, and another on Good and Bad Fortune, are scarcely less bombastic. The sentiments display neither truth nor depth of thought. They are merely a show of words, on some given subject The author pre-determines his view of the question, and never examines the arguments for the purpose of discovering the truth, but of vanquishing the difficulties which oppose him, and of making every thing agree with his own system. His letters, of which a voluminous collection has been published, which is, however, far from being complete, are, perhaps, more read than any other of his works, as they throw much light upon a period which is well worthy of being known. We do not, however, discover in them either the familiarity of intimate friendship, or the complete openness of an amiable character. They display great caution, and studied propriety, with an attention to effect, which is not always successful. An Italian would never have written Latin letters to his friends, if he had wished only to unfold the secrets of his heart; but the letters of Cicero were in Latin, and with them Petrarch wished to have his own compared. He was, evidently, always thinking more of the public than of his correspondent; and, in fact, the public were often in possession of the letter before his friend. The bearer of an elegantly-written epistle, well knew that he should flatter the vanity of the writer by communicating it; and he therefore often openly read it, and even gave copies of it, before it reached its destination. We find, in his correspondence, that several letters were lost in consequence of their too great fame.

It is difficult to say, whether the extended reputation which Petrarch enjoyed, during the course of a long life, is more glorious to himself, or to his age. We have elsewhere mentioned the faults of this celebrated man; that subtlety of intellect which frequently led him to neglect true feeling, and to abandon himself to a false taste; and that vanity which too often induced him to call himself the friend of cruel and contemptible princes, because they flattered him. But, before we part with him, let us once more take a view of those great qualities which rendered him the first man of his age; that ardent love for science, to which he consecrated his life, his powers, and his faculties; and that glorious enthusiasm for all that is high and noble in the poetry, the eloquence, the laws, and the manners of antiquity. This enthusiasm is the mark of a superior mind. To such a mind, the hero becomes greater by being contemplated; while a narrow and sterile intellect reduces the greatest men to its own level, and measures them by its own standard. This enthusiasm was felt by Petrarch, not only for distinguished men, but for every thing that is great in nature, for religion, for philosophy, for patriotism, and for freedom. He was the friend and patron of the unfortunate Rienzi, who, in the fourteenth century, awakened for a moment the ancient spirit and fortunes of Rome. He appreciated the fine arts as well as poetry; and he contributed to make the Romans acquainted with the rich monuments of antiquity, as well as with the manuscripts, which they possessed. His passions were tinctured with a sense of religion which induced him to worship all the glorious works of the Deity, with which the earth abounds; and he believed, that in the woman whom he loved, he saw the messenger of that Heaven, which thus revealed to him its beauty. He enabled his contemporaries to estimate the full value of the purity of a passion, so modest and so religious as his own; while, to his countrymen, he gave a language worthy of rivalling those of Greece and of Rome, with which, by his means, they had become familiar. Softening and ornamenting his own language by the adoption of proper rules, he suited it to the expression of every feeling, and changed, in some degree, its essence. He inspired his age with that enthusiastic love for the beauty, and that veneration for the study of antiquity, which gave it a new character, and which determined that of succeeding times. It was, it may be said, in the name of grateful Europe, that Petrarch, on the eighth of April, 1341, was crowned by the senator of Rome, in the Capitol; and this triumph, the most glorious which was ever decreed to man, was not disproportioned to the authority which this great poet was destined to maintain over future ages.

INDEX.

END OF THE FIRST VOLUME.

LONDON: PRINTED BY S. AND R. BENTLEY, DORSET STREET.

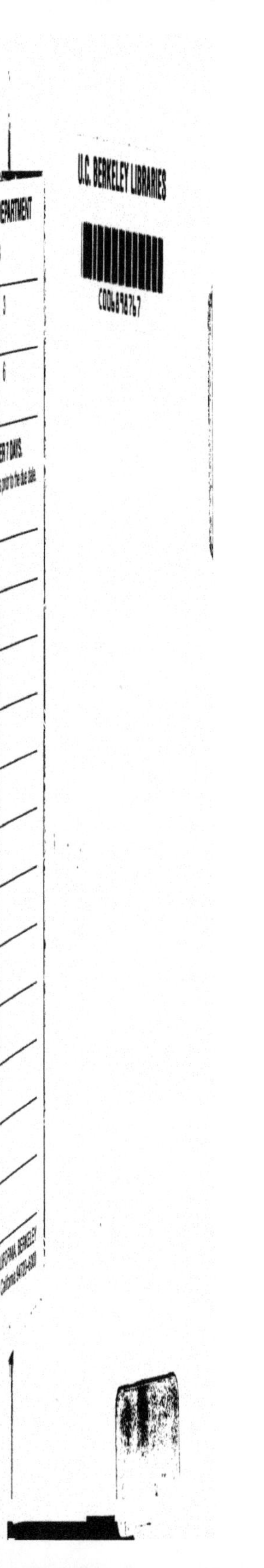

CPSIA information can be obtained
at www.ICGtesting.com
Printed in the USA
BVHW081247250819
556642BV00035B/1881/P

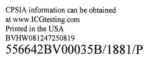